Punk Anarchism

ALSO AVAILABLE FROM BLOOMSBURY

Anarchism Today, Randall Amster
Punk Rock, Simon Stephens
Punk Style, Monica Sklar

Punk Anarchism

An Anti-Politics of Resistance

Sean Parson

BLOOMSBURY ACADEMIC
LONDON • NEW YORK • OXFORD • NEW DELHI • SYDNEY

BLOOMSBURY ACADEMIC
Bloomsbury Publishing Plc, 50 Bedford Square, London, WC1B 3DP, UK
Bloomsbury Publishing Inc, 1359 Broadway, New York, NY 10018, USA
Bloomsbury Publishing Ireland, 29 Earlsfort Terrace, Dublin 2, D02 AY28, Ireland

BLOOMSBURY, BLOOMSBURY ACADEMIC and the Diana logo are trademarks of Bloomsbury Publishing Plc

First published in Great Britain 2026

Cover design: Ben Anslow
Cover images: AdobeStock

A catalogue record for this book is available from the British Library.

A catalog record for this book is available from the Library of Congress.

ISBN: HB: 978-1-3505-3732-3
PB: 978-1-3505-3733-0
ePDF: 978-1-3505-3734-7
eBook: 978-1-3505-3735-4

Typeset by Deanta Global Publishing Services, Chennai, India
Printed and bound in Great Britain

For product safety related questions contact productsafety@bloomsbury.com.

To find out more about our authors and books visit www.bloomsbury.com and sign up for our newsletters.

Contents

Acknowledgments

Every creative work, from a song to a book, only emerges due to a mixture of dialogue, cultural sampling, and intentional or unconscious theft. This book is, of course, no exception. Every sentence, as much as I wish it was a result of my unrestrained genius or an authentic expression of my trauma, wasn't. Instead, it is a curation, chaotic and ugly as it may be, of countless conversations with family, friends, colleagues, accomplices, and enemies about the world we all inhabit. This can range from the wonderful friends of mine in our local academic book/writing club (Andrew, Emily, Eyal, Ira, Luis, Paul), who read an early draft and provided profound comments to my good friends who have listened to me rant and rave for ages (Chelsea, Danielle, Dunya, Joanie, Garrison, Jeff, Mara, Mike, Nihilia, Rose, Sarah and countless others), to the friends I meet up with at conferences who pushed and prodded me to make better arguments and who have inspired my thinking more than they can imagine (Emily Ray, Brian Lovato, Cedar, John Hultgren, Mary Witlycl, Peter, and so many more), to my mom, who has heard me lament the messed up nature of this world for decades (likely wondering where she went wrong in raising me!), to the masked protestors I have met in the streets, and the houseless neighbors that I have made friends with over the years of walking my dogs. Each interaction, discussion, or monology has shaped me and made this book what it is. In short, if you hate this book, and you might, blame them, not me!

But they are not the only ones to blame. Much of this work results from my conscious and unconscious theft of ideas from TikTok, memes, gallery art pieces, anonymous zines, fantastic novels, underground manga, comics, and songs. These uncredited sources have as much of an influence on my view of the world as the academic philosophers, theorists, and artists that I cite and reference throughout the book. Maybe even more. Their catchy little phrases, mashups of pop culture and radical politics, jokes or angry songs, fictional heroes and antiheroes, and weird tentacled monsters all live rent-free in my brain. Likely, other aspects of media—from commercials and TV sitcoms to Mariah Carey's Christmas ballad—have also wormed their way into my gray matter and likely shaped my worldview in ways that I will never comprehend. Hell, the fascistic rambling of figures like Tucker Carlson or the genocidal gaslighting by politicians and CEOs throughout the world has also shaped this book. It is common to only acknowledge the positive forces that contribute to a book, but, at least in this book, my political and narrative enemies also contributed. Every fossil fuel CEO, sitting on a pile of money while they actively burn the planet, and every politician who defends the bloody violence of the state, all so that the wealthy and power can thrive, shaped this book. If this book is a love poem, co-written with my friends and colleagues, it is also a letter bomb to every one of the bastards who is trying to grind us down. If you hate or even love this book, blame these CEOs and politicians. They are the villains in this story and in every story, no matter how hard the media tries to make us think of them as heroes.

But this is how life in the spectacle (or spectacles) functions. Everything we produce is a mashup of everything around us. Every book is a product of our relationship to images and mass culture, as are our most intimate relationships. This is why writing an acknowledgment while embedded in the spectacle is impossible. The logic of capitalism, and of property and ownership in general, likes to construct a story that everything results from individual creativity, will, or passion. We want to assume and associate individuals with ideas, as if the individual, as a philosophic reality, exists in the first place. But this is the logic of ownership under capitalism. The boss owns the factory, though the workers make the wealth, and the writer owns the novel or book, while it is at best a curated expression of the world they inhabit and, therefore, co-written. Writing and publishing, as such, reify the idea of the individual, erasing the memory and complexity of creative creation. An authorial version of the fetishism of commodities. The concept of authorship, or even the individual, is a lie, though it might stabilize a world that otherwise is swirling chaos. If nothing else, the idea of the author as creator might limit the likelihood of there being even more pretentious things like this. But it likely breeds entirely different forms of pretension.

Honestly, though, and from the bottom of my heart, I want to acknowledge how much my friends, colleagues, family (blood and found), and broader community influenced me. No acknowledgment could ever express how deeply you all mean to me.

An Anti-Introduction

A *Leap into* the Void

Modern philosophy has explored the socially constructed nature of this world but has rarely embraced a politics that takes social construction and its critiques seriously. Judith Butler, for instance, in *Gender Troubles* (Butler 2006), shatters the essentialist claim that gender and sex are linked and that either expression is related to any form of biological foundation. She writes that "the apparatus by which the production and normalization of masculine and feminine take place along with the interstitial forms of hormonal, chromosomal, psychic, and performative that gender assumes" (Butler 2004: 42). Gender is a social construct, and, as such, to Butler, we can perform gender however we see fit, highlighting the radical power of drag and other forms of queer gender performance. Sadly, most of the current discussion around queer and trans politics centers not on the construction of gender and sexuality but on an exploration of identity and authenticity politics. Phrases like "I was born this way" neuter the political radicalism of anti-essentialist philosophy. Alyson Escalante, a radical trans philosopher, in their short piece, *Gender Nihilism: An Anti-manifesto*, embraces the spirit and passion of this book when they write:

> At the heart of our gender abolition is a negativity. We seek not to abolish gender so that a true self can be returned to; there is no such self. It is not as though the abolition of gender will free us to exist as true or genuine selves, freed from certain norms. Such a conclusion would be at odds with the entirety of our antihumanist claims. And thus, we must take a leap into the void. (Escalante 2015: 316)

Escalante here takes Butler's logic of gender as a social construction and embraces the radicality of this claim. In seeking to imagine a world without gender and seeking to abolish gender as a social category, Escalante forces us to follow them into the void.

This book explores leaping into that void, searching deep within our hearts for a desire to abolish, negate, and destroy that which is oppressive. Moreover, an urge to destroy and dismantle is at the heart of the lessons that Judith Butler, Michel Foucault, and the famed horse defender Nietzsche[1] put forward in their work. The systems of gender and race, of capitalism and states, are not products emerging from the crust of the planet or created by an all-loving and knowing God but are merely illusions, animated, and armed by state officials and social bootlickers. While socially formed, these constructs leave bruises and mass graves dotting our bodies and the planetary landscape, but that does not make them eternal.

The idea of negation has been a part of radical political thought, but like the political implication of social construction, negation has rarely been embraced to its full extent. For instance, Marx develops his theory of alienation in the Economic Manuscripts of 1844. He writes, "Just as in religion the spontaneous activity of the human imagination, of the human brain and the human heart, operates independently of the individual—that is, operates on him as an alien, divine or diabolical activity—so is the worker's activity, not his spontaneous activity. It belongs to another; it is the loss of his self" (Tucker, Marx, and Engels 1978: 111). The process of alienation, to Marx, occurs in four different ways under capitalist modes of production: from the products of laboring, from the process of laboring, from our collective species being, and from other workers. Through alienation, the worker's identity and their acts of expression are tainted and corrupted by the commodity process.

---

[1]There is a famous but likely apocryphal story about Nietzsche that on January 3, 1889, while walking through the streets of Turin, he witnessed a horse being beaten by the carriage driver. Nietzsche, famously, threw himself over the horse, protecting it from the attacks. This story is often used to highlight when Nietzsche finally went insane, but instead of reading this as a moment of insanity, I think it is best to view this as the most profound and radical act of Nietzsche. As the book will later argue, most of Nietzsche's work focuses on the "powerful" and the desire to greatness, and this story illustrates a more useful, playful, and radical version of nihilism in which the focus is not on "greatness" but on solidarity and connection with the oppressed.

The worker herself has their humanness erased and, through an alchemy of exchange, becomes a mere commodity. Or, as Marx phrases it, "the worker sinks to the level of a commodity and becomes indeed the most wretched of commodities; that the wretchedness of the worker is in inverse proportion to the power and magnitude of his production" (Tucker, Marx, and Engels 1978: 106). According to Marx, our individual and collective inner nature is blocked from flourishing, and we become a hostile force to our essence. In early Marx, we can dream of unalienated existence.

This dream never gets fully implemented in the writings of Marx as the struggle against alienation directly conflicts with the productivism found in Marx's Capital. In his unfinished third volume of *Capital*, which Engel edited from Marx's notes, the section "Realm of Necessity and Freedom" illustrates the tension between alienation and productivism (Tucker, Marx, and Engels 1978). The common reading of this section shows that Marx, still enamored with industrial production, contends that only through industrial production we can minimize the amount of time needed in the "realm of necessity" (alienated labor).[2] Thus, if we maintain industrial production, we might not be able to eliminate alienated labor, but we can maximize our time in the "realm of freedom" and have more of our daily lives structured around unalienated labor. The dream of abolishing alienated labor dies; with it, we are forever haunted by the commodity form. Alienated labor is not a requirement. Marshall Sahlin, in his book *Stone Age Economics*, analyzes hunter-gatherer societies and contends that before the rise of civilization they had already created social relationships free from alienated labor. Sahlin writes:

> Hunter and gatherers have, by force of circumstance, an objectively low standard of living. But taken as their objective, and given their adequate means of production, all the people's material wants usually can be satisfied. The evolution of the economy has known two contradictory movements:

[2]I want to avoid claiming that Marx himself was enamored with productivism at the time, since *Marx in the Anthropocene* provides a compelling claim that Marx himself was already disillusioned with productivism at the time he wrote this section. But, if he was or was not still primarily a productivist, this section either (1) shows the difficulty of squaring the circle that Marx created with his theory or (2) shows the ways by which Engel's shaped and molded our readings of the late Marx's work.

> enriching but at the same time impoverishing, appropriating in relation to nature but expropriating in relation to man. (Sahlins 2017: 34)

So why couldn't Marx, a clever historian and political thinker, imagine a life outside of alienation? Because Marx wanted to maintain the productive system of capitalist industrialism, which contradicts the value and desire to abolish alienation. Happiness is denied so the factory can continue humming.

In recent years, scholars like Kohei Saito (Saitō 2017, 2022) and Kevin Anderson (Anderson 2020) have explored the collected notebooks of Marx through the Die Marx-Engels-Gesamtausgabe. In their detailed dive into Marx's post-*Capital* notes, they find that ecology and precapitalist peasant history dominated the elder Marx's focus. According to these theorists, the lessons Marx took from such work changed the foundations of Marxism. Saito writes that "Marx's final vision of an alternative society can be developed only based upon a full synthesis of Marx's engagement with political economy, ecology, and pre-capitalist societies in his last 15 years of life" (Saitō 2022: 173). Anderson and Saito contend that Marx's engagement with Russian revolutionaries and his increasing attention to German and Russian peasant communes led the great thinker to shift away from his earlier conception of historical materialism, Eurocentrism, and his fetish for industrial production. This leads Saito to declare that "Marx's last vision of post-capitalism is *degrowth communism*" (Saitō 2022: 208; italics in the original). This opens up a form of Marxism that might take the question of abolishing alienation seriously. It is also a form of Marxism that rejects and counters the vile authoritarianism of Lenin, Stalin, Mao, Castro, and others. Saito writes:

> Hierarchal control is incompatible with Marx's vision of providing more autonomy to the associated producers, but without hierarchy, it takes more time to mediate between different opinions and reach a consensus. Since the increase of productive forces under capitalism relies upon the undemocratic and top-down character of the production process with the concentration of power in the hands of the few, democratic decision-making in the workplace inevitably slows down the process of production. The USSR was not able to accept this and imposed bureaucratic control upon social production. (Saitō 2022: 241)

In rejecting industrialism and productivism, Saito's reading of Marx exemplifies what a politics of anti-theoretical negation might create.

This book centers on the politics of negation—looking to reject all politics of reification. Horkheimer and Adorno contend that "reification is always an act of forgetting," reminding us that as we naturalize any social systems, we forget there is no natural foundation to said institution. Capitalism, nationalism, and even anthropocentrism are not byproducts of nature but are social systems, constructed by humans. As we reify, we forget that truth and defend the institutions surrounding us instead of actively working to deconstruct or abolish them. Among the radical tradition, few writers engage with the issue of reification more deeply than John Zerzan, the anarcho-primitivist author. Throughout his long durée as a writer, Zerzan has argued that symbolic thought and language function as a form of reification. Zerzan writes, "There is no agreement as to when language began, but no evidence exists of speech before the cultural 'explosion' of the later Upper Paleolithic. Instead, it seems to have acted as an 'inhibiting agent,' a way of bringing life under 'great control' stemming the flood of images and sensations to which the pre-modern individual was open" (Zerzan 2012: 9). In general, Zerzan contends that symbolic activity, from speech to art, serves not as a bio-natural aspect of the human species but is instead a techne developed by primitive human societies to constrain and regulate human and nonhuman nature. As such, language itself is a reified idea, a concept that we assume is natural, but, in reality, we might be simply forgetting what life was like before the advent of symbolic exchange. Or, as Zerzan puts it, "the emergence of symbolic culture, with its inherent will to manipulate and control, soon opened the door to the domestication of nature" (Zerzan 2012: 10). To Zerzan, the forces of civilization seek to domesticate human and nonhuman worlds, in order to make the world more calculable and controllable. The systems of civilization reify the logic needed to domesticate, forming a feedback cycle of control.

Zerzan is critiqued for putting forward a political project that is not at all practical. Michael Albert, the long-time editor for Z Mag, an American-based leftist/activist periodical, critiques Zerzan by writing:

> The most obvious way to discern the unwarranted leap in Zerzan's claim is to note that without technology humans would have no clothes, no source of power outside their own muscles, and not even agriculture to renew their muscles. Life would be brutish, isolated, and short. The disease would be rampant. Communication, mobility, knowledge, music, art, play, and pretty much everything else would be harshly limited. (Albert 2010)

The critique that Albert provides of Zerzan is not to reject the theoretical arguments but to instead center the pragmatism of the political implications.[3] I am using this debate between Zerzan and Albert not to contrast "the good" negationists (Zerzan) versus "the bad" modernist (Albert), as such an analysis is trite, but to highlight how terrifying and unsettling negation can be, even to an openly radical activist and thinker like Albert. That said, just because an idea is unsettling does not mean that it is wrong, nor does it mean that it is correct. Instead, I want to contend that these negationist theoretical exploration open up the space to radically reimagine politics.

As we critique the hegemonic order of scientism, the dangers of irrationalism haunt our dreams, and the superstitions and the magical mystification of the world return. In a World currently shaped by reactionary and irrational far-right politics, a politics that has questioned the validity of science (for climate change, Covid, and everything in between) and is working to undermine

---

[3]This is not to say that Zerzan and the anarchist tradition of primitivism are not open to theoretical or political critique. Zerzan, for instance, embraces a conception of nature rooted in the logic of authenticity and essentialism. His work conceives that there is a natural way for humans to interact within this world, and if we can deconstruct reification to its endpoint, we can find that authentic way of living. Such an authentic life is what is essential for living "sustainably" on this planet. However, later chapters will go more in-depth; the concepts of nature and humans are wrought with philosophic confusion, and there is a need to deconstruct these concepts as well, which leaves, at the bottom of reification, not turtles but the endless void of nothing. As such, the philosophical critique of Zerzan's position is not that he misunderstands the benefits of technology, civilization, and reification of nature, humans, time, or symbolic thought but that he assumes that there is a base of Truth at the core that will allow humans to live their correct and authentic lives. Politically, there are many additional critiques of the primitivist position that do not rest on an uncritical acceptance of a Hobbesian state of nature but, instead, how authenticity and myth function as a means of providing a radical Palin defense logic, which can easily be linked with "blood and soil" far-right politics. Again, this is not to say that Zerzan or even most primitivists have links with fascism, merely that there are links there that can be politically troubling. For more examples, explore how Derick Jensen has found inroads with reactionary and neofascists and trans-exclusionary radical feminists.

liberal representative institutions to implement fascism, there is a knee-jerk reaction for those on the left. While these concerns are valid, the arguments against revolutionary change reek of what Wendy Brown (1999) calls "Left Melancholia." Brown contends that post–Cold War left is nostalgic toward past movement successes like the Russian Revolution and the Civil Rights movements and that the left fears they lacks the power to implement change. Under such melancholic politics, the left defends the status quo, becoming a conservative force in society. Brown writes:

> If the contemporary Left often clings to the formations and formulations of another epoch, one in which the notion of unified movements, social totalities, and class-based politics appeared to be viable categories of political and theoretical analysis, this means that it literally renders itself a conservative force in history-one that not only misreads the present but installs traditionalism in the very heart of its praxis, in the place where commitment to risk and upheaval belongs. (Brown 1999: 25)

The lack of revolutionary imagination of the left has led to the stagnation of thought and an unwillingness to confront the neoliberal order. Instead, the political imagination is tied to the past, such as the call for a Green New Deal by the progressive wing of the democratic party in the United States. While their approach nominally rejects some aspects of neoliberalism, the proposal does not critique capitalism or provide a lens of analysis for shifting how we engage with the climate crisis. Instead, it wraps progressive policy demands with the shroud of the past, focusing on acceptability and nostalgia for the FDR administration's response to the great depression, forgetting the bourgeoise, white supremacist, and patriarchal logic that underscored his political project. Every act of reification is an act of forgetting. Similarly, we see knee-jerk reactions to defend liberal institutions, scientific technocracy, capitalist property relations, and the biosecurity apparatus of the state, not because these are good positions to take but because if we do not protect the status quo from the growing far-right, we fear becoming the handmaidens of fascism. But, the neoliberal disintegration of communal life as well as the inherent limits of capitalism and liberalism are the source of the growing fascist threat. In short, liberalism is also a form of fascistic politics.

The World we live in is breaking, and the future, if there is one, will look nothing like the present. The World, the colonial project of modernity that Western nations imposed on the planet, is doomed. The crisis is felt in our bones, and the longer that practicality reigns in restricting theoretical imagination and the radicalization of political demands, we cede critique and rebellion to the right. Instead of left melancholia, Brown highlights that we need "a spirit that embraces the notion of a deep and indeed unsettling transformation of society rather than one that recoils at this prospect, even as we must be wise to the fact that neither total revolution nor the automatic progress of history will carry us toward whatever reformulated vision we might develop" (Brown 1999: 26). At this moment, this means a politics that embraces the end of the World. Only in the ashes of our World is there any path for life to continue. Before constructive theory can build and imagine new worlds to come, first we need a theory that focuses on negation and destruction. At a time when we need an antiworld politics, we need to develop an anti-theory.

Anti-Theory: Dada, Situationism, Stirner, and Punk Theorizing

Boris Groys describes antiphilosophy as "a readymade philosophy that ascribes universal philosophical value to certain already existing ordinary practices, in the same way, which practices of artistic readymades ascribe artistic value to ordinary objects" (Groĭs and Fernbach 2012: X). Groys applies the logic of anti-art found in the Dada movement to a range of philosophers. Like the Dadaist understanding of anti-art, he understands antiphilosophy as existing in a dialectic relationship with philosophy. He primarily focuses on the Dada use of readymades and contends that anti-art does not seek to destroy the concept of art but instead attempts to democratize the artistic, removing the aura and "great man" identity that art has. Of course, Groys, in looking to the readymade as the exemplar of Dada anti-art, deradicalizes the potentiality of what antiphilosophy could be. If we take the more radical aspects of Dada as an inspiration for an anti-theory or antiphilosophy, we see a shift from democratization to negation. In the 1918 Dada Manifesto, Tristan Tzara writes:

> Every product of disgust capable of becoming a negation of the family is Dada; a protest with the fists of its whole being engaged in destructive action: Dada; knowledge of all the means rejected up until now by the shamefaced sex of comfortable compromise and good manners: Dada; abolition logic, which is the dance of those impotent to create: Dada; of every social hierarchy and equation set up for the sake of values by our valets: Dada: every object, all objects, sentiments, obscurities, apparitions and the precise clash of parallel lines are weapons for the fight: Dada; abolition of memory: Dada; abolition of archaeology: Dada; abolition of prophets: Dada; abolition of the future: Dada; absolute and unquestionable faith in every god that is the immediate product of spontaneity: Dada; elegant and unprejudiced leap from a harmony to the other sphere; trajectory of a word tossed like a screeching phonograph record; to respect all individuals in their folly of the moment: whether it be serious, fearful, timid, ardent, vigorous, determined, enthusiastic; to divest one's church of every useless cumbersome accessory; to spit out disagreeable or amorous ideas like a luminous waterfall, or coddle them—with the extreme satisfaction that it doesn't matter in the least—with the same intensity in the thicket of core's soul pure of insects for blood well-born, and gilded with bodies of archangels. Freedom: Dada Dada Dada, a roaring of tense colors, and interlacing of opposites and of all contradictions, grotesques, inconsistencies: LIFE. (Danchev 2011: 144)

Tzara's Dada is about much more than the democratic and anti-elitist logic of the readymade; in fact, the readymade isn't even worth his mentioning. Dada was not about democratization; it was about abolition. In his 1916 Dada Manifesto, Hugo Ball writes, "How does one achieve eternal bliss? By saying, Dada. How does one become famous? By saying, Dada. With a noble gesture and delicate propriety. Till one goes crazy. Till one loses consciousness. How can one get rid of everything that smacks of journalism, worms, everything nice and right, blinkered, moralistic, Europeanized, enervated? By saying Dada" (Danchev 2011: 128). What we see with Ball is not just a desire to erase from art the aura of the creative genius but a mocking tone, a critique of art that desires to blur the boundaries of what is or is not art to the point in which art itself has no space to justify its existence separate from the world as it is—

irrational, meaningless, absurd, and chaotic. Walter Serner, a Dadaist radical that Hans Richter said "was the incarnation of revolt in what would now be called existential form (Richter 2016: 36)," stated, "Since we have no meaning (the void), we succumb to the delusion that we have meaning, or, the more agreeable case, to the delusion that we are not deluded. We are thus incurably demented." With Serner, and most of the original Dadaist, the institution of art is viewed as an elitist space that helps to curate the bourgeoisie notions of society. Only in the rubble of the art World can creativity be liberated.

This negationist logic is expressed in Louis Aragon's manifesto published in 1920 under the "twenty-three manifestos of the Dada movement." This collection of manifestos, which often contradict each other, functions to decenter any one voice from gaining control over the logic of Dada while also creating confusion about the politics of Dada. Aragon writes:

> No more painters, no more writers, no more musicians, no more sculptures, no more religions, no more republicans, no more royalists, no more imperialists, no more anarchists, no more socialists, no more Bolsheviks, no more politicians, no more proletarians, no more democrats, no more bourgeois, no more aristocrats, no more armies, no more police, no no more anything, nothing, nothing, nothing, nothing. (Danchev 2011: 167)

Similarly, Francis Picabia, in their "Dada manifesto," contends, "The Dadaists are nothing, nothing, nothing, nothing, and they will certainly succeed in nothing, nothing, nothing, nothing" (Danchev 2011: 162). This focus on nothingness and negation within Dada relates to their understanding that contemporary politics, philosophy, religion, and art could not bring about a world free from alienation and horror. If anything, the values the world hold have led to the brutal violence of the First World War.

In the logic of Dada, modernity was a block to the paths of liberation, and the negation of modernity pulls the curtain to show the void at the heart of contemporary life. This differs from the work of Surrealism. Andre Breton, in his surrealist manifesto, assumed that "Everything leads us to believe that there exists a spot in the mind from which life and death, the real and the imaginary, the past and the future, the high and the low, the communicable and the incommunicable will cease to appear contradictory" (Danchev 2011:

268). Breton, a firm believer in the unconscious theories of Freud, searched to find the hidden truth through an engagement with the dreamlike nature of irrationality. This assumes a certain level of authenticity and a Jungian logic of archetypes. In contrast, Dada rejects that primordial authenticity exists. Guy Debord wrote of Dada and Surrealism: "Dadaism sought to abolish art without realizing it; Surrealism south to realize art without abolishing it. The critical position since developed by the situationists demonstrates that abolition and the realization of art are inseparable aspects of a single transcendence of art" (Hemmens and Zacarias 2020: 28). But Dadaism should not be the only basis for an antiphilosophy. There are other forms of philosophy and art that, in their dialectic, attempt to negate though. For instance, we have the situationists, the work of Max Stirner, and the punk movement.

Debord, who was inspired by Dada, wished to negate what he called "the spectacle," a new form of social relations mediated through the image of mass culture, life. In his analysis, everything had become a commodity; as such, there was nothing to life but alienation—at work, in leisure, in your interpersonal relationships. The project for revolutionary art and activists, to the situationists, was to counter the spectacle. Since mainstream art was already a tool of the spectacle, the museums and art schools were nothing but complicit institutions. Similarly, the representative political organizations that existed, ranging from unions to the communist parties, were also coopted by the spectacle and function as extensions of state apparatuses of control. Revolutionary art must abolish the hierarchies the spectacle places on art and, through its performance, create situations that undermine the legitimacy of the spectacle. In Debord's "situationist manifesto," he describes the "constructed situation" where art desires "the production of the new cultures, independent of the political and union organization which currently exist, as we dispute their capacity to organize anything other than the management of that while already exists" (Danchev 2011: 349). This is done by shattering the spectacles separation and alienation. Instead of a World in which there are artists and consumers of art, "everyone will be an arists, i.e., inseperablly producers-consumer of total cultural creation, which will help the rapid dissolution of the linear criteria of novelty" (Danchev 2011: 350). In short, the creation of artistic situations should not reify the system, nor should it be something passively consumed; instead, the artistic situation will simultaneously negate the logic and value of art while also being an expression of art itself. Through art, anti-art through theory, anti-theory.

The anti-theorist par excellence is Max Stirner, whose book *The Unique and Its Property* provides an impressive and thorough critiques of systemic thought and philosophic ontology. Stirner, the primary inspiration for individualist anarchism, rejects all attempts to create abstract and representational logic within political, philosophic, and social life. In this critique, Stirner refers to all representational concepts as either ghosts or phantasms since concepts, like humanity, are not "real" but haunt politics, philosophy, ethics, and economics. This critique of the representational goes beyond the general anarchist critique of the state to also encompass any abstracted thoughts or principles. For instance, Stirner, who places all foundations for the world in the self—that is, the ego—rejects all systems that exist above the ego.[4] Concepts such as "the people," "humanity," and "community," as well as political terms like "property," "freedom," or "rights," are phantasm and only exist because of the power we give to that state—which exists only through coercive violence, theft,

[4]Using Stirner and his metacritique of modernist philosophic and political theory work does not mean an uncritical acceptance of all of his work. Building on the critique of Stirner that Gustov Landauer develops in his work "on socialism," Stirner can be critiqued for not adequately using his critical assault on the values he holds—primarily the assertion that the self or the ego is an existing thing. Though Landaeur overstates this critique of Stirner, who does claim that even the self is a spook, or phantasm lacking inherent Truth, Stirner never explores the implications of this assertation to his argument. Much of the work of twentieth-century post-structuralism is rooted in a decentering of the individual and the radical critique of the concept of the self, another specter that haunts our philosophic world. If I use Strirner, I do so in his critique of the meta-system of analysis and not in his embrace of egoism. I would agree with Stirner that the ego (or the self) is as much a fiction as is the concept of the people or humanity. There is no self, no unified ego, or even a human. Instead, all humans are also an assemblage of countless species, as gut bacteria and nonhuman cells play as necessary a role as human cells in the making each of "us" unique. Similarly, there is a problem in assuming that the dividing line between "me" and another is not as clear as Stirner might like. My sense of self is a product of multiple nodes of experience, thought, biological life, and interpersonal connection, and, as such, the self cannot be guaranteed from the world of others—both human and nonhuman. This thought does not undermine Stirner's broader claim about abstract systems of thought but radicalizes it more. If even the self is a specter, then there is nothing to ground our authentic expression of ourselves. This opens up more chaotic, nuanced, and liberatory politics, one in which the self is in a dialectic tension between other human and nonhuman life, and, therefore, the problematic egoism that most anarcho-communists critique of Stirner is addressed while maintaining that his brutal critique of their project is still left in place.

and ideological control. In a section criticizing liberal ideological thought, he contends:

> Because liberalism is a religion since it separates my essence from me and sets it above me since it exalts "humanity" to the same extent that some other religions would God or idol since it makes what is mine other-worldly, since it generally makes out of what is mine, out of my qualities and my property, something alien namely an "essence;" in short, since it places me beneath the human and thereby creates a calling for me. But liberalism also declares itself a religion in form when it demands this highest essence, humanity, a religious zeal. . . . So also, for every member of the state-community, this community must be sacred, and the concepts that are highest for the state must also be the highest for him. (Stirner 2018: 165–6)

To Stiner, liberalism constructs the concept of "humanity," which becomes a category that then links all people into a unified community. This community, the abstract concept of the human, then imposes on individuals a series of rules and regulations that undermine the individual's rights by imposing the abstract principles of "humaneness" onto us. With the creation of "the human" an opposite must also be formed, "the antihuman." To maintain the borders of humanity the antihuman must be punished, repressed, and excluded. Stirner writes that "Even though every inhuman monster is a human being. Still the state excludes him, i.e., locks him up, or transforms him from a state-comrade to a prison-comrade (a lunatic asylum or hospital-comrade for communism)" (Stirner 2018: 165). Revolutionaries should not run from such framing by the state but instead embrace the categories of inhuman, criminal, underclass.

Similarly, "the People" are not a representation of actual individuals but an ideological ghost that distorts the ability of us to relate to each through traits and characteristics that we as individuals might have. Stirner writes,

> *People* is the name of the body, *state* the name of the spirit, of that *ruling person* that gas suppressed me up to now. Some have wanted to transfigure people and states by expanding them to "humanity" and "universal reason," but enslavement would only become more intense through this expansion;

> philanthropists and humanitarians are as absolute masters as politicians and diplomats. (Stirner 2018: 228)

The state, modernity, and the tools of universal reason, much like the theocratic projects of Christendom, are nothing but tools of oppression, imperial projects seeking to control. In modernity, this control is done through reason, liberal or communist values, and supposed humanism, while in the past it was the imposed idea of Christian brotherhood. Like the Jews and Muslims, forcibly converted through torture in Spain or killed through pogroms and crusades, those who reject or resist the expansion of modernity will also be purged. For society to be defended, antisocial people must be removed or reformed.

Stirner critiques ontology, leaving nothing but the ashes and ruins of philosophy. His critique goes further than Marx, who, though critical of Hegal, does not burn the philosophy to the ground. Instead, Marx flips Hegel on his head, assuming that the antithesis of Hegel's idealism will serve as a valuable foundation for Marxian materialism. Stirner rejects all attempts to build up institutionalizing foundations for political and philosophic reality, leaving the individual instead and, through his idea of associationism, unmediated politics as the only legitimate foundation for one's worldview. Stirner reminds us that all ideas, as they calcify and become "authorities" in themselves, cease to be revolutionary. All that exists must melt into the air as the solidity of thought, institutions, and hierarchies will always lead to the construction of new jails and tighter chains.

Moving from the anti-theoretical to the anti-praxis fusion of anti-theory and action, we have the musical genre, and movement, of punk. According to Mark Achterman (Bestley et al. 2021), the complexity of punk makes it difficult, if not impossible, to provide a cohesive definition. He notes that a few common themes have emerged in all the attempts to define punk, such as a DIY ethos, leftist politics, and focus on conflictual relationships with authority. Worley notes the same issue when he writes, "Punk's politics were messy. They could be contradictory and formative; implicit and explicit; liberatory and reactionary. Meanings were projected onto punk, but also cultivated from within" (Worley 2017: 255). Skov (2023), in his art history analysis of Punk art, similarly contends that Punk, because it has actively refused and resisted set identification markers and because the movement is so locally and historically contingent, is impossible to define. He notes that punk tends to universally have two qualities: a focus on negation and DIY creation. Seeking to destroy, as Iggy Pop sang, punk needs to destroy the dominant institutions of music and culture while also building up unmediated spaces for direct relationship to thrive. To both Achterman and Skov, limiting punk to a music genre is a mistake as the concepts within punk are more of an embodied form of lived values and, as such, blur boundaries—between public and private, between art and life, destruction and creation—and that the punk modifier can be stretched and expanded to incorporate a range of nonmusical practices. Anti-theory is a form of punk theory. And the punk theory is always a form of praxis, a praxis of negation and of nonmediated construction.

To provide an example of the punk-anti-theory praxis fusion, we turn to the anarcho-punk collective Crass. Crass was an art collective formed in 1977 in Essex, England. Based at the anarchist commune, the Dial House, the collective produced music, poetry, and collage art. The group is best known for songs like "Do They Owe Us a Living"[5] and "Banned from the Roxy"[6] and for their situationist-inspired pranks. For instance, in 1983, right before the UK election, the collective released a tape where they created, through collage splicing of political speeches and interviews, a fake conversation between Thatcher and Reagan purporting to show Thatcher admitting to intentionally sinking the HMS *Sheffield* in order to start the Falklands War (Staff 2014). The tape hoax, which most news outlets caught before they released the tape, worried the CIA and M15 as both security institutions initially believed the tape to be part of a coordinated Soviet disinformation campaign. "Crass argued that thought the tape was fake." According to Skov, "what it showed was true: cynicism, lies, war mongering, and abuse of power" (Skov 2023: 115). Thatchergate can be seen as a form of the constructed situation in which the collective, through tape collage, attempts a détournement (rewriting or hijacking), of Thatcher and Reagan's words to undermine the legitimacy of the British state. In these

[5]Of course, they fucking do.

[6]This wasn't too big of an issue since they never liked playing there anyways.

pranks, as well as their music, Crass's anarchist values and politics and their focus on disruption, conflict, and negation are centered.

However, Jim Donaghy highlights that the early anarcho-punk bands, like Crass, embraced anarchism but did so with little knowledge of the anarchist canon. Yet even without the legacy of the canon, or maybe because of their lack of connection to the canon, the anarcho-punk movement was "a force for real social change: a genuine revolutionary movement" (Donaghey 2020: 169). Traditional socialist and anarchist organizations, such as Class War, a UK-based anarcho-syndicalist group, regularly criticized Crass for their politics. Crass's hostility toward labor organizing, mass movement building, and the like was seen as being rooted in bourgeois values and not radical or revolutionary praxis. In neither knowing nor caring about the legacy of anarchism, Crass's politics seemed confusing, especially to those entrenched in the history of anarchism and radical politics. For example, in the song "Big A Little A Bouncing B," they sing, "Be exactly who you want to be, do what you want to do / I am he, and she is she, but you're the only you." This song, which embraces a Stirner-esque ethos, rejects the labels of right and left and can be seen as an early example of post-left anarchism, a position that rejects the left-right label project and often embraces an egoist or individualist anarchist analysis.

The album that best expresses their nuanced and heterodox anarchism is not *Stations of the Crass* (1980) or The *Feeding of the 5000* (1979), both of which are classic punk albums, but their album *Penis Envy* (1981). *Penis Envy* was controversial on its release. Before its release, the band created a national controversy when they released a single, "Our Wedding," through the teen magazine *Loving*, which did not know the song was a prank. The single "Our Wedding" was a straight-faced mocking version of a traditional wedding song. Joy De Vivre and Eve Liberation, on the song, sing, "All I am I give to you/ You'll honor me, I'll obey you/ Rich or poor or come what may/ We'll forsake all other love/ Just we two, one flesh, one blood/ In the eyes of god/I am yours to have & hold/I'm giving you my lie." In 2005, Penny Rimbaud, the drummer and a central member of the collective, wrote in *Vice News:*

> We were recording an album called *Penis Envy*, the last track of which was "Lipstick On Your Penis," based on the old standard "Lipstick On

> Your Collar." The band's women fronted Penis Envy; it was a very feminist album, and "Lipstick" was about the institution of marriage as little more than prostitution. Having recorded that track, we realized it would almost certainly lead to copyright prosecution, so we completely rewrote the lyrics. What we ended up with was so convincingly schmaltzy that we had the idea of trying to sell it to a teenage romance magazine called Loving. It was one of those magazines which fed lies to young girls and set them up with ludicrously impossible fantasies which they can't follow, won't follow, and don't follow. Magazines like that just create heartache; they remove young people from themselves and set them up to be knocked down.
>
> Anyway, we called in at *Loving*'s IPC offices as Creative Recordings and Sound Services (CRASS) and said, "We've just made this recording and think it would be suitable for your publication." They jumped at it, saying, "It's great, fantastic. We're about to do a special bride [bribes] issue. How about us doing it as a free Flexi?" Which is precisely what it became. They advertised it as "Our Wedding"—an "absolute must for your wedding day." They'd bought it hook, line, and stinker, but the lyrics were frightful, banal shit about the social fantasy of marriage, you know, things like never looking at other girls or guys once you've fallen for it. It was total rubbish, but they happily gave it away with their magazine. Now, what kind of love is that? Shortly afterward, a friend in Fleet Street exposed the scam, and *The Star* printed the glorious headline "Band of Hate's Loving Message." I think there were a few sackings at *Loving* magazine. (Rimbaud 2005)

Following the hoax and media fallout, the band released *Penis Envy,* and shortly after, the Manchester police confiscated copies of the record, claiming that the album was obscene. The obscenity charge was later overturned, but the year-long legal battle cost the band significant resources and led to their breaking up in 1984. The obscenity charge and the national coverage of the prank help solidify *Penis Envy* as more than just a musical album, but a constructed situation meant to amplify tensions and serve as anarchist propaganda.

Penis Envy, like all Crass albums, was accompanied by collage art and poster work provided by Gee Vacher and drummer Penny Rimbaud. These pieces of art, all collage projects, are similar in format and style to 1920s Dada collage projects using similar styles and approaches. The front and back cover of the album appropriated readymade images of blow-up sex dolls and a hunter showing the corpses of his victims and, in doing so, radicalizes the viewer by the images by placing lyrical propaganda around the images. Death and patriarchal violence are thus juxtaposed, bringing to mind the absent referent that Carol Adams decries in the sexual politics of meat (Adams 2017). In contrast, in the included poster Crass's collage decries the gendered binary of male/female and claims that it is a tool of the current state and a handmaiden to capitalist violence by asking if "masculine/feminine perfect alliance?" Beyond the art, the album expands and explodes the logic of gender, linking patriarchal violence to nuclear Armageddon, violence, and control while condemning left and right political projects for undermining creative and free thought through intellectual authority figures.

In the song "Where Next Columbus," a mocking title rejecting the legacy of "great men" and the position that thinkers "discover" truths, Eve Libertine critiques the authority of Marx and other prominent thinkers, such as Mussolini, Jung, Einstein, Jesus, and Sartre. A mix of left and right, philosophers and scientists, psychologists and religious figures, are all mocked. In turning the authority of these voices into a form of oppressive control, Crass rejects the abstract logic and ontology of Western thought. The song exposes the ideological power of thought as a tool of comfort; it provides a frame for understanding the world, but ideology also limits possibility and expression in structuring the world. And why? Because there is nothingness at the core of our world.

The critique of patriarchy is found in the songs "Berketex Bride" and "Bata Motel," "Smother Love," and "Our Wedding." These songs together provide an argument against gender and highlight a constructivist logic, in which gender socially functions as a tool to maintain the system's structures and to allow for the exploitation of both men and women. This is years before the groundbreaking work of Judith Butler's *Gender Troubles* (1990). In "Smother Love," Crass focuses on how gender norms link to the capitalist logic of property. In politicizing the personal and marriage and linking those personal politics to the broader systemic nature of capitalism and the state, Crass refuses to allow the person to remain personal, and, even as they are accused of being "individualists," they always link the individual to the systemic in exciting ways. They expand their gender analysis in "Berketex Bride" when they highlight the ways that the norms and language around gender construct what it means to be a woman but in a way that avoids gender essentialism but instead is more rooted in a more queer and nonbinary approach that is close to the gender nihilism that started this chapter. As Alysson Escalante writes: "The negation of all things, ourselves included, is the only means through which we will ever be able to gain anything" (Escalante 2015). Gender, as performative practice, crashes into the structural logic of state power as Crass critiques the institution of marriage. The bride (which they sometimes exchange with the word bribe) provides the socially productive labor needed to keep the husband a functional worker for the capitalist system.

The bridge between enforced gender norms, patriarchy, and the state with the logic of exploitation and death of the capitalist system is found in the song "Systematic Death." "Systemic Death" tells the story of a boy and girl's intertwined lives from childhood to marriage to their untimely death during a nuclear war. The lives of our two characters are haunted at all points by indoctrination. While the boy is indoctrinated with masculinity and liberal workerism, the girl is brainwashed with the logic of femininity, defining her value primarily through her sexual proclivities and domestic labor. "They'll fuck her mind so they can fuck her silly," Eve sings as the marching drums bang and the distorted guitar loudly weeps. As the story continues, the two marry and move to the suburbs, where the man works his life away for a wage, and the woman sacrifices her life to maintain the stability of the home. Capitalism sucks away life, turning both of them into alienated and unhappy beings who can only find the simulacra of joy and happiness through consumption.

As the spectacle encircles their life, consumption replaces joy and passivity replaces agency, and they trade their life force for stability, but even that stability is a lie. In poking at the futility of life under capitalist production, the song confronts the spectacle logic of bourgeois life. Showing that the American or British Dreams and the claim of capitalist progress are all ideological lies, the song crashes to an end with the wreckage of a bomb falling on the couple's half-bought home. Like many punk songs, it ends abruptly, as abruptly as lives ends when nations bomb cities. The abrupt ending serves as a way to reinforce the violent chaos of contemporary life and also as a tool to jar and unsettle the listener; to not allow them to be too comfortable in genre norms or expectations. In contrast with the politics of sacrificing your life for the lie of bourgeois comfort, the listener is brought into a constructed situation and asked to be a coconspirator with Crass against the system. If the world is going to be destroyed—be it by nuclear war or climate change—why should we, or anyone, not live life to the fullest? If we could die as abruptly as the song ends, why are we wasting our lives working full time to enrich people who have zero concerns if we live or die?

The first generation of punk was part of what Richard Hell called "the blank generation," and, as a whole, "punk rejected the perception of progress; the notion that society was moving forward toward something better—socially, economically, and culturally. No future" (Skov 2023: 145). The threat of nuclear Armageddon during the Cold War, the economic collapse of urban spaces in the 1970s, and the failures of the 1960s revolutionary pushes led early punk to believe that there was no path forward. The no-future logic, and the focus on crisis, collapse, and failure, is also found later in Crass's album, as contemporary life is framed as a form of collective and individual suicide. In "Healthy Surface," the suicidal impulse in a life structured around the current state becomes a critique of the entire system. This functionally attacks the assumption of liberal society—that it functions differently from the authoritarianism of Soviet communism and that the liberal project was leading toward uplift, progress, and liberation—and is instead weaponized as evidence of the inherent unsustainability of the modernist project.

Crass here is used as an example of a negationist, anti-theory, approach to politics. The negationist nature of Crass's art and politics puts them into a direct conflictual relationship with the canon of anarchism, rock, art, and political activism. This does not mean that they disengage with these canons merely that they relate to the canon in a dialectal way that seeks not to build on the old traditions but to instead torpedo them. While most of the focus has been on their lyrics, which forge a militant anarchism that is closer to Stirner than to the more classical anarchist political groups in the UK, their use of pranks as a form of constructing situations is intended to use the spectacle of consumer capitalism as a weapon to undermine that institution. The last part to discuss is their music itself. Crass, while clearly a punk band, has less in common with many of the more traditional rock influenced groups of their era—bands like the Clash and the Sex Pistols—and more of a focus on experimental noise and anti-music. Most Crass songs actively combine military march-style drumming, discordant percussion, tape and noise collage, high-pitched distorted guitars, with monotone or half-spoken and half-yelled political sloganeering. The music is more in line with experimental noise rock such as Lou Reed's *Metal Machine* or the genre of "japanoise." Novak (2013), in his book on the Japanese Noise subculture, contextualizes noise as a genre breaking form of "music" that cycles and feedbacks onto itself and to the culture more broadly. He claims:

> As a universal opposite, Noise frames many dialectical forms of knowledge:
>
> Noise is the opposite of music, as the antithesis of beautiful things admissible as art; this noise pertains to aesthetics and affective modes of cultural expression.
>
> Noise is the opposite of classification, in its violations of categorical objectivity; this noise stands at the margins of musical history and typologies of style and form.
>
> Noise is the opposite of communication, against meaningful transmissions of information; this noise embeds discourse in a binary signal-to-noise relationship.
>
> Noise is the opposite of the natural world, and its silence; this noise emerges from the urban industrialized environment and in technological conditions of social production, regulation, and control.
>
> Noise is the opposite of public consensus and corporate and state-ordered collectivity; this noise relates to the mediation of subjectivity by overlapping projects of globalization, cultural nationalism, local infrastructure, and subcultural identity. (Novak 2013: 229–39)

To put it another way, state and capitalist relations desire stability and predictability and noise undermines this project, highlighting the violent nature of modern technodystopian society and in making the listener uncomfortable breaks the spell of the spectacles spectatorship logic. Of course, all new sounds are first described as noise—think of the hostility toward hip-hop by many white suburban older listeners—and as they become culturally accepted, they become "music." Noise, as an experimental approach, attempts to resist that genre capture. Crass, as a noise punk rock band, made their music impossible to play on radio stations and even hard for bands to cover.

The discordant and jarring quality of their music can actually be most clearly heard, not by Crass themselves, but by anti-folk artist Jeffrey Lewis's album *12 Crass songs*, where he does folk influenced covers of Crass songs with vocal support from Helen Schreiner. This album of covers was made, according to Lewis, because "At a certain period in history it might have been crucial for Crass to get those songs across by tying them to a certain attitude and style, but in a different period that attitude and style becomes a barrier to the songs, it holds the songs back instead of pushing the songs onwards." Yet even with the more soft indie rock quality of the album, the jarringness of the music is still clear. Vocals mix like oil and water with the guitars, and the drums trash about as if they were almost made for a different song. Crass, either through Lewis or their original noise and punk records, are a form of anti-music made for antisocial radicals. And are a form of political project that is, at its core, anti-theoretical.

At this point, much of politics is seemingly foreclosed in the West, where capitalist realism has made revolutionary or anti-capitalist thinking nearly impossible. Anti-theory rejects the sacred and scientific logic of progress and in undermining the root ontological foundations of contemporary political life cracks open spaces for new radical visions. This book will be including a range of thinkers often excluded from the worlds of respectable philosophy and theory. This will include fringe or forgotten academics, activists, punk musicians, artists, and film and television. In addition, this book will reject most of the ontological assumptions of liberal, and even radical, political thought. The carnivalesque quality of this project finds the power and the beauty in the excluded grotesque and relishes the chattering of the absurd while also developing into the pits of existential despair and the guerilla camps of insurrectionary playfulness.

An Outline of Things to Come: From Anti-Theory to an Anti-Introduction

Horkheimer and Adorno, in *The Dialectic of Enlightenment*, provide a profound and unrelenting critique of how the mass consumer entertainment industry has, in conjunction with industrialism and capitalism, created a world increasingly less creative, expressive, and magical. In place of creativity, the cultural industry imposes on capitalist society a series of norms and conventions that homogenize culture. They write, "The cultural industry has finally posited this imitation as absolute. Being nothing other than style, it divulges style secret: obedience to the social hierarchy" (Horkheimer, Adorno, and Schmid Noerr 2002: 102–3). While they were writing about music, television, film, and the like, the same logic also applies to academic work, which is structured around norms and genre conventions. For example, most social science and humanities academic books use cookie-cutter introduction formats. Instead of a traditional introduction, this section will deconstruct the prevalent genre norms within academic introductions by engaging with the introduction for my first book, *Cooking Up a Revolution: Food Not Bombs, Homes Not Jails, and Resistance to Gentrification (Parson 2019)*. The goal of the analysis is not to contend that these genre norms are "good" or "bad" but to explore the ideological and political function that the norms reinforce. The two norms explored are the personal narrative and the outline of chapters.

My first book starts with a personal introduction where the author contextualized life story and experience within the logic and topic of the book. The introduction claims:

> I was intellectually curious but stuck, learning within a boring and hierarchical education system. I had no idea what to believe; all I knew was that I hated the conservative and apathetic political climate I found in San Diego. That culture, the overreliance on cars to traverse the web of highways, and the high cost of rental space meant that there were few radical community centers or info shops that a careless kid could get to. (Parson 2019: 1)

This personal narrative is a selective story that highlights specific traits in telling about my lengthy experience within the anarchist activist community and how *Food Not Bombs* helped educate me on the politics of mutual aid, prefigurative politics, and the social implications of gender, class, and race. The story, while not a fiction, is not the full version of myself. Like all memoirs, personal stories are embedded within the politics of masking in which all of us present our framing as an authentic representation of the self. Jello Biafra sang, on the Dead Kennedy's song "Halloween" about the social role of masking, contrasting the freedom of dressing up on Halloween with the day-to day-life of hiding our complex selfs, asks, "Why not everyday, are you so afraid, what will people say?" The social norms of neoliberalism fuses with the network of self-panoptic social media to create a complex arrangement of branding as identity. It does not take long, as Wendy Brown in *Undoing the Demos* writes, "neoliberalism thus does not merely privatize—turn over to the market for individual production and consumption—what was formerly publicly supported and valued. Rather, it formulates everything, everywhere, in terms of capital investment and appreciation, including and especially humans themselves (Brown 2015: 176)." In short, neoliberalism dictates that we all act within the bounded logic of the market, this shapes our expression of ourselves, pollutes our relationships with others, and even shapes our own internal narratives of the self.

The personal narrative in the introduction to my first book served competing purposes. First, the narrative was provided to bring the reader into the story. Connecting with a personal story or creative nonfiction prose is more accessible than academic texts' more abstract and alienating language. The impulse to counter academic language's obscure and gatekeeping intellectual phrasing is valuable, but the counterproject is often shallow. Since my book returned to the jargon used in academic institutions, the personal prose served as an oasis from the desert of academia that swallowed up most of the book.

Second, the personal narrative at the start of my book provided a space for expressions of performative identity. This norm, which can be traced to the critique of academic objectivity by postcolonial, feminist, and critical race scholars, played an important historical role, but since then the radical critique of early intersectional identity politics has been coopted by neoliberal performance. Originally intersectional personal narratives functioned as critiques of the zero-point epistemology of enlightenment science and Western colonial projects while also rejecting the positivist and supposedly objective scientism of social science and humanities. As a critique of the "truth" of Western scientific epistemology, these narratives served an important function. But, I am skeptical that these narratives function the same way today. Instead, I notice an attempt to share identity markers so that a reader can use that as a shorthand to know if your analysis can tap into Truth. This wrongly assumes that Truth is the product of academic work, but it is not. Truth is an illusionary goal and a dangerous phantasm. To link Truth to identity also shifts politics to personal ontology, a new form of zero-point epistemology rooted in essentialism. Olúfẹ́mi O. Táíwò, in *Elite Capture*, explores the nuanced way that such focus on identity as ontology, when embedded with neoliberalism, actually allows for the further capture of institutions by elites. Táíwò writes:

> Deference as a default political orientation can work counter to marginalized groups' interests. We are surrounded by a discourse that locates attentional injustice in the selection of spokespeople and book lists taken to represent the marginalized rather than focusing on the actions of the corporations and algorithms that much more powerfully distribute attention. This discourse ultimately participates in the weaponization of attention in the service of marginalization. It directs what little attentional power we can control at symbolic sites of power rather than at the root political issues that explain why everything is so fucked up. (Táíwò 2022: 72)

In academia, an institution that is essentially captured by elites, identity performance can be a tool to shield the author from critique and to obfuscate the way that their work and their analysis play into the broader politics of capitalist accumulation and the maintenance of empire. This does not mean that there are not intense class divisions within academia. The neoliberal shift in education has led to the precarity of adjuncts and the increased exploitation of teaching faculty. However, the personal narrative of academic books rarely focuses on the relationship between the individual and the broader institutions of social control—including higher education. If such a personal narrative does such work and puts pressure on the entire institution of academia, it is an actual radical use of the genre norms, as it undermines the logic of meritocracy and the lie of democratic inclusion that higher education advertises.

Instead, most personal narratives, including the one in my first book, provide space for a particular performance. In my case, the intro was meant to show that my research was not just an intellectual pursuit but that my academic work is intimately linked to my work on the ground. I provided evidence of my feminist and radical bonafide, letting the reader know that someone with good politics and values is writing the book.

In its performative forms, the personal narrative is analogous to the "confessional" that served as an oppressive control apparatus in Foucault's *History of Sexuality*. The confessional, Foucault writes, "By virtue of the power structure immanent in it, the confessional discourse cannot come from above, as in the ars erotica, through the sovereign will of a master, but rather from below, as an obligatory act of speech which, under some imperious compulsion, breaks the bonds of discretion or forgetfulness" (Foucault 1990: 62). The confessional, introduced into Christianity during the Lateran Council of 1215, shifted power relations. Where previously guilt was beaten out of a person through acts of torture, now the guilt of consciousness was freely expressed by subjects to those with power over them. In exchange for the self-declaration of sin, the logic of forgiveness allowed for penance—expressions of wrongness and offering a path for redemption. To Foucault, the confessional shift was tied to the overall shifting discourse of sexuality. The overall discussion of sexuality was later medicalized, turning sexuality into a more nuanced and complicated system of control. Much like the confession, the personal essay, as it often functions in social science and humanities work, provides quick labels that allow the reader to effectively place the writer within the broader nexus of social power while it allows the author to perform idealized expressions of the identities. To ask for forgiveness or express their potentially solidarity with the oppressed for whom they speak for.[7]

[7]Similarly to social media, personal narratives create an avatar of the writer, a public persona meant to create feelings of authenticity between the reader and the author. Since much of modern political and social life is overrun with simulacra and simulations, there is a quest for the authentic and embracing "real," and the personal essay functions as a form of authorial hyperreality. By making the reader feel the writer is authentically expressing themselves, the author is closer to Truth.

In an essay for the *New York Review of Books*, Merve Emre turns to Theodore Adorno and Walter Benjamin to criticize the personal narrative and complicate the ideological project it provides. Her critique confronts the political role of the "I" in the liberal conception of the world. She writes:

> The private individual is not a particular person with a particular story to tell, no matter how distinctive, original, or purely bizarre that story may be. . . . Rather, it is the idea that animates all these figures, the powerful, unobtrusive concept that gives the personal essay the appearance of ventriloquizing a singular and spontaneous subjectivity. . . . What if individual subjectivity were as much a fiction as the "I" with which it so prettily speaks? What if stressing the artifice of the first person were, as Louis Althusser argued, a strategy for masking "the internal limitations on what its author can and cannot say"? What if the real limitation of the genre were its glittering veneer of expressive freedom, of speaking and writing as a self-determining subject? What if no performance of stylish confession or sly concealment could shake this ideology loose? What if these performances only intensified the enchantments of subjectivity? (Emre 2022)

The personal narrative reinforces the author as a unique figure and embraces the neoliberal fiction that, as Margaret Thatcher stated, "There is no such thing as society." However, what if there is no "I" to speak of? At the core of the liberal ontology is understanding the individual as the foundation for social life. For instance, John Locke's defense of property starts with an assumption that the individual owns their own body, and this self-ownership is why, to Locke I gain ownership over whatever my labor, or money, tended, including the labor of workers I employ.

Similarly, Rene Descartes's famous declaration of "I think therefore I am" is often described as a defense of the body/mind dualism, which it is, but it is also a declaration of the importance of the self. If, as Descartes argues, I have no evidence that others exist, they could be illusions planted there by a devil. Then all I know, for a fact, is that I exist. Others may or may not. There is a lack of certainty, so should I not shed a tear for the horrific violence of vivisection on nonhumans Descartes engaged in. The assurance of the individual functions simplifies casual relationships and allows a specific form of autonomy to form. In *Ugly Freedoms*, Elisabeth Anker persuasively links this conception of autonomy to the Barbados slave plantation economic zones under British imperialism, which Locke was intimately connected to and helped manage and regulate. In this plantation autonomy, the individual property owner was given limited autonomy to regulate and control their property and workers. They function like mini-kings, and consider their plantations as feudal playgrounds. Anker writes:

> Locke writes that the West Indies planter is the master of a "voluntary" society, which means that all the people he controls, including servants and slaves, are thereby "consent." Locked designates the plantation as a consent-based society. Slaves have, according to Locke's just-war theory, consented to the terms of their enslavement, even as Locke suggests in the Second Treatise that colonial enslavement is not oriented by conquest, so they would not be subject to just war norms. Thus, even though the planter does not head a political society, he still heads a voluntary one that others have chosen to join and consented for him to lead. Crucially, part of what grants the West Indies planter the power to make war is his very ownership of land and slaves. (Anker 2022: 60)

The liberal autonomy of the plantation owners highlights how the individual only exists to do the exploitative relationship of control with others. The liberal political system, and its focus on the individual as sovereign, actively rejects the autonomy of those in lower social positions. The autonomy of the property owner is like that of the king, and the workers, slaves, and family members are placed into a relationship of sovereign control.

Last, there is an argument that the personal narrative undermines authorial power and makes the work more "dialogic." If I express myself and tell my story, then the reader is brought into my story, and connections between us can be formed. This is the idea of the book as a consciousness-raising project. If the introduction did such a thing, I would proudly scream its praises from the top of every mountain—and being in the mountain west, there are many mountains to scream from. Books, though, are not dialogic spaces. There is no back-and-forth. You read my story and can personally react to it, but there is no back-and-forth with me. I cannot learn from your reading of my book, or from your life experiences. Books function like television and film. They are a one-way exchange of emotion and information. This is the limit of books and why books are best served when discussed in groups. The book club fulfills the dialogic function of the book by taking the text and creating a dialog in an unmediated space of exchange. My narrative has no relation to that process unless I am in that room discussing it with you. Books can prod, make one question and link ideas together, and evoke emotions. But they cannot be dialogic. To be made real and powerful, the ideas in books must be weaponized through unmediated relationships.

The band Jawbreaker start their song "Boxcar" by singing: "You're not punk and I'm telling everyone. Hold your breath I never was one." The self-reflexive nature of the song, and the willingness to not view oneself as above or beyond their critique applies here as well. While this introduction has centered on a critique of the genre of the introduction, primarily playing on my first book's introduction, the introduction you are currently reading is not exempt from the same market forces, neoliberal platitudes, and performative expressions of the self. If my first introduction was centered around making you, the reader, feel that I, the author, was trustworthy and authentic in my engagement with anarchist mutual aid networks and in solidarity with the homeless, this introduction is meant to highlight how I am taking the role of the critic, the postmodern thinker, or, if you hate what I am doing, the sophist. It is an expression of smug distance, of the performativity of transcending the networks of forces of social control. "You don't know what I'm all about, like killing cops and reading Kerouac," Jawbreak finishes the first refrain of their song. I can say with certainty that I have never killed a cop, including the cop within my own head, and, frankly, I cannot stand Kerouac.[8] All words on a page, expressed through a reflection of personal stories, speaking for a subaltern, or through semicolon-fused sentences of postmodern scholarship, are all embedded within the same networks of power and the neoliberal need to self-brand and impress. The limits of language crash into the superstructures

---

[8]Of the beats, I have always found more in the heroin-addled words of Burroughs or in the Jewish melancholia of Ginsberg. In fact, in the deeply heartbreaking hours after my dad succumbed to the cancer that ravaged his body, I sat down and read all of Ginsburg's "Kaddish" before with my mom reading the Mourners Kaddish in broken Hebrew.

of economics and governmentality, highlighting that there might not be a way past some sort of reification. Similarly Foucault wrote, "Don't ask me who I am or to remain the same. Leave that to the bureaucrats and our police to see that our papers are in order" (Foucault 2010: 17). Most importantly, ontological truth is not linked to any author's identity, self-expressed or perceived, because authenticity is not a shortcut to truth and is always bound into the larger matrices of powers that shape the self.

The second-genre convention that my first book embraced was the detailed outlining of the chapters to come. In my first book, the section "Our Path from Here" previewed the remaining chapters and their arguments. I wrote:

> Chapter 2 provides an introduction to Food not Bombs, by providing a brief history of the group, from their involvement in the anti-nuke movement in Boston to their role in providing disaster relief after Hurricane Katrina. . . . Finally, this chapter provides an analysis of the Food, not Bombs political project. While figures like Howard Zinn have stated that Food Not Bombs' politics are simple to forward fight against militarism and feed people—I contend that their political project is much more nuanced and complicated. (Parson 2019: 17–18)

The list of chapters serves a few practical functions. First, it provides a roadmap for the reader, allowing them to understand the book's trajectory. While this can be seen as helpful, a deeper question is: Why must roadmaps be provided? Academic books are not trip ticks; they are not Google map directions; they are explorations of ideas and thoughts. They are curated experiences meant to provoke thought. As a culture, there is a norm against "spoiling" movies or novels, but, apparently, there is no such norm against spoiling every twist and turn within an academic manuscript. In fact, that is encouraged! This is directed mainly by political economy, as academic presses regularly offer options to purchase book chapters separately. Like songs on an album, book chapters have become ala cart consumables. The totality of the album has already been degraded by the shift to parceling out music via streaming and song purchasing, and academic books are following this same trajectory. Instead of an album, books are collections of self-contained chapters to be consumed.

While selling individual chapters is relatively new, the norms against reading books as cohesive documents have been prevalent since, at least, when I attended graduate school where some classes required so much reading that completing it all was impossible. This was a teachable moment; I was advised to read only the intro, the conclusion, and, at most, one chapter from the book. With this approach, books could be crossed off from my reading list while only knowing enough about the book to write the sentence or two needed for a paper. This "fast thought" is similar to fast fashion or fast food in that it combines accessibility, consumer choice, and a checklist logic of experience. Ideas are meant to be condensed into "elevator pitches," and universities provide training for three-minute dissertation or thesis proposals. Talks are modeled after TED talks or short YouTube clips of pop analysis. There is, of course, nothing wrong with accessible, short, playful, or entertaining forms of thought as these are the traits of good radical propaganda. But, the same is true for consumer clickbait. The power of the spectacle has turned everything into a consumable, including experiences and learning, so it is no surprise that books have been shaped and altered. However, that does not mean the process should happen without reflection and a critical tone. In my first book, the different chapters were sold piecemeal, and that was a tool that allowed increased access to the book. I played along with it. The goal here is not to prove that I am "pure" and that others are "corrupted." We are all corrupted under late-stage capitalism, and the desire for "purity," like the desire for "authenticity," leads to a dead end.

This book will provide no outline or road map. I intend it to be like a haunted house. Each chapter has jump scares, which work best if you go along for the ride. So sit down, make sure the bar is safely placed on your lap, and enjoy. Or don't.

1

The Crisis of the Liberal Representational Order

The destruction of everything is the beginning of something new
Your new world is on fire and soon you'll be too
—REFUSED, "THE APOLLO PROGRAM WAS A HOAX" (1998)

In his famous twelve theses on Feuerbach, Marx stated, "The philosophers have only interpreted the world in various ways; the point is to change it" (Tucker, Marx, and Engels 1978: 145). If this is the case, woe is the history of philosophy. We have gained few insights into Truth for the thousands of years of Western philosophical thought, and our methods of interpretation have barely grown. We shifted our representational and symbolic orders from that of religion to that of the state and science. God becomes the Sovereign, the psalms, the scientific method, and we yell from the mountain that we are the new masters of this world. If we have failed to understand how to interpret the world, our projects to change and transform the world are even more disarming.

"The Earth Dies screaming while I lay dreaming," Tom Waits (1992) serenades as the edifice of Western industrial systems—politically, socially, economically, and philosophically—crumbles. The Western industrialists, including their coconspirators of violence in the developing world, have built elaborate set pieces, like Mussolini lining the areas outside the trains with fake buildings to project order and progress. Banal cheerleader for the status quo, Stephen Pinker (2012), even claimed that "As one becomes aware of the decline of violence, the world begins to look different. The past seems less innocent; the present less sinister" (xxvi), while industrial pollutants kill at least nine million a year (Wallace-Wells 2022). At the same time, tree roots break through the concrete, the ocean waters reclaim the lands ceded to the air during the last ice age, and our cultural institutions distract our attention away from the scream of the world. We need a philosophy that does not merely seek to interpret the world but to decompose the artifices of industrial society.

The original vision of the Enlightenment was, as Adorno and Horkheimer assert, to liberate humanity from the domination of nature and myth via the rationality of science and reason. Like agent orange, the tools of the Enlightenment burned away the forests which hid the parts of the world humans feared and could not comprehend. The Enlightenment did nothing to help humanity win the war against fear and the unknown but did poison the world, incinerate flesh, and imprison human and nonhuman spirits within a planetary prison. Auschwitz's smokestacks, Bhopal's fumes, and Fukushima's radiation are examples of the dark side of the Enlightenment's legacy. The tools of modernity did not liberate us from domination. On the contrary, the power of domination has only grown.

Reason and rationality have not even dethroned their primary target, God. The more the world becomes demystified, or we perceive it as demystified, the more intensely people cling to the irrational, the mystical, and the absurd. Science has not replaced God but has merely taken the place of the Meshhit, the Jewish angels of destruction. In some branches of Judaism, these angels are created by the sins of humanity and sin we have done! Oppenheimer, as he saw the devastation he created with the atomic bomb, famously quoted the Bhagavad-Gita when he declared: "Now I become Death, the destroyer of worlds." And Death he became. Analytic thought and positivism have done little to provide us with valuable lenses of interpretation; the world of humanities—the poetic, the musical, the creative—has done more. However, even those worlds of poems and prose, of oil on canvas or clay in hands, and those means of tapping into the unconscious—from psychedelics to tarot—can provide us glimpses, not of truth, but something more profound: they tap into the untruth that is the world we inhabit.

Progress, progress, progress, the priests of technocratic rationalism chant, but only by mortgaging the future. The climate crisis threatens the ability of human civilization to thrive on the planet's surface but even in extinction entrepreneurs can find a means to accumulate profits. It is, of course, hubris to assume that our science accurately describes the world we inhabit, but while we should reject the claims of Truth that science makes, we should not reject all of the lessons it teaches, much like we should not reject the entirety of religious or spiritual traditions. As flawed as the logic that implies that modeling science provides us access to the Truth of the world, the models do highlight a potentially catastrophic future. Science is not the only proof of this. The devastation of the world is felt in our bones and exists everywhere in our cultural productions. It manifests in many ways, including our apathy and anger toward our political institutions and the desire to find and slaughter scapegoats. Politicians and activists are bemoaning voter apathy, celebrity saviors are lecturing the "masses" about their climate footprint before enjoying gourmet meals on private planes, capitalists and bankers are trying to squeeze every dollar from the corpse of the planet, and our entire cultural apparatus is working overtime to quell anxiety and keep the tattered ideological superstructure of capitalist realism alive and well. The status quo conceptions of political life—liberal democracy, capitalism, the state, sovereignty, and industrialism—are doomed to fail as the distance between the representational claims of state institutions and the absurdity of capitalist commodity relationships contrast with the unknowable "real" that is roaring back. As the real crashes into the ideologically mediated illusions of modernity, nihilism, anger, resentment, and neurosis spread.

The Mediated Reality, the Hyperreal, and the Crisis of Representation

We only experience the world mediated through sensory organs that cannot provide an unmediated image of the "real." For instance, our eyes can see only within a specific light spectrum; even within that spectrum, our vision is limited. Many animals—for example, the mantis shrimp—experience the visual world with much more complexity and nuance than we do. The same is true for all our senses. In addition, the chaos of the world and the range of complex and interacting forces go beyond our ability to map and understand. As Deleuze and Guattari argue in *What Is Philosophy*, much of what we call philosophy, and with it science and art, are attempts to simplify the world's chaos, to make the chaos manageable for our consciousness. In simplifying the chaos, we inevitably construct conceptual categories. These categories are not "real" but are attempts to model the real within our head. They write, "We require just a little order to protect us from chaos" (Deleuze, Guattari, and Deleuze 1994: 201). However, in the need to protect our minds from chaos, the world's reality slips through our hands like mist.

Thomas Hobbes, in the first book of *The Leviathan*, interspersed between wrongheaded assumptions of human nature and an ahistorical analysis, correctly criticizes the inability of humans to explore and understand the reality before them objectively. Hobbes writes:

> Whatsoever we imagine is finite. Therefore there is no idea or conception of anything we call infinite. No man can have in his mind an image of infinite magnitude; nor conceive infinite swiftness, infinite time, or infinite force, or infinite power. When we say anything is infinite, we signify only that we are not able to conceive the ends and bounds of the thing named, having no conception of the thing but of our own inability. . . . Also, because whatsoever, as I said before, we conceive it has been perceived first by sense, either all at once or by parts, a man can have no thought representing anything not subject to sense. No man therefore can conceive anything, but he must conceive it in some place; and endued with some determinate magnitude; and which may be divided into parts; nor that anything is all in this place, and all in another place at the same time; nor that two or more things can be in one and the same place at once: for none of these things ever have or can be incident to sense, but are absurd speeches, taken upon credit, without any signification at all, from deceived philosophers and deceived, or deceiving, Schoolmen. (Hobbes and Gaskin 2008: 19)

This limit of the human to understand the infinite and the distortions of reality conducted by our senses is why, to Hobbes, philosophic arguments must start from agreed-upon first principles and why his book so painstakingly defines root concepts. If we cannot trust that our experiences are universalized, we must define concepts clearly and develop arguments via reason, not via senses. Hobbes's claim, of course, is rooted in a long tradition of philosophy going back to Plato, whose allegory of the cave describes the mere shadows that humans understand through our sensory experience. Hobbes, though, expands this line of analysis, highlighting the material and biological reasons (at least as was apprehended at his time) for why reality is beyond our ability to perceive.

In a way, our mind functions much like digital imaging algorithms. Davide Panagia, in a piece on algorithmic political ontology, describes the digital image:

> The virtual life of the digital image is vexing because something other than representation and transcription is at stake; perhaps (though I would say "almost certainly") we are dealing with an operation of transcoding that Johanna Drucker calls "capital." The digital camera does not photochemically transcribe an image; it captures a datum of light, converts it into electronic impulses called picture elements (i.e., pixels), transcodes these as digital information, and arranges them to produce an algorithmic image. But—and here is the crucial point—the captain of information need not have a physical correlate in the empirical world. (Panagia 2021: 12–13)

In short, digital images are representational models in which small pieces of visual data are overlayed with algorithmically constructed pixels to create a facsimile of the real. Ontologically, the digital image is not a "picture" of the world, as it is but a representation of the world mediated through computer code. Our sensorial experiences of the world, of course, function similarly, as our brain, like the code, overlays points of data with layers of best guesses.[1]

This all implies that the human can never experience or view "the real." In that case, we can move to criticize the political and personal projects that

---

[1]This does not mean that the brain is a biological computer. The analogy between the brain and the computer obfuscates the actual complexity of the material world and instead centers a Cartesian framework on the world by turning the brain into a complex machine. The brain is not a machine, at least not one analogous to a machine that the human hand and consciousness create. It is also worth noting that "nature" is not a machine either.

focus on the tapping into the real like the authentic and the natural. The concept of wilderness is in many ways similar to the concept of the authentic, and, following Cronon's influential criticism, we can see the anthropocentric forces that frame the concept (Cronon 1996). By structuring the world along the binary of natural/artificial, certain strands of environmental thinking promote a quest for the authentic, a legacy of the influence of transcendental religious thought and its de-Christianized German equivalent, the work of Martin Heidegger. Such a position seeks to experience the sacralization of the natural world in which God, or dasein, exists. The authentic thus exists in a consumptive relationship of experience with the world. This goes against the general narrative of authenticity, which requires uncovering an otherwise hidden essence, but there is no essence to uncover. Instead, the quest for authenticity is a continuous process in which the different layers of the world are mined and consumed to fill the spectacle's hollow void. We will fill that void with consumption and tourist experiences, like a prisoner trying to tunnel his way to freedom.

The expansion of capitalist logic of accumulation, and enlightenment visions of domination and control, led to the commodity form colonizing all aspects of life in industrial nations. As Guy Debord contends, the spread of the commodity form leads to a situation in which "those societies in which modern conditions of production prevail presents itself as an immense accumulation of spectacles" (Debord 1994: 12). Debord highlights that the mediated nature of contemporary capitalism further abstracts the world through systems of representation. If authenticity existed or was experienced, it was before the layering of "second nature" onto the world, or, as anarchist thinker John Zerzan claims, before humans had formed symbolic thought and language. But as Steven Vogel contends, "Smart tool-users that we are, as soon as we show up in an area, we start to change it, building shelters, hunting and developing agriculture, clearing land and domesticating animals, constructing villages and cities . . . in a way that radically transforms the world that environs us so that it no longer looks like 'nature'" (Gabrielson 2016: 151). The quest for this pre-symbolic and representational human existence is a quest to grasp the illusory authentic. If our phenomenological experience of the world is mediated through a range of senses and human-constructed apparatus, then the *real* always exists outside our grasp. As such, we can never hold, gaze at, or embrace the authentic reality of the world. The quest for authenticity—in character, identity, experience, or politics—is a Sisyphean task, an impossibility that always ends in your liver being ripped out of your body and eaten.

The search for the authentic is a byproduct of modernity and industrialization. Before the violence of the Enlightenment, the natural world was shrouded in mystification. Worlds of shadows, spirits, and magic existed as a mirror to the world in which humans moved and acted. At the edge of towns, forests filled with monsters and witches threatened to consume the children of the goodly Christians. "Here be monsters," warned old maps, and the warning was not the musing of the ignorant but an accurate foreboding of what lies beyond. Before the hubris of science allowed humans to feel superior to the more-than-human-world, the world was to be feared, not mined for resources or authentic experiences. It was only with, as Francis Bacon states, humans "recover that right over nature which belongs . . . by divine bequest" that the shroud of mystification was replaced with the growing logic of administrative rationalism (quoted in Merchant 1989: 172).

Hobbes helped desacralize the sovereign shifting justifications for state violence from the philosophy of the divine right of kings, and, in doing so, the secular and religious were transmogrified to a mechanistic logic centered around a selfish quest for power. Foucault contends that this shift in the logic of sovereignty elucidates why we see a shift from punishment as a spectacle of suffering to supposedly redemptive punishment that transforms and domesticates the soul. The religious character of sovereignty was not destroyed but merely hides behind secular authority. Sovereignty was first shrouded in the mystification of the world and later sacralized in the logic of rationality and reason; as such, secular sovereignty is haunted by the ghosts of the religious. As Carl Schmitt argues, "All significant concepts of the modern theory of the state are secularized theological concepts not only because of their historical development . . . but also because of their systematic structure, the recognition of which is necessary for a sociological consideration of these concepts. The exception in jurisprudence is analogous to the miracle in theology" (Schmitt 2005: 36). The sacred, though, always needs its counter, the blasphemous, whose oppression and subjugation are the border that defines the sacred.

If the modern is merely the secularized religious order, then, at its core, modern nation-state sovereign is inherently monarchical. In a democracy, it is not the people as a multitude that is sovereign but "the people" as an abstract category. The category thus functions no differently from that of the king, highlighting again that the state is the foundation of sovereignty, and the people merely a category imposed on the multitude and maintained through the coercive power of the state—that is, its military, policy, and legal apparatus. Hardt and Negri noted this, stating:

> Sovereignty can properly be said to exist only in a monarchy because only one can be sovereign. If two or three, or many were to rule, there would be no sovereignty because the sovereign cannot be subject to the rule of others. Democratic, plural or popular political forms might be declared, but modern sovereignty really has only one political figure: a single transcendent power. (Hardt and Negri 2003: 85)

The monarchical nature of sovereignty is why the executive branch of the United States is protected from criminal charges, why states around the world maintain the logic of a symbolic emperor, and why, as Schmitt contends, it is not "the people" but the executive that has the power to declare a state of emergency.

With the supposed death of the divine rights of kings, legitimacy for the political shifted to the will and desire of "the people." There is no "we the people," only a multitude constructed into a people through the apparatuses of state power and the linguistic act of constitution writing. In his analysis of the US Constitution and the inherent trouble in creating a republic, Derrida writes, "[The people] do *not* exist as an entity, the entity does not exist *before* this declaration, not *as such*. If it gives birth to itself, as a free and independent subject, as a possible signer, this can hold only in the act of the signature. The signature invents the signer" (Derrida 1986: 49). As such, the representative signs as a representative of the collective will, but the collective people do not exist prior to the declaration of the will. Speaking for a subject is the moment the subject being spoken of is formed. The original absurdity of this act haunts the systems of representative government as that representational sleight of hand serves as the primary force of legitimating the secular state. It is this tension between the liberal representative logic of the "people" and the monarchical and sacred logic of the state that creates the gap of representation that puts the entire edifice of the liberal order in crisis.

The will and desire of the people, a constantly redefined fiction, must be constantly appealed to maintain the state. Rituals of democracy, such as voting, protest, and lobbying, are deployed much like the Eucharist is for catholic mass. The ballot is the body and protest the blood of our political lord. Amen. Through cannibalistic consumption, mediated through rituals of voting, we are constantly codified as members of the flock. This does not mean, as some anarchists contend, that not voting will undermine the legitimacy of that state; on the contrary, those who refuse the Eucharist are not exempt from the institution's violent power but are instead its primary target. Under the guise of representational logic lies the same sovereign power of the spectacle of violence. At its best, a collective strategy of refusal can remove the mask of representation showing the untrue reality of democratic sovereign power; at worst, it can spur a fascistic project to replace the mask of democratic representation with the mask of representational violence.

It is in this disconnect between our mediated, representational world—democracy—and the actual reality of state power—coercive state power—that much of the current malaise with democratic institutions of the state can be found. To maintain the illusion of representation, there is a constant desire to search for the authentic representative who truthfully represents the "people." Much like any quest for the authentic, this quest is impossible, as the people do not exist except through a discursive sleight of hand and, as such, cannot be represented. This reality was understood by Rousseau, who contended that "as soon as a nation appoints representatives, it is no longer free; it no longer exits" (Rousseau 2019: 221). But, of course, it was wrong for Rousseau to assume that sovereignty resides within the people in the first place or that a "general will" is any less a fiction. What happens when representatives are elected is not the elimination of sovereignty, which permanently resided in the spectacle of power and violence, but the creation of the illusion that the people ever existed. Once the simulacra of the sovereign people are forged, the multitude seeks to be represented in that simulacra. Therefore, the representational liberal state is always on the cusp of sliding into a fascistic state. Kojin Karatani, in discussing

Marx's *18th Brumaire*, states, "Representative democracy emerges via the elimination of the absolutist monarch, yet it contains within it a hole that can never be filled. The 'repetitive compulsion' within the system of modern democracy is faced with the task of filling that hole in times of crisis" (Karatani and Lippit 2012: 15–16). Karatani contends that liberal political institutions inherently fail at providing actual representation, and, as such, the desire for representation crashes into the failure of the system, opening up space for a fascistic takeover of state power. We are currently witnessing the "farcical" repetition of history as liberal institutions are reaching crisis points.

The Collapse of the Postwar Spectacle

When you support these fucking bastards the results remain the same
The starving are still hungry
The suffering still in pain
The poor still have no money
While the rich drink their champagne

—AUS ROTTEN, "WHEN YOU SUPPORT THESE FUCKING BASTARDS" (1996)

Previously, liberalism was saved from itself only through embracing the radically unliberal value of the enemy/friend dichotomy. As Schmitt highlights, the use of the enemy creates an internal cohesion that allows for a hegemonic narrative founded on opposing an existential threat (Schmitt and Schmitt 2007). Colonialism, racial apartheid, the Cold War, and the war on terror shaped the enemy/friend relationship during the history of liberal statecraft and constructed a form of liberalism that Achille Mbembe refers to as "the nocturnal body of democracy" (Mbembe and Corcoran 2019: 15). The nocturnal space requires colonial violence to maintain the democratic order. He explores how lynching and black exclusion from politics were essential in constructing the American state and that colonial violence was essential for constructing Europe. By highlighting this interconnection of imperial violence and the formation of the liberal state, he highlights how the cohesion of liberal society only existed with the colonization and oppression of the other.

To Mbembe, the violence of colonialism and slavery are not mere historical moments but are fundamental to the liberal democratic state. He writes, "But the brutality of democracies has simply been swept under the carpet. From their origins, modern democracies have always evinced their tolerance for certain political violence. They have integrated forms of brutality into their culture, forms borne by a range of private institutions acting on top of the state, whether irregular forces, militias, or other paramilitary or corporatist formations" (Mbembe and Corcoran 2019: 17).

The nocturnal nature of liberal democracy and its requirement for surrogacy to function has provided the backdrop for endless enemy/friend dynamics to create internal cohesion for the Western democratic order. Using the enemy/friend has effectively erased the democratic nature of liberal regimes and provided a means of ignoring the representational crisis inherent in liberal democratic state formation. The existence of this threat has meant that, pragmatically, states have enacted states of exception (Agamben 2005). These exceptions illustrate the undemocratic nature of the supposedly democratic state since, as Schmitt contends, sovereignty lies in the ability to decide on the exception. Since the Second World War, the exception—especially concerning national security—has become the norm. The hiding of information to protect the state is not new, but following the horrors of the camps found at the end of the Second World War and the development of the Cold War, the liberal state had to shift its discourse to create a new enemy/friend dynamic. The liberal state defended freedom and equality and opposed the authoritarianism of fascism and state communism. This heightened tension as former internal enemies, like the black community, could appeal to liberal values. This act illustrated the contradiction between reality and the representation of the state and is one of the reasons for the success of the civil rights movement, the growth of antiwar activism, and great society's attempts to rectify historical inequality and injustice (Klinkner and Smith 1999).

In the postwar era, we see the development of what Guy Debord calls the spectacle. The spectacle is "a social relationship between people that is mediated by the image" in which there is a "concrete inversion of life, and as such, the autonomous movement of non-life" (Debord 1994: 12). The spectacle is encapsulated with the rise of TV and commercial culture and mass production of goods. The newly formed relationships between humans and the new communication technologies shape our thoughts, actions, and conceptions of time. Debord contends that "the origins of the spectacle lie in the world's loss of unity, and its massive expansion in the modern period demonstrates how total this loss has been" (Debord 1994: 22). The loss of unity is part of the project in which liberal democracy lost its cohesion as the new enemies led to the shattering of internal order and the increasing of social tensions. The spectacle becomes a mediation tool in which the tensions of representation are depoliticized in the West, and the citizen or subject is transformed into the consumer. The diffuse spectacle followed the logic of capitalism. It existed as a logic of choice—Coke or Pepsi, Dominos or Pizza Hut, Republican or Democratic—but undergirding the logic of choice was a web of structures that channeled politics and decisions away from the political and the social to that of consumption. In contrast, the concentrated spectacle of Soviet rule, there were no citizens, only subjects. Subjects' identities were linked to the images and narratives of the leader. Stalin and Mao exemplify this centralized spectacle as their visage—and the fear and adoration it engendered—shaped the subjectivity of those living in the Soviet or Chinese communist states. The citizen ceased to exist in either the diffuse or the concentrated spectacle. The death of the citizen also meant the death of the revolutionary and the hollowing out of political subjects, leaving a gaping void in the center of representational politics that can only be filled by consumerism.[2]

---

[2]Meaning and purpose are fraught categories, and we should not fetishize them. The core of Nietzsche's work illustrated that meaning is a constructed category, and contemporary work from figures like Eugene Thacker highlights the lack of inherent meaning in life. The cosmos is not organized around us; we are unimportant to the universe. There is even an argument that there is no reason to value life versus nonlife on a cosmic scale. But what is important here is that humans seem to want a meaning to exist reflexively. For Nietzsche, this meaning could be found in the individual will to power, but that meaning is not universal, inherent, or true in any grand scheme. It is merely a conditional meaning that gives a form of purpose to individuals. However, for most humans—being the social animals we are—meaning is more collectively formed. In his piece "Neutralization and Depoliticization," Schmitt highlights that the move to neutralize politics through the lens of science or technology (and here, I would add the consumer spectacle) leads to the hollowing of meaning and, with it, a profound nihilism. I would contend that at the core there is no meaning only an empty void and attempts to hide that brutal untruth via nationalism, revolutionary subjectivity, religious or spiritual beliefs, and practices; the occult is unstable and therefore needs to be constantly created and recreated.

The stability for the consumer capitalist spectacle was predicated on a system of continual economic growth, the imperial expansion of empire, and the creation of a "managed democracy" (Wolin and Hedges 2017). This golden age of consumer capitalist stability has since fallen apart, and the diffuse spectacle of the 1960s has shifted to that of an integrated spectacle. "Once it attains the stage of the integrated spectacle," Debord explains, "self-proclaimed democratic society seems to be generally accepted as the realization of a fragile perfection" (Debord 2011: 21). The fragility of this representational system has led "the controlling center has now become occult: never to be occupied by a known leader or clear ideology. And on the diffuse side, the spectacle has never before put its mark to such a degree on almost the full range of socially produced behavior and objects" (Debord 2011: 9). In short, we see the diffusion of the spectacle to cover all aspects of social and political life and, with it, a further obfuscation of the ideological underpinning of the society. The integrated spectacle can thus be understood as embracing the core values and logics of neoliberalism, which, Wendy Brown states, is "a governing rationality through which everything is 'economized' and in a particular way: human beings become market actors and nothing but, every field of activity is seen as a market, and every entity (whether public or private, whether person, business, or state) is governed as a firm" (Brown 2017: 30). Neoliberalism colonizes and imposes a market logic on all aspects of our life, to Brown, which is another way of asserting what Debord claimed in the 1960s. We are no longer just workers who sell our labor as commodities and then, in turn, consume with our wages, but we view our entire being as that of a commodity and brand, selling and endless hustling.

The disappearance of a political enemy, and the failure of the United States to forge another existential threat in Islamic fundamentalism or China, has opened space for the crisis of representation to reemerge. At this point, consumer spectacles are not able to maintain the stability and order that liberal representative democracy requires. McKenzie Wark calls this a shift to the "spectacle of disintegration." She writes, "Let's call the endpoint reached by the integrated spectacle the disintegrating spectacle, in which the spectator gets to watch the withering away of the old order, ground down to near-nothingness by its own steady divergence from any apprehension of itself" (Wark 2013: 3). The disintegration of the spectacle does not lead to the ending of a spectacle of consumer capitalism, merely the fragmentation of the messages and the expansion of the message makers. At first, this disintegration seemed potentially liberating, as can be seen by the early advocates of the internet hoping that it would democratize. In a way, they were right: the disintegrating spectacle opened space for the mass democratization of spectacles, replacing one singular narrative or reality with a nearly endless stream of competing meanings. "Everywhere one seeks to produce meaning, to make the world signify, to render it visible," as Baudrillard states, "we are not, however, in danger of lacking meaning; quite the contrary, we are gorged with meaning, and it is killing us" (Baudrillard 2012: 63). The breakdown of the Cold War elite consensus, the expansion of competing meaning claims facilitated by the internet, and the neoliberal capture of political life have amplified the crisis that Baudrillard noted. The only force keeping the crisis of both representation and meaning in check for the history of liberal politics has been the presence of a political enemy to forge a fascistic cohesion of the social.

In previous crises of liberal politics, from the election of Bonaparte to the takeover of power by Hitler and Mussolini, there was a hole in the center of politics because the system could not represent everyone. That hole was filled with an authoritarian and mythical figure that, much like the old kings, represented "the people" through a spectacle of power. The weak felt powerful because of their relationship with the sovereign, but that figure did not represent them but merely represented the power that the people wished to hold. Today, the crisis of representation, much like the commodity form, exists throughout society. The original crisis still exists—as we see the endless debate about finding "authentic candidates" who represent the people and gleeful and sadistic appeals to strongmen—but there is a second crisis, the identity crisis. In this crisis, the partisan becomes a representation of the personality of the political leader, and, as such, they not only seek to be represented by the spectacle of politics, but they also must represent the spectacle in their own identity. From that crisis, the partisan identity fuses with our consumer identity, which has been trained by brand capitalism to exist as both the consumer and the advertiser. There is a hole at the center of our society and a hole in the center of ourselves. These chasms will only grow as the spectacle society reaches its breaking point.

The Current Crisis of Representation

The State is like a vast slaughterhouse and an enormous cemetery, where under the shadow and the pretext of this abstraction (the common good) all the best aspirations, all the living forces of a country, are sanctimoniously immolated and interred.

—MIKHAIL BAKUNIN

The liberal political institutions are taking the current world as the baseline for what is possible, and, as such, they fall into the trap Fisher calls "capitalist realism." According to Mark Fisher, "Capitalist realism" occurred after the Cold War when the capitalist economic system expanded to the entire planet. At this point, capitalism had reified the market to such a degree that there is no outside to the capitalist system (Fisher 2009). Without a viable outside to the capitalist project, the spectacle of neoliberal capitalism has cannibalized the outside. The last outposts of radical imagination are churned into brands, identities, and consumer products. Any critique that points its finger at the core values of the current system, from markets to the concepts of sovereignty or representation, must be ignored. The liberal inability to imagine a world postcapitalism leads, no matter how much they scream pragmatism, to engage in irrationally rational claims. Industrial capitalism is the source for most of the problems facing our planet, but since the market has been reified and naturalized, the only solution that are deemed pragmatically available are those that already dominate the liberal toolbox. This means a doubling down on the capitalist logic of exchange. Liberalism, at this moment, functions as a form of unconscious accelerationism, because in all their attempts to fix the crisis, they speed up the contradictions causing the crises in the first place. At the altars of capital accumulation, the capitalist and financiers pile up the skulls higher and higher, while the blood flows and drown the world in sorrow. Expressing a similar critique, the Salvage Collective, a group of pessimist Marxists, correctly claims that "to avert planetary disaster is to inflict an earth-sized blow on capitalist industry. It is to choose between burning a planet of value and burning the planet itself. But the death cult is so strong, so pervasive, that, against all resistance, the choice has already been made" (Allinson et al. 2021: 12). There are no tools within liberalism that can serve as anything but a stopgap. In other words, liberalism is a form of slow suicide.

Suicidal logic is what bridges liberal and fascist politics. Fascism, as Adorno and Horkheimer contend, "is not a relapse into the old barbarism but the triumph of repressive *egalite*, the degeneration of the equality of rights into the wrong inflicted by equals" (Horkheimer, Adorno, and Schmid Noerr 2002: 9). Fascism is not counter to the logic of enlightenment's desire for *egalite* but the full embrace of the dark barbarism that exists in the shadows of this concept. Fascism is not a rejection of modernity or an alternative to the logic of liberal representation, but is instead the taking of this logic to the point in which the humanist façade of the Enlightenment cracks, showing the camp guard that hides beneath. Unlike liberals, the fascists are aware that their politics are a suicide pact. Gleefully, the Trump administration's National Highway Traffic Safety Administration, in responding to California's attempt to increase fuel standards for cars, admitted that the planet faces a catastrophic future due to climate change. Instead of lamenting this reality, pretending to care, or even denying, the administration embraced the catastrophe and used it to justify not changing fuel standards (Eiliprin, Brady, and Mooney 2018).

Fascists have always prayed at the altar of death. While the Holocaust is the obvious example, Hitler's 1945 "Nero Decree," in which the Nazi dictator called for the destruction of all of German institutions—from infrastructure to cultural heritage—is an even better example. With the war nearing its end, it was better for Germany to have never existed than to have lost the war. The decree is an example of the end stages of fascism, where the leviathan cannibalizes its own body, and with it the political subjects of the state. The logic of fascism is always the logic of the camp. In this case, the fuhrer wanted to expand the showers to include the supposed Aryans, and the guards refused. This does not mean that the street-level fascists did not fetishize death. They did, in intimate and personal ways, which is seen in the misogynistic and necro-sexuality that Theweleit found in the journals and novels of freekorp members. Theweleit, in analyzing the more macro culture of fascism's death politics, writes:

> Human productions as a rule invest their objects with life. It is the living labor of the artisan that allows a table to be created from a tree, the worker's living labor that forges a tool out of raw metal; the "mother's" living labor that enables a newborn infant to become a person. The production of our men acts conversely. It divests social products, both people and things, of the life that has entered into them, especially in war. Their mode of production is the transformation of life into death, and dismantling of life. I think we are justified in calling it an antiproduction. This antiproduction has a destructive and a creative aspect. It builds new orders from a reality that is devivified. (Theweleit 1987: 216)

Fascism is nothing but a megamachine that efficiently and callously transmogrifies life into death. But, that is also the logic of capitalist accumulation, as the billions of animals slaughtered in industrial slaughter houses, or the capitalist response to the Covid crisis makes clear. Unlike the liberals, the fascists fetishize the death politics as can be seen with the Spanish Falangist mantra of "long live death" or even the mocking phrase "ARBEIT MACHT FREI" (work shall set you free)," which adorned the gates of Auschwitz as the bodies burned.

Death cult logic emerges when the gap between an ideological position's assumptions about the world crashes into the material reality. When this happens, the adherents and priests of the faith are confronted with a fraught situation: accept the incorrectness of their ontology or direct the trains toward the camps. Ideologies are abstracted logics that attempt to map themselves onto the contours and fissures of the planetary. But the only way for an ideology to map the world perfectly is to create a perfect 1:1 model of the world, as we see in Borges' short story "on exactitude in Science" (Borges and Hurley 1998). Maps require simplification and are inherently shaped by politics, culture, and power. Good maps provide guidance and support for traversing the world, but bad maps lead to confusion and potential death. Ideologies are similar. But, even the best ideological positions will have faulty assumptions requiring the navigator to be flexible, creative, and open-minded. In a sense all future trajectories are unmapped. While the fascists are willingly directing us to death, like hunters leading bison over a cliff, liberals are lost; their map is telling them that progress is just around the next curve but material life is showing something much different. Like the Nazis, who, in 1944, saw their dream of a thousand-year Reich crumbling under the steady march of Soviet troops and tanks, liberals are unable to throw away their map and reject the assumptions that are causing the world massive harm.[3] Liberalism though is not alone, and we see all contemporary ideologies slowly transforming into death cults.

In "Capitalism as Religion," Walter Benjamin contended that the cult of capitalism differs from previous cultic logic. He writes, "Capitalism is entirely without precedent, in that it is a religion which offers not the reform of existence but its complete destruction. It is the expansion of despair, until despair becomes a religious state of the world in the hope that this will lead to salvation" (Benjamin, Bullock, and Jennings 2004: 289). Capitalism, unlike other religions, has no dogma or doctrine; it is a religion in which "there is no day that is not a feast day," and it feeds off Christianity and other faiths parasitically. It is a cult that corrupts and alters all values and systems. Benjamin, always the astute observer of the world, was correct in his lambasting of the cultic tradition of capitalism but confused the specific rituals of exchange, fetishizing them while ignoring the logic of industrialism. Horkheimer and Adorno expanded Benjamin's analysis in their critical reflection on the Enlightenment. The same values Benjamin saw in the cult of capitalism imbue all systems that grow from the tree of enlightenment domination. Both liberalism and fascism, as well as most forms of communism and socialism, are examples of the corrupting influence of industrialism and the Enlightenment. These ideological apparatuses view the world, which humans are part of, through instrumental rationality. In this view, the entire world is modeled, dissected, manipulated, and transferred via the logic of equivalence. As such,

[3]The Nazis also knew that postwar justice would have them hanging from the gallows, and therefore they had nothing but pain in their future no matter what paths they picked. Unable to accept the reality of their punishment for the atrocities they had committed, they decided on suicide. Both individually—as we saw when Hitler's brains splattered against the wall of his bunker—and collectively with the Nero decree. The liberal political establishment will do anything to maintain their hold on power, for much the same reason that Donald Trump ran for president in 2024, to avoid the violent justice that they deserve. The victims demand justice and the architects and defenders of the the system warrant punishment. But, collective suicide is preferable to the elite, who are dead anyway.

all modernistic political systems are different sects of cults competing for adherents. All are death cults, either consciously (fascism) or unconsciously (liberalism). They champion and require sacrifices—via either the extraction of resources from the earth or the draining of life force through industrial work—and require a logic of homogenization. The world becomes nothing more than a plantation, a prison, a camp, a factory. As such, all industrial projects are death cults, washing their altars in blood. For capitalism, people die for the abstract fetish of the market, for fascists for the mythical illusion of the state and mythic past, and for communists as offerings to ward and protect the proletariat. Industrialism, and its denominational offshoots, require the construction of a representational world that abstracts away from the real. A separation between the real and illusions is foundational to any priestly caste, which uses that separation as a justification for its existence. The politicians, capitalist, academics, and bureaucrats all mediate between "the people" and either the "market" or the "nature." To Debord, modernity has always been a spectacle, as modernity and the Enlightenment require a logic of representation and equivalence. The contemporary spectacle is merely augmented, broadcast with the amplifiers of technology.

At times, the separation between the real and the augmented simulation we exist in becomes painfully clear, like a person tripping over a curb as their eyes are peeled to their phone. In moments of crisis and catastrophe, the lines blur, and the spectacle loses its ability to maintain. What we glimpse is not "the real" but the untruth of the world that our ideological frames have created. The climatic disasters ravaging the world, filling our lungs with smoke and flood water, exemplify this phenomenon. Economic crises, likewise, bring the separation between the simulation and reality into conflict, as the fetish of the market starts to lose its luster as wealth melts into the air. As does war. There are no atheists in a foxhole, as the cliché says, because the pain, suffering, and fear of death makes the absurd meaningless of the violence so clear that few can maintain eye contact with that untruth. We turn to religion in the foxhole, not because of the truth that religion provides but because religion blocks our view of the deep and endless void of nothingness. Liberal demands for market reforms and democratic institutions, the fascistic image of a mythical past and unity through blood, and even the socialist vision of a worker's paradise organized through the priestly party are similar to each other. The more intense the crisis, the harder it is for the spectacle to obfuscate the violence essential to the system, and, at some point, the market (liberalism) will no longer be strong enough to distract and the state will turn toward fascism. To avoid the coming fascism, the nihilistic impulse to burn the edifice of oppression to the ground must be fueled. As the anarcho-punk band Chumbawamba (1994) sang, "Nothing ever burns down by itself, every fire needs a little bit of help."

Past, Present, Future, and the End of History

The crisis of contemporary politics is rooted in the failures of the representational political project. Representation always fails to actual represent and a hole grows at the center of the system, a hole that is easily filled with a fascistic impulse to have a leader represent sovereignty. In the history of Western liberal democracy, the worst aspects of the representational crisis were averted in at least two ways. First, by the construction of an enemy/friend dichotomy that allows for social cohesion in the face of failed representation. Second, by the creation of the colony either at the fringe of the liberal state empire or, in the case of the United States, with internal colonies. The violence committed against the other allowed for the cohesion and seeming safety of the liberal order for those behind the drone consoles.

The next chapter explores the second, existential crisis, the ecological one. Industrialism serves as a megamachine that transforms life into death and is inherently unsustainable, as it destroys the material foundations of the world. Ideologically, the logic of industrial production has become hegemonic; this hegemonic order comes into conflict with the ideological frames that justify and naturalize industrial production. Unable to reject the hegemonic logic, industrial society instead transforms itself into a death cult, doubling down on the violent causes of our ecological crisis and praying that more of the same will remedy the problem. For instance, the solution to the climate crisis is the development of industrial CO_2-removing technology, not the burning of the factories to the ground. Likewise, as liberal state institutions fall apart, the only solution offered is to endlessly attempt to patch the holes in the system. In this never-ending process of repair, there is neither energy nor vision left to move away from a system that is clearly collapsing.

The structures of the present cannot exist for much longer. The lack of sustainability that undergirds industrialism never bothered liberal political imaginations, as, according to Horkheimer and Adorno, capitalism has always positioned itself as a constantly repeating present. However, the crises of the twenty-first century—climate, inequality, social cohesion—create a ghost that haunts the zeitgeist of modern liberal society. "It is easier to imagine the end of the world than the end of capitalism" has become a truism because, as Mark Fisher contends, we inhabit a period of capitalist realism. With no alternative to capitalism and no future with a capitalist economy, we exist in a liminal space between the apocalypse and the need to continue going to work.

2

Fetish and Prophylaxis

A Cultural and Theoretical Genealogy of the Gas Mask AKA How I Learned to Hate Industrialism

On March 4, 2020, freshman congressman Matt Gaetz, a Trump loyalist, neofascist insurrectionist, and alleged sex trafficker, wore a gas mask onto the floor of the House of Representatives to mock newly enacted Covid restrictions. His wearing of the gas mask was not random. The mask is embedded with a wide range of symbolic meanings. As with other items of modern industrial life, the gas mask has a history of shifting meanings linked with society's structural logic. On specific faces, such as the soldiers and civilian populations in the First and the Second World War battlefields, it represented the preparedness of a national military or a militarized population. While on another person's face, such as an anarchist protestor clouded in tear gas, the gas mask symbolically represents a coordinated and militant resistance to state power. The gas mask is a consistent signifier of a toxified and dangerous landscape no matter the relationship. The gas mask reminds us that the air is not safe to breathe. The act of breathing, to theorist Bifo, is a powerful metaphor for the suffocation of contemporary life ravaged by alienation, anxiety, and oppression. He writes that "physical and psychological breathlessness everywhere, in the megacities choked by pollution, in the precarious social conditions of the majority of exploited workers, in the pervading fear of violence, war, and aggression" (Berardi 2018: 15). For those victims of capitalist production, the mask becomes the worn embodiment of one's relationship with industrial production. In these instances, the gas mask is a prophylactic put in place to protect life and make breathing possible. But the gas mask is also adorned on the face of those agents of state oppression—the police, military, paramilitaries, and political figures like Matt Gaetz—and in these cases, the gas mask represents the state's desire to make a landscape oppressive and suffocating. In these moments, the gas mask is a fetishistic symbol of the state's attraction to death.

Unintentionally Gaetz's attempts at humor highlight the perfect symbol for our modern times. The gas mask—and its cousin, the filtered face mask—exemplifies the danger of the air for contemporary life. According to a recent UN special report by David Boyd, seven million people die annually from air pollution and an additional two to three million from polluted water and soil. These nine million excesses deaths a year equal the high estimates of the global death total in the first eighteen months of Covid. Yet, the Covid deaths represented a form of spectacular violence before becoming "cultural endemic." Since becoming endemic, Covid deaths, like air pollution more generally, are merely the accepted slow violence of industrial capitalism. Once forms of deaths become accepted as part of everyday life, they are no longer a threat to the global economy but are instead an intimate and essential example of the sacrifices needed for the global economy to work. Remember, that reification always requires forgetting and erasure. The gas mask serves as a medium for which the ghostly image of the dead haunts the symbolic meaning of the present.

Industrial Objects and the Materiality of Symbolic Anxiety

Flowers that decay on the graves that are fresh
The problem got buried alongside the flesh

The contamination of body and soul
By nuclear waste dumped a long time ago

—SUBHUMANS (1985), "SOMEONE IS LYING"

Living and breathing in a contradiction, industrialism has two faces—interwoven and corrupted by each other. These faces look in different directions and represent the mirage of two experiences of industrialism: an ashen haze of pollution and the uncanny sanitized world of the perfectly packaged mass consumer product. Industrialism embraces a desire to cleanly separate the spheres of death from spheres of purity. However, borders do not stop pollution, which travels through the porous reality of actually existing life. This, of course, does not mean that industrialism affects everyone equally. The anarchist theorist David Watson, in his short piece "We All Live in Bhopal," reminds us that we are all impacted by the pollution and destruction of industrial production. He writes, "A powerful image: industrial civilization as one vast, stinking extermination camp. We all live in Bhopal, some closer to the gas chambers and the mass graves, but all of us close enough to be victims" (Watson 1998: 45). The bifurcation of the world into sacrifice zones and purified zones is thus both a utopian fiction and a lived reality of inequality.

The products and benefits of industrialism litter most of the major cities of this world. The web of connection facilitated by the internet and cell phone technology, the mass production of cheap food, and the success of modern pharmaceuticals can blind us to the violence embedded within these technologies. Those living comfortable do not want to look at the mass graves that industrialism requires but this does not mean that the graves are not there. Marx warned of the danger of commodity fetishism, which hides the social relations of labor that underpin capitalism, but this fetishism also obscures the sacrifices needed to make accumulation possible. No matter how much investigative journalists, academics, and global NGOs try to unmask the fetish of commodities, their reporting is always limited by the overwhelming power of the spectacle. Visibility is not a panacea under the spectacle. Debord argues that "the language of the spectacle is composed of *signs* of the dominant organization of production—signs which are the same time the ultimate end-products of that organization" (Debord 1994: 13). The mediated reality we live in—shaped by mass media, technology, and the apparatus of ideology formation—aids the power of commodity fetishism. They are obfuscating the mass graves of industrialism with a shallow pile of dirt and portraying the whistleblowers as madmen. Debord, in his short piece "Sick Planet," highlights that "The rate of production of nonlife has risen continually on its linear and cumulative course; a final threshold having just been passed in this progression, what is now produced, directly, is death" (Debord, Nicholson-Smith, and Debord 2008: 85). Yet, the deaths haunt the living world. No matter how well the myth of Promethean logic and technological progress is manipulated, the ghosts manifest themselves in symbols, like the gas mask, which create paradoxes in our understanding of the industrial world.

The symbols of industrialism, much like industrialism itself, are bound in contradictions. This is because industrialism oscillates between two poles, like celestial bodies caught in a gravitational pattern—zones of sacrifice and zones of accumulation. The paradoxes of industrialism are interlinked and create a relatively stable system of production that is, ironically, always on the verge of utter collapse: a world of shrink-wrapped objects, cellophane-covered corpses of nonhuman animals, and environmental slums like Ghana's infamous Sodom and Gamora e-waste sites. The best metaphor for industrialism might be found in one of industrialism's most significant "discoveries"—nuclear power. In a nuclear reaction, two competing forces—implosion and explosion—balance each other. If either force gets unbalanced, the entire system enters a feedback cycle known as a nuclear meltdown. Nuclear reactions, much like industrialism writ large, follow the same logic as the forces of environmental collapse, and the expanding global economies pressure each other and, ideally, create a system kept in a chaotic balance. The industrial system destroys through its pollution, and the capitalist system attempts to clean up the waste.

A part of the process of spectacle capitalism is to naturalize disaster as an inherent part of industrial production. Paul Virilio, in explaining the complex relationship between "invention" and "disaster," states:

> If, in fact, invention is just a way of seeing, of grasping accidents as signs, as opportunities, it is high time to open up our galleries to the impromptu, to that "indirect production" of science and technoscience that is the disaster,

> the (industrial or other) catastrophe. If, according to Aristotle, "accident reveals the substance," the invention of the substance is also the invention of the "accident." Seen this way, the shipwreck is indeed the future "invention" of the ship, the air crashes the invention of the supersonic plane, and the Chernobyl meltdown, the invention of nuclear power stations. (Virilio 2003: 6)

Industrial disasters are the "future invention" of industrialism. The catastrophes of the modern age are not accidents—an unexpected event or mistake—but a thoroughly expected, actuarial risk accepted via political and economic decisions. Industrial disasters are inevitability under an industrial system of production. Once the airplane is developed, air crashes are unavoidable. Once industrialism emerges, Bhopal is inescapable. Once the nuclear bombs are dropped on Hiroshima and Nagasaki, Fukushima becomes predestined. Industrialism is a system of massive productive power—the ability to shape and alter the entire system of the planet—but everything industrialism touches dies and withers on the vine. The destructive impact of industrialism cannot be cleaned or erased through its production. This is not a new realization. Industrialism is an alchemical attempt to transmogrify the blood of those sacrificed into mass consumables. Cannibalism is at the heart of our entire economic system. Next we turn to a geneology of the gas mask, unpacking the way that the symbol has always been connected to the Janus faces of industrial production.

A Genealogical Analysis of the Gas Mask: From Plague Doctors to Anti-State Protestors

It's the pinnacle of ecstasy
The spiral into blight
One shivering gasp of air

—POISON RUIN, "PINNACLE OF ECSTASY" (2023)

The feudal world was brought to its end by the spread of the bubonic plague from 1348 to 1351. During the black death, up to 60 percent of European populations and up to 50 percent of China's population died from the flea-spread disease. The bubonic plague, some scholars claim, killed between 100 million and 200 million people during its long durée. In Europe, the epidemic marked a tectonic shift for the feudal regimes, as Silvia Federici highlights in her seminal work *Caliban and the Witch*. She writes:

> Social hierarchies were turned upside down because of the leveling effects of the widespread morbidity. Familiarity with death also undermined social discipline. Confronted with the possibility of sudden death, people no longer cared to work or to abide by social and sexual regulations but tried to have the best of times, feasting for as long as they could without thought of the future. (Federici 2014: 44)

The shift in labor power that surviving peasants experienced pressured feudal masters, and led to the witch trials and other assaults on women, to regulate social production.

In a world shaped by death, the most famous image of the plague was the plague doctor (see Image 1)—a haunting visage that lurked in the waking dreams of the Covid pandemic. The visage of the doctor is described by Charles de' L'Orme, a sixteenth-century physician who codified and centralized the uniform of the plague doctor, as:

> The nose[is]half a foot long, shaped like a beak, filled with perfume with only two holes, one on each side near the nostrils, but that can suffice to breathe and carry along with the air one breathes the impression of the[herbs]enclosed further along in the beak. Under the[waxed]coat we wear boots made in Moroccan leather [goat leather] from the front of the breeches in smooth skin that are attached to said boots, and a short-sleeved blouse in smooth skin, the bottom of which is tucked into the breeches. The hat and gloves are also made of the same skin...with spectacles over the eyes. (Mussap 2019: 672)

This early outfit was pragmatic as well as symbolic. The outfit protected the doctor from miasma, what the doctors at the time assumed caused the plague, through a bundle of herbs in the beak. Medical researcher Christian Mussap defines miasma theory as contending that "noxious vapours arising from

Image 1 *Plague doctor.*

decomposing organic matter as the mechanism for disease transmission" (Mussap 2019: 673). The herbs supposedly filtered and cleaned the air. The mask, and its focus on cleaning the air, makes this a precursor to the modern gas mask and represents how symbolic meaning around protective masks are linked with the guiding logic of culture. The birdlike structure of the mask harkens to local animistic religious strands which still influence. Magic and the supernatural were essential components of the feudal imagination. Federici describes this feudal magic,

> At the basis of magic was an animistic conception of nature that did not admit to any separation between matter and spirit, and this imagined the cosmos as a *living organism*, populated by occult forces, where every element was in a "sympathetic" relationship with the rest. (Federici 2014: 141–2)

Understanding the magical conception of the Middle Ages, and how spirit and matter, nature and human life, and the cosmos all interacted, provides a means for symbolically understanding the plague doctor mask.

Claudie Lévi-Strauss argued that figures like the crow functioned as a symbolic mediator between the realms of the living and the realms of the dead (Lévi-Strauss 1963: 224). As scavengers, crows congregate at locations of death. A murder of crows is a reference to their connection to death and were a harbinger of ill omens. In this context, the plague doctor became a stand-in for the crow and as a mediator between the realm of the living and the dead. As the person tasked with providing for those dying, plague doctors became crows, modeling their appearance with that of the corvid: long beaks and head-to-toe black leather. The image of the plague doctor is a totemic response to the black death, a symbol that links the doctor with the witch as both existed in the liminal space between human and animal and between life and death.

The plague doctor symbolically highlights the cognitive landscape of preindustrial European life in the transition from feudalism to capitalism. They symbolically existed as a figure in direct relations to the dominant modes of production and the cultural power of naturalism and magic in the Middle Ages. The feudal production system was primarily localized, and the commons were a central component of social and economic life. The existence of the commons offered a location for peasants to alleviate some of the difficulties of social reproduction. The commons also created space for resistance to proto-state power and places for outcasts from society—the rebels and witches—to hide. The existence of the commons and the closeness of feudal peasants to the land also strengthened the power of animistic and totemic spirits. The plague doctor emerges in this context and embodies aspects of local magical and animist traditions while also embodying aspects of an increasingly professionalized medical community and the expansion of state power.

Foucault links the development of the modern state to the plague. To maintain power, the cities, and European proto states, used quarantine procedures and the new tools of statistics to regulate and manage people as a population. He writes that "(. . .) in order to see perfect disciplines functioning, rulers dreamt of the state of plague" (Foucault 1995: 355). Through plague management, the logic of governmentality formed helping usher in the era of disciplinary control. The plague doctor, unlike the peasant healer, thus played a central role in the creation of the disciplinary society. As an employee of the city state and part of the growing apparatus of state control, the plague doctor was a liminal figure with one leg in the mid-evil world of animism and magic and the other in the rational and patriarchal world of modern science and medicine.[1] The plague is a tool of the modern colonial state, and the expansion of industrial production and the destruction of ecosystems by capitalism only make plagues more likely.

With the enclosure of the commons, the expansion of factories, and the dawn of the era of industrial production, the animist symbolism of the plague doctor disappeared. In the Western world, the Enlightenment and the rise of rationalism attempted to demystify the realm of magic to structure the world along the logic and lines of the growing factory system. The rise of industrialism led to the spread of new social problems: industrial pollution. As states forced the enclosure of the commons, peasants were displaced from their homes and forced into cities where they became workers. The influx of new urban inhabitants led to an increase in urban fires, as housing was being built cheaply and poor areas faced severe overcrowding. It was in the context of a world being turned into a factory that American brothers Charles and John Dean, in 1823, designed their "smoke helmet" (Image 2). They intended for the smoke helmet to protect firefighters from inhalation; but it was never implemented because it cost more than the industry was willing to spend. But, the smoke helmet served as the prototype for their underwater diving helmet in 1828. Both these helmets used pump technology to shift and move air from a clean location to an at-risk person in a burning building or the ocean floor. These early air filtration systems were expensive and cumbersome and, as such, were not financially viable for regular use in dangerous industries. This changed with the advent of the first "inhaler or lung protector" by chemist John Stenhouse in 1848 (Image 3). In this new filtration system, a person would cover their mouth and nose with a cloth mask fitted with a "charcoal-filtered air device." Stenhouse's invention happened as the European world was shook by the failed revolutions of 1848 and the publication of Marx and Engel's *Communist Manifesto*, two events representing the growing frustration

[1]Similarly, the Chinese collective Chuang (2021) in their book on Covid, *Social Contagion*, expand this analysis and highlight that plagues serve as a tool for the expansion of colonial power, capitalism, and state capture. They highlight that plagues played an important role in the process of European colonization. For instance, animal plagues throughout the African continent and germ warfare enacted by European colonists in the Americas helped undermine indigenous social relationships and connections to the land.

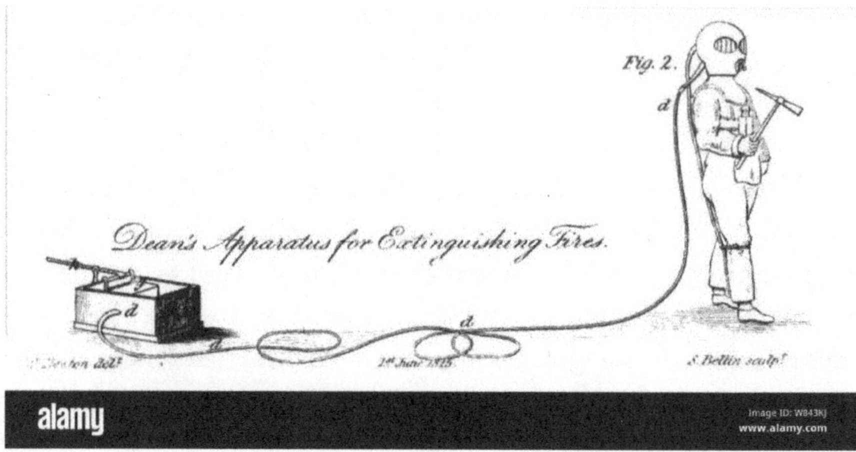

Image 2 *1824 smoke helmet.*

and disillusionment with the newly formed capitalist system of production. The filtration mask was a solution to a problem unique to the industrial age; it was a band-aid meant to limit industrial exposure at the site of production while doing nothing to limit the toxification of the world.

The underwater diving helmet and the cloth filter represent two interconnected ideological needs for early industrialism: desire to colonize environments that had historically been blocked by natural limits, such as the mine and the ocean floor, and the protection of workers struggling in newly toxified environments. Industrialism's expansion and colonization into worlds previously not hospitable to human exploration was part of a Western manifest destiny that desired the transmogrification of the entire world into a commodity. The underwater helmet provided the fantasy of human colonization of the deep seas, as seen in *20,000 Leagues under the Sea* by Jules Verne, even if it took nearly a century before access to the ocean floor was technologically possible. The cloth filter assuaged worker fears about industrial pollution, a panacea offered to the newly emerging antipollution movements in the UK.

Baudrillard writes that "The true revolution of the nineteenth century, of modernity, is the radical destruction of appearances, the disenchantment of the world and its abandonment to the violence of interpretation and of

Image 3 *1848 lung protector.*

history" (Baudrillard 1994: 105). This nineteenth-century revolution banished the magical world of the plague doctor and altered the structure of symbolic meaning regarding the mask, instead of the supernatural and animist, the world of the crow—symbolizing a space between life and death—the proto gas mask linked to industrialism's logic. Jean Baudrillard contends that disaster and catastrophe function as a threat to the established order because disaster undermines the sovereign rationality of politics. In this instance, the industrial catastrophe—the invention of the industrial mode of production—inevitably creates unstable ground for the sovereign power of the modern nation-state. He writes:

> This unreason is intolerable, since reason wants to be sovereign and can no longer even think of what escapes it; it is unresolvable since for us there are no longer any propitiating or reconciling rituals: the accident, like death, is absurd, that's all there is to it. It is a piece of sabotage. An evil

> demon there to make this beautiful machine always break down. Hence this rationalist culture suffers, like no other, from a collective paranoia. (Baudrillard 2016: 282)

With the rise of industrialism, we then see the invention of the industrial accident, and with it a built-in logic of crisis that threatens the social order of industrialism. The technology of the mask is a way in which the tools of industrial logic is used to protect against the harms of the industrialization process. Industrialism constructs a wobbly and unstable system, and an endless process of innovation is needed to constantly replaster the rotten foundation. The same logic is found in the modern era, where figures like Elon Musk call for the creation of an industrial "carbon dioxide purifier," effectively calling for industrialism to manufacture a tree, while globally expanding deforestation to feed the ever-growing need for growth.

The industrial factory, which expanded during the nineteenth century, seeped into the social factories of Europe on April 22, 1915, during the second battle of Ypres, Belgium, when the German army launched chlorine gas canisters at Canadian and French troops. This marked the first modern use of chemical weapons and changed the trajectory of the war. Shortly after, the Allies ramped up the production of their gas weapons, and an arms race began. Within the year the modern gas mask was developed by scientists at the Kaiser Wilhelm Institute of Chemistry and Electrochemistry Berlin. This mask covered the soldier's entire face, sealing tight on the face with a canister filter at the bottom. While effective when worn correctly, gas masks require training and discipline. All nations, but most aggressively the German nation, implemented mandatory gas mask training for all their soldiers. The training created a cyborg assemblage in which the soldier fuses with the gas mask in much the same way that in the factory the worker became nothing but an expansion of the industrial machine.[2]

[2]In Rebecca Campbell's sci-fi/horror novella, *The Talosite*, scientists during the First World War learn how to transform the dead bodies of soldiers into automata. The dead bodies of the soldiers are thus expended twice, once in life and once in death, as part of the war effort. The process, which transforms the dead body of the soldier into a machine that follows simple orders, terrifies and disgusts the living soldiers who all, correctly, understand that they are nothing but parts of a growing war machine.

According to historian Peter Thompson (2017), the First World War marked a significant step in making the industrial subject. He writes:

> gas was a uniquely ephemeral weapon, and its physical presence was not always necessary to inspire action, fear, or reflection. As a tool of resistance and survival, the gas mask encouraged the same fears of being gassed while also exposing a soldier's level of faith in the ability to control or defend against the new modern condition either through technological armoring or individual discipline. (252)

The gas mask and its link to industrialism—a mass-manufactured good and defense against industrial chemicals—led to a unique relationship between the soldiers and the object. Thompson highlights how German soldiers resisted the implementation of this device, even in the face of death and injury from noxious gases. For some soldiers, exposure to gas was a better option than fighting in the trenches. Soldiers would remove the mask and scar their lungs, making themselves no longer fit for battle. Moved to military hospitals, these soldiers would spend months away from the front line.

Other soldiers refused to wear the mask because of its perceived feminine qualities.[3] Thompson writes:

> Some saw this new technology as un-masculine or ungentlemanly in relation to the inherited rules of war. Others found gas masks particularly comical or alien in form, referring to them as "stink hoods, mouth drums, pig snouts, muzzles, and carnival veils." Certainly, there was something rather dehumanizing and disturbing about the concealment of the face. When the masks were donned, the trenches were no longer filled with friend and foe, and they became outlandish landscapes populated by bug-eyed ghosts incapable of entirely expressing emotion or humanity. (Thompson 2017: 253)

This feeling that linked the feminine with the aesthetic of the alien marked the social shifts in gender norms that had emerged when women replaced

[3]A direct link can be made here between the fragile masculinity of the soldier in the First World War with the fragile masculinity of many during both the Spanish flu and the Covid plague.

men in factory production. In wearing the gas mask, the soldiers ceased to be human but instead transformed into an alien other—a faceless mass, which they associated with femininity. The mask symbolically functioned as an expression of their profound alienation. The mask's dehumanization mirrors the factory life's alienation while also highlighting the fear of empowered women wrestling back their social reproductive power.

While the poisoned air of the trenches altered the soldiers' relationship with industrial technology and the state, the transformation did not end at the trench but altered the role of citizens on the home front. German women, starting in the First World War and throughout the Nazi regime, took a leading role in training and disciplining the community for air raids and gas attacks. In many ways, German women gained political power and agency by taking on the part of civilian coordinators by linking their role as home protectors to community protectors. Women made up the bulk of block wardens and building caretakers, all through the coordination of the Reichsluftschutzbund (German national air defense). At first, many fascists and even pacifist figures in Germany rejected training women to use gas masks because they believed women were not qualified. However, the framing changed after a massive gas leak at a chemical plant in Hamburg. It was an industrial factory disaster, and not the use of chemical weapons against urban centers, that led the Nazis, in 1935, to pass the Air Defense Act, which required all civilians—men, women, and children—to be trained in using a gas mask. Most civilian agents involved in the society-wide training program were women who functioned as the "new women of the metropolis" (Thompson 2020: 357).

Similarly, the ultranationalist Japanese state during the 1930s also developed gas mask training programs for the public. The first air defense raid drill in Japan happened in Osaka in 1928 before being expanded to Tokyo and most other major cities by 1933 (see I 4). In Japan, Boku (僕), or air defense, fused with shisu (死す), or "defense to the death," to transform the entire populace into a soldier. The mask served a few primary roles: first, as a symbol of the cohesion and discipline of the Japanese population, as seen in the children's marches (Image 8); second, via a sexualization of the gas mask. Weisenfeld writes "that the gas mask did much more than merely express or inculcate fear. It excited the imagination, particularly in the context of a widespread Japanese

Image 4 *Japanese students march in gas masks.*

popular culture movement known as" (or erotic-grotesque-nonsense, often shortened to ero-guro) (Weisenfeld 2014: 181). In Japan, the gas mask was not just a tool but became a culturally constructed sexual fetish. In promoting air defense and civilian protection, the state-created ads showing sexualized women donning or holding gas masks. Slogans such as "Tactics spread poison gas all around; beautiful young women wear gas masks" (190) link preparedness with sexuality and beauty. In addition, the link contrasts the death of chemical weapons with sexuality, which is seen in a tag for a poster that highlighted that "Amid poison gas, you cannot kiss." The long history of Japanese sexual fetishization of the grotesque linked the gas mask and the fear of death and destruction with a sexualized female subject. Weisenfeld writes that "War sublimated the sexual liberation of Japanese modernity into martial labor" (190). As such, the gender roles of Japanese society, at threat from the rise of industrialism and modernization, were eroticized in a way that shifted sexual freedoms and liberation to be a tool of expanded domestic labor and public support for the total war effort.

The sexualization of the gas mask eroticized industrial modernity, transforming mass society's physical isolation, international alienation, and anonymity into desirable traits. Weisenfeld writes:

> The alienation of the modern subject from their environment on the militarized Homefront, which necessitated the application of commodity prostheses for survival, eerily paralleled the general processes of modernity that were gradually alienating the modern consumer-subject from the natural environment and replacing his relationship with commodity fetishes that similarly denaturalized the human body. (Weisenfeld 2014: 180)

This project thus attempts to link the libidinal logic of sexual fetishization for the gas mask as a stand-in symbol for the violence to the body that industrial modernity caused. The Japanese eroticism of the gas mask is an example of George Battaile's claim that "the two primary taboos affect, firstly, death, and secondly, sexual functions" (Bataille 1986: 42). While death and reproduction are diametrically opposed forces, they are also intimately linked and the primal desire for both, when fused with moments of sadomasochistic energy, can devolve into an "orgy of annihilation" (Bataille 1986: 61). With the ever presence of death during war, the erotic gas mask is an expression of such an orgiastic desire for destruction. The chemicals of modernity, the weapons of war, and the cog-like practice of the factory penetrated the body, making it hard to understand where the body ended and the industrial world began. Moreover, with total war the boundaries between civilians and the military were blurred, as the public and the private, the pure and the poisoned, all fused.

During the Second World War, the Japanese and the Germans placed the most focus on civilian defense and public training in gas mask usage. This is the case even though Germany and Japan were the only two nations that regularly used chemical weapons, both for the war effort and as a war crimes against prisoners and civil populations, which makes the fetishization of the gas mask also a symbol of their fears of reverse colonization. Japan, which began its widespread colonization of the Asian continent in 1910 with its violent conquest and suppression of Korea at the peak of the war effort, had colonial control over Korea, Manchuria, Taiwan, and a significant amount of the Pacific Island nations, justified their colonial project as the "East Asian Co-prosperity Sphere." The fascistic Japanese state defended the East Asian Co-prosperity Sphere as a necessity to defend Asian nations from Western imperialism. During the Meiji Restoration, which was spearheaded by the imperial demands, backed by the US warships of Matthew Perry, the Japanese state modernized and industrialized rapidly to protect itself from colonization. In a projection of Western state logic, the Japanese state viewed the colonization of other Asian forces as a strategy to deflect European attempts to colonize. In short, the Japanese state colonized much of Asia under the supposed defense of Asia against European colonization. As the Second World War expanded, the Japanese state, in desperate need for access to natural resources, like rubber, which was essential for the war effort (as well as the making of the gas mask), advanced into what is now Indonesia. The success of the Japanese state in colonizing these rubber plantations was, in part, according to Tully, a central reason why the United States and the allies developed petrochemical forms of rubber (Tully 2011).

Naoki Sakai, in his analysis of the competing imperial nationalism of the United States and Japan, contends, "From the outset, Japanese nationalism was by definition assumed to be an exceptionalist ethnic particularism exclusive of other identities, while American nationalism always manifests itself in universalist orientation toward multiethnic integration" (Sakai 2005: 164). While the inclusive nature of American nationalism is limited, as it only applied to ethnic groups associated with whiteness, it was still more open than the ultranationalist Japanese assertions of Japanese ethnic superiority. To Sakai, the Japanese version of exclusion created a complicated relationship for colonized Japanese subjects. They were both a part of the Japanese nation and given incentives to assimilate or support the Japanese imperial project while being excluded from being included in the Japanese people. Sakai quotes a historian of Japanese colonization, who writes, "It would be an impossible demand: you ought to behave as loyal subjects of the emperor, even though you must be aware you can never be Japanese" (Calichman 2005: 165). The short stories that Sakai analyzes, all written by colonized subjects of the Japanese empire, shows the conflictual identity and logic of being a colonized subject. Similarly to Fanon in *White Mask, Black Skin*, the internal sense of self-respect found in those colonized by the Japanese empire gets linked to an endless attempt to perform as Japanese. Sakai writes, "the humiliated desperately perform the expected role of patriotic subject in order to recover their self-respect by gaining recognition from their masters" (Calichman 2005: 185). The only path of safety for the colonized then was to become a defender of Japanese imperialism and actively exclude or condemn all those who resisted colonization.

That the Japanese state prioritized the training of Japanese civilian populations in the use of the gas mask while at the same time using chemical weapons against the colonized subjects resisting state power reinscribes the fear of reverse colonization. Anna Lee Newitz, in reading Lovecraftian stories, contends that the fear of reverse colonization is one when

> Yet even the most simplistic and racist of these stories also reflects the moral confusion of a nation that feared, yet desired, an end to colonialism in the world and at home. White in these stories is haunted by knowledge of a distant past when people of color were free and powerful. And they anticipate a future where whites have become ghosts doomed to drift unsubstantially among formerly colonized people who have regained their sovereignty. (Newitz 2006: 90)

While Newitz is writing about the US imperial fear of the colonial other, the logic applies to the Japanese nationalists and their fear of Korean, Chinese, and other Asian resistance to their imperial project. The gas mask training thus did at least two things. First, it constructed a logic of fear in the minds of the populace, who regularly awaited chemical weapons while the Japanese states used such weapons against the empire's enemies. Second, it provided an apartheid-like separation between the Japanese and non-Japanese populations. Only certain people should be protected against chemical weapons, while other bodies are expected to choke and die.

As for Germany, the populace was being trained to defend against the nonexistent allied gas attacks while the state slaughtered trainloads of Jews, Roma, queer folks, communists, and disabled people in concentration camps throughout central and eastern Germany. Giorgia Agamben in *Homo Sacer* contends that the Nazi state epitomized the logic of biopower and illustrated how the modern state is predicated on the logic of the state of exception and the extermination camp. To Agamben, the *Homo Sacer* is a figure that is both excluded and included in the broader network of state power by the logic that "It is not permitted to sacrifice this man, yet he who kills him will not be condemned for homicide" (Agamben 1998: 71). Agamben contends that the *Homo Sacer* is a subject that is stripped of all the qualities that are reserved for human or political life and that exists solely via bare life. Those with bare life are exceptions to rules that protect citizens and humans and can be killed with relative impunity.

Under the industrial state, the logic of exception has become the norm, and the logic of camp has become embodied in all the decisions of statecraft. Agamben writes, "There is a line in every modern state making the point at which the decision on life becomes a decision on death, and biopolitics can turn into than to politics, this line no longer appears today as a stable border dividing two clear distinct zones" (Agamben 1998: 122). The blurring of lines of division between safe and unsafe, dirty and clean, and purity and corruption are inevitably blurred by the logic of industrial production. The human body becomes an extension of machines, be it in the factory or as a soldier in the state's military apparatus. The gas mask training, like the yellow stars and upside-down pink triangles, attempted to construct and police the line separating the Aryan citizen and the murderable other. However, as the Nero decree highlights, the lines between the inside and the outside of the camp were always blurred, and through decrees the state of exception could be expanded to the broader population. Alternatively, as Agamben puts it, "The fracture that was believed to have been overcome by eliminating the people (the Jews who are its symbol) thus reproduces itself anew, transforming the entire German people into a sacred life consecrated to death, and a biological body that must be infinitely purified" (Agamben 1998: 179–80). The gas mask was one of the many symbols that demonstrated who was and was not within the confines of the Aryan state and who was or was not protected by state power. Being trained and used in the gas mask was also a part of linking and connecting the people into the industrial apparatus of the fascist state and, therefore, a potential victim of the fascistic death drive.

In criticizing the Japanese imperial project, Takahashi Tetsuya criticizes not just the fascist state but even the modern liberal state for embodying a supposedly kinder and less-overt form of assimilationist exclusion. He writes, "To the extent that nationalism is nationalism, however, we cannot deny that it possesses an essential tendency to fabricate a nation's oneness, homogeneity, and identity, thus excluding the heterogeneous other" (Calichman 2005: 209). The issue for Takahashi is the logic of exclusion central to nationalism and not the specific nationalism of the Japanese fascist state. He calls for a *Democracy without nationalism* or a democratic spirit opposed to exclusions as the basis of a just and democratic political space. Similarly, Agamben contends that the lessons of the rise of the Nazi state are a broader critique of the modern state form. He writes, "Only a politics that will have learned to take the fundamental biopolitical fracture of the West into account will be able to stop this oscillation and to put an end to the civil war that divides the peoples and the cities of the earth" (Agamben 1998: 180). During the period of world wars and genocide conflicts, the gas mask was one of the primary symbols of the bio and necro political powers of the modern state. Thus, the mask is a symbol of state protection and the power of the state to kill en mass.

In the postwar era, the symbolic role of the gas mask shifted again as the logic of preparedness in the United States fused with conservative anti-communism. During the Cold War, in the United States, the mask became linked with a prepper and survivalist's vision while also being coopted and used as a symbol of resistance against state power by protestors. The two-faced nature of industrialism and the modern state, once again, is seen in the symbol of the gas mask. On the one hand, the mask was used to show one's preparedness and symbolically positioned one as an anti-communist; on the other, the mask was a symbol of resistance to state power, especially the police, who increasingly began to use weapons of war—tear gas and pepper spray—as tools of oppression to maintain order.

Starting in the 1960s, the far-right in the US linked the gas mask-wearing individual with the politics of hyper patriots, like the John Birchers, who took individual responsibility to prepare themselves to protect the nation from communist invasion. Since the Cold War ended, the narrative of the gas mask-wearing patriot has not gone away. Instead, we see how the neoliberal subjectivity fuses with reactionary patriotism, with the figures of the individual- or family-level preppers preparing for a range of potential catastrophes, from natural disasters to the breakdown of social organization, to EMP blasts from enemy nations. Emily Ray makes clear that we cannot separate pre–Cold War prepping from post–Cold War prepping through the lens of consumerism. Even in the 1950s and 1960s, the US state linked the ability of individuals to become consumers of bunkers and dehydrated food, and so on as a part of what it meant to be a "good patriot." Instead, we see a shift from a conservative belief in the state to a right-wing military hostility to the state. Ray writes:

> The average consumer is unlikely to buy a Preppi bag and hopes this signals the end of democracy. Nevertheless, this consumer has already conceded that democracy is unreliable and cannot guarantee a political environment for collective organizing and mobilizing the state's resources for equitable public distribution in the face of disaster. The only path to survival, and later to thriving, is through one's preparation, ingenuity, and the ability to access a responsive marketplace that will persist beyond any environmental collapse. The fear of state failure is legitimate, just as worrying about the inability of the state to respond adequately to any number of disasters justifies some degree of preparation. However, preparing alone, or just within a family unit, is not the only choice available, but one framed by a neoliberal ideology that champions individual responsibility to public needs. (Ray 2021: 4)

As Ray highlights here, the shift is not about consumerism or patriotism but a change from a right-wing nationalism founded on a powerful central state to one that has defanged many aspects of the state and either awaits or champions the collapse of the liberal government and its replacement with a theocratic or overtly white supremacist state. Unsurprisingly, this shift happened during the 1960s and 1970s, the short period in which the US state actively put policies in place to end and redress some of the wounds of slavery and Jim Crow. The 1960s saw the end of de jure racism by law with the passage of the voting rights and equal housing acts. As the federal government turned hostile to overt displays of racial entitlement, even using the national guard to integrate southern schools, the state became an enemy to conservative whites. As the state became, at least in principle, more openly multicultural, the far-right shifted from defending the state to opposing the state and calling for a return to a primordial period of "greatness" in which the state was the marker and defender of white, male Christendom.

The most absurd example of the reactionary use of the gas mask is seen through the use of the gas mask in the online propaganda of the neo-Nazi accelerationist group Atomwoffen Division. The group, which has already been linked to seven murders in the United States, looks to accelerate the social tensions around race and bring about a race war. The group's name, attomwaffen, is a shorthand for the Nazi atomic weapon division, and the group propaganda regularly shows signs of industrial infrastructure—factories, smoke stakes, pipelines, and the like—and shows members, often armed, wearing either gas masks or skull mask gators over their face. While practically these outfit choices are meant to protect the identity of the group members, they are also used to create an imposing image of white men, armed and ready to fight for the white race in the despoiled environment of a collapsed US state.

The difference in preparedness between the "prepper" and the "protestor" relates to their relationship to certain power hierarchies. The prepper is preparing for a societal collapse and is worried about returning to a "state of nature." In a way, their preparedness is a defense of the state's sovereign power. A formal embodiment of Hobbesian logic is expressed through the body, machine, and assemblage that individuals create with the gas mask. While the protestor is that figure who resists specific logics of hierarchy—may be racial, gendered, or class—

and as such, the difference is not in tactics but in the target of said tactics. Hence why the Black Lives Matter protests in the wake of the George Floyd lynching differs from the protests and caravans organized by the far-right against Covid, drag performances, or the "Stop the Steal" rallies. The reactionary defense of existing hierarchies differs from attempts to dismantle said hierarchies.

The mask operates as a symbol marking spaces of industrial death and pollution. In the short-lived but critically well-regarded FX TV show *Y: The Last Ma*n, which was based on the critically acclaimed comic of the same name, in the first scene we see a man walking around an empty and dilapidated New York City. His gas mask hides his face as he looks into abandoned cars and travels around the city with his pet monkey. After following this masked figure, we finally see him remove his mask, and the audience is meant to be anxious—unsure if the air might kill him. In this scene, we know a disaster has happened to the people of New York, but we do not yet know what. The gas mask highlights that the air itself might be toxic. We see this same image in many other works of dystopian fiction.

Similarly, based on the real eco-horror of the nuclear meltdown, we see hazmat-clad figures regularly in the miniseries Chernobyl. They are reminders of the toxic environment. They are meant to create a sense of anxiety for the characters, especially when dangers like chemical attacks and radiation are invisible to the human eye. This invisibility requires that the threat is transposed through an object—In this case, the gas mask or hazmat suit. Here, much like the symbolic role of the gas attacks in the trenches of the First World War, it highlights the threat we cannot see. When we see individuals walking around the radiated spaces not protected, we are meant to fear for their life and safety, as the presence of the mask on others lets us know that the space is deadly. In contemporary political culture, like at all times, the gas mask has a symbolic function that links it with the two sides of industrial power. It is a fetish that legitimates or justifies certain forms of state power while highlighting the dangers of the state's power to toxify the air.

Industrialism as Suicidal Blackmail

In *Symbolic Exchange and Death*, Baudrillard contends that the development of capitalism shifted the social and symbolic role that death played in

European societies. He writes, "little by little, the dead cease to exist. They are thrown out of the group's symbolic circulation. They are no longer beings with a full role to play, a worthy partner in the exchange, and we make this obvious by exiling them further and further away from the living" (Baudrillard 2016: 232). He noted that the dead, who originally had a resting place in the center of European cities, with the development of capitalism, were pushed to the outskirts. This shift was due to dramatic changes in how Europeans understood worth and value. Under capitalism, our productive capacity is the store of value that we, as individuals and as a collective, have, and the dead are the epitome of unproductive labor. If our labor is all we value, then those who cease laboring are worthless. At the same time, the laboring process under capitalism entails transferring life force and energy from the worker to the product itself. As industrial production systems colonize the space of life, "The cemetery no longer exists because modern cities have entirely taken over their function: they are ghost towns, cities of death" (Baudrillard 2016: 232). The gas mask symbolizes what it means to traverse and survive in the necropolis world that industrial production and capitalist exchange relationships have built. Capitalism during these apocalyptic times is selling us safety from the industrial toxicity that it produced. When the air is poisoned, those who sell the masks reap massive profits. Go to Whole Foods and witness the anxiety purchases of the middle class striving to find sustenance that they believe will not poison them. Organic produce and vegetables, free-range chicken eggs, and ethically murdered animal carcasses are surrounded by unverified supplements claiming to solve all the problems that snake oil once cured.

However, there is no question that the mass-produced food, laden with petrochemical insecticide and fed a steady diet of pharmaceutical antibiotics, is, killing us. While not as overt, wild, or frankly aesthetically attractive, the organic label functions much like a gas mask; the label is a prophylactic symbol of safety in the poisoned trenches of industrial life. Of course, our safety is related to our economic capacity as the rich can avoid the worst aspects of industrial positions. Most importantly though, our consumer choices enrich people like Jeff Bezos. This is the most nefarious aspect of industrial production: as capitalism destroys the world, we must pay the elite for the privilege of having them poison us less. "Though they broke my legs, they gave me a crutch to walk," sang the anarcho-punk band Chumbawama (1987). Nowadays, only the wealthy can access crutches. The rest of us have to limp.

Not only have the wealth elite further accumulated wealth by providing us protective talismans for the disasters they have caused, but they have also found ways to gain extra wealth from the death of their workers. James Tyner, in *Dead Labor: Toward a Political Economy of Premature Death*, lays bare the corporate strategies currently being used by corporations to profit off of premature death. For instance, corporations like Walmart have taken out life insurance policies for floor workers, allowing them to profit if they die prematurely. Tyner writes:

> Throughout the 1980s and 1990s, due to intensive lobbying on behalf of the insurance industry, most American states expanded the concept of insurable interest to include low-level, low-skilled, non-essential employees. These are euphemistically termed "dead-janitor" or "dead-peasant" policies and constitute a fetishized form of violence unique to advanced capitalism. No longer concerned with protecting one's corporeal investment in key employees, dead-peasant policies were (and are) taken out on any and all employees, regardless of the length of employment or the "value" of their services. Moreover, policies often remain in force after employee termination or retirement, and indeed, companies frequently use the database of deaths maintained by the Social Security Administration to track employees by social security number after termination or retirement, and thus are able to receive COLI death benefits upon their death. (Tyner 2019: 99)

Thus, the same corporations that fight expanding health care coverage and increasing the minimum wage are able to capitalize off the premature deaths of their workers. The insurance policy functions as a fetish, a magical object, a devil's contract that allows Walmart to turn their workers' cancer deaths into corporate profits. Alchemy, or necromancy, has never been so financially lucrative.

Industrialism has led to a massive increase in capacities for production and the spreading of a cloud of death that has slowly encapsulated the entire planet. However, more often than not the focus on industrialism is centered on its productive capacity, which is, in fact, impressive. Nevertheless, to explore industrialism without including the darker side of industrial production is at best misinformed and at worst genocidal. Industrialism functions by turning life into death. The darkest humor of industrialism is that we feel that there is no solution to our problem, but the further expansion of industrial production. Without industrial food production, we are told, millions will starve. This may or may not be accurate in the short term, but industrial production consumes the soil, leaving us with around fifty years of topsoil. Once that soil is gone, how many millions will starve? Since there is no solution but industrialism, we have to assume that technological progress will allow us to overcome the crisis of soil depletion. Likewise, nuclear reactors poison the entire world. Not only when they meltdown—like we saw with Chernobyl and Fukushima—but in their daily operations as radionuclides leech out of reactors and the toxic waste piles up with no long-term solution. However, shutting down and decommissioning a nuclear reactor is intensive, taking up to sixty years and costing at least $400 million. If not done safely, the decommissioning process is potentially catastrophic, but if left running like usual, the results are also catastrophic. In this way, industrialism has held us hostage, and every year we pay the ransom with our labor, our lives, and our planet.

This hostage logic is at the core of most aspects of contemporary politics, partly because any attempt to upset the social, political, and economic structures of society inevitably opens up the potential for catastrophic changes. But, the maintenance of the status quo is inevitably catastrophic. Every day that the same old continues, the noncatastrophic options diminish. The situationist Raoul Vaneigem contended that one of the primary problems of contemporary mass society was what they called "survival sickness." In his analysis, the spectacle mediates our lives to such a degree that we continue in the fog of a never-ending present. While the present we inhabit is, in fact, horrible, it lulls us into a sense of complacency. He writes:

> The fact is that people possess both the means to eliminate the causes of despair and the power to mobilize these means in order to rid themselves of it. No one has the right to ignore that the sway of conditioning accustoms them to survive on one-hundredth of their potential for life. So general is

> survival sickness that the slightest concentration of lived experience could not fail to unite the largest number of people in a common will to live. The negation of despair would, of necessity, become the construction of a new life. The rejection of economic logic (which only economizes on life) would, of necessity, entail the death of economics and carry us beyond the realm of survival. (Vaneigem 2012: 289)

In the current moment, we see a form of despair-oriented survival sickness. Apathy and frustration are prevalent, and few believe that the governing institutions of liberal life or that the mechanism of the mythically free market will solve any problem.

Survival sickness overlaps with how George Ciccariello-Maher understands George Sorel in his book *Decolonizing Dialectics*. To Ciccariello-Meher, Sorel's understanding of dialectical struggle is frozen. "He [Sorel] found a dialectic blocked not only by material development," Maher writes, "but crucially by an ideology of social harmony to which his contemporary socialists were not immune, and which many were even willing to participate" (Ciccariello-Maher 2016: 24). Because of these blockages Sorel was hostile to a dialectical analysis of the present and developed a politics rooted in "jump-starting" the dialectic relationship. To Sorel, this was accomplished through proletarian violence and political barbarism against the ruling classes. Maher writes that "against the common opposition that Luxumberg and many since have posed between 'socialism or barbarism,' Sorel's reply would be characteristically provocative: socialism through barbarism" (Ciccariello-Maher 2016: 40).

What does it mean to jump-start the dialectical conflict around industrialism? Since industrialism will, left to its own devices, continue to cannibalize the world and, in doing so, straightjacket any attempts at reform or transition, the answer has to be found in active resistance and sabotage of industrial networks. Andreas Malm's book *How to Blow Up a Pipeline* offers a glimpse into the politics needed here. Malm's book critiques the logic of nonviolence that climate activists in the West have embraced and calls for a more critical and militant stance against fossil fuel industries. He writes, "So here is what the movement of millions should do, for a start: announce and enforce the prohibition [against fossil fuel use]. Damage and destroy new CO_2-emitting devices. Put them out of commission, pick them apart, demolish them, burn them, blow them up. Let the capitalist who keeps investing in the fire know that their properties will be trashed" (Malm 2021a: 67). This is, of course, what we see among indigenous resistance to fossil fuel extraction worldwide. For instance, in the Niger Delta, the Movement for the Emancipation of the Niger Delta from 2004 to 2014 engaged in arson, kidnapping, and targeted assassination against oil industry workers who were destroying the land for the accumulation of profit. In a communique, the organization wrote: "It must be clear that the Nigerian government cannot protect your workers or assets. Leave our land while you can or die in it. . . . Our aim is to totally destroy the capacity of the Nigerian government to export oil" (Tattersall 2008). During their campaign against the oil industry, the rebels decreased the amount of oil extracted by a third.

What the environmental movement calls "frontline communities" are often the groups most willing to use radical and revolutionary tactics against industrial extraction and production. It is assumed that these groups and communities, which are having their ways of life decimated for capital, are resisting the destruction of their ways of life, and their resistance is tied to their connection to previous ways of living. We need to realize that we are all on the front lines of industrial death and destruction. The entire planet is being burned alive to extract wealth, and living beings—human and nonhuman—are consumed by the machines of industrialism. We all live in Bhopal, some might be closer to the vents spreading the poisoned gas, but sooner or later, we will all choke and, as Franz Fanon said: "When we revolt, it's not for a particular culture. We revolt simply because, for many reasons, we can no longer breathe" (Fanon 2008).

3

The Climate Is Not Real

On the Joe Rogan podcast, psychologist and alt-right academic hero Jordan Peterson said:

> Well, that is 'cause there is no such thing as climate, right? Climate and everything are the same word, and that's what bothers me about it, technically. It's like climate is about everything. Your models aren't based on everything. Your models are based on a set number of variables. So that means you've reduced the variables—which are everything—to that set. Well, how did you decide which set of variables to include in the equation if it's about everything? That's not just a criticism; that's like, if it's about everything, your models aren't right. Because your models cannot model everything. (Boyle 2022)

This exchange between Jordan Peterson and his slack-jawed host was panned online, with the criticisms highlighting the self-help guru misunderstanding of climate science. These criticisms, especially since Peterson is a climate denier and right-wing troll with close ties to oil and gas lobbies, ring true as Peterson's discourse functions to muddle the public discussion about climate change, sowing doubt and confusion. With that said, Jordan Peterson, like a broken clock, unintentionally engages with a fundamental problem with the politics of climate change: the hyperreal, spectacular nature of climate modeling. In discussing the First Gulf War in 1991, Jean Baudrillard said, "We prefer the exile of the virtual, of which television is the universal mirror, to the catastrophe of the real" (Baudrillard 1995: 28). That war, which was mediated through twenty-four-hour cable news and filtered through the US defense department lens, felt like a nonwar for those of us on the spectator side of the screen. It did not follow Clausewitz's famous dictum that "war is politics through another means" but as "absence of politics by another means" (Baudrillard 1995: 30). Of course, the Gulf War did happen, and it had profound material impacts as an estimated 100,000 people died due to the war.[1]

The climate and the First Gulf War are both mediated via state agencies and corporate media, and in their mediation the harmful material effects of both disappeared for those in "their safe European homes."[2] Those on the other end of the bombs, depleted uranium shells, rising seas, fires, and draughts, are not able to ignore the material violence. For both the climate crisis and the war, the obfuscation of the harmful effects via mediation is harder the closer one is to the violence. We must never forget that, as Crass claimed, "the Generals sip bacardi while the privates feel the pain." And, the vast majority of us on this planet are privates, and never will be generals.

The Intergovernmental Panel on Climate Change (IPCC) provides expert mediation of the science for our collective understanding of the climate crisis. The experts at the IPCC then have the power to shape the political discussion as experts, and only experts are required to parse out the complex models that serve as the backbone of the field. As mediators of an already-abstracted process, the hyperreal nature of modern media and science shape climate politics, which, as Baudrillard highlights in *Simulacra and Simulation*, leads to a crisis of an overabundance of competing meanings. The abstraction of our climate experience allows the climate to become nothing but an empty

[1]In addition, the Gulf War was the first war that used depleted uranium weapons, ammunition made out of repurposed nuclear waste (from reactors and nuclear weapon production). Between the first and the second US-led wars in Iraq, an estimated 259 million tons of depleted uranium armaments currently litter the sands, buildings, and waterways of Iraq. Rob Nixon writes, "The result is a seductive kind of alchemy: weapons manufacturers magically cut their production costs while the Defense Department magically rids itself of a five alarm waste product that no American wants buried in their backyard. The result is a kind of antienvironmental recycling that converts highly toxic waste into even more deadly explosive forms" (Nixon 2013: 2012). While depleted uranium is known to be toxic, the US military had aggressively denied that the weapons have caused any long-term effects to either US soldiers or Iraqi civilians. Rates of birth defects, cancers, and other health effects related to radioactive exposure, as well as internal reports from the US military itself, seem to refute such claims.

[2]Effectively, for anyone in their safe homes, protected from the worst aspects of these crises.

signifier allowing climate scientists, state officials, and climate change deniers the power to provide whatever meaning they want. One of the central problems of climate politics is that the climate is not a uniformed material thing; it does not exist as something we can hold, touch, or see. Instead, the only way we comprehend the climate is a socially constructed abstraction, defined and shaped via scientific measurement models. Much like the way technocrats contrast "populations," the climate is a haunting specter formed when statistical analysis turns a complex system into a unified symbolic entity. The simulacra that is the climate, then, as Baudrillard highlights, are regulated and monitored by state institutions that supposedly represent us. As the climate is mediated away from our lived experience, political discussions become hollow debates about the correct forms of consumer purchasing, the joys of biking to work, and how best to express your support for climate on social media platforms. The space for radical and revolutionary political exchange is frozen, allowing the status quo to continue, making catastrophe a near inevitability.

The Simulacra and Disaster Management: The Environment and Climate

In social science and the humanities, there has been a general acceptance that many of our social, political, and historical concepts are socially constructed, but there is less acceptance of the idea that scientific values and principles are as well. Gender is a social construction, a sociologist or a political theorist might argue, but the concept of the environment is not. The environment is a material thing, something I can touch, hold, and smell, and therefore is not a construct. However, all scientific concepts, like their social brethren, are socially constructed. This does not mean there is no material Real, merely that we view and experience the world from a socially constructed space.[3] According

[3]This does not mean there is no material real, merely that we view and experience the world from a socially constructed space. However, there is a problem within environmental and political theory in assuming that social construction manufactures the material world. What we shape is our perception of the world, but not the world itself. As an example of this move, Jason Moore writes, "Nature is co-produced. Capitalism is co-produced. Limits are co-produced." In this version of monism, which

to David Bond, "the environment" was socially constructed during the mid-twentieth century when the pollution from oil, the production of plastics, and the slow creep of radioactive nuclides illustrated "a web of life—or death," as Rachel Carson provocatively said. The original work of ecological thinkers—Carson, Commoner, and Bookchin—structured their analysis through a lens of "negative ecology," which critically explored how US imperial power was linked with the natural world's destruction. For example, Barry Commoner, at the first Earth Day in 1970, told the crowd: "You are the first generation in the history of man to carry Strontium-90 in your bones and DDT in your fat: Your bodies will record in time the full effects of environmental destruction of mankind" (Bond 2022: 35). This focus on the existential threat to humankind shifts when the state institutionalizes ecology and formulates the environment. Bond writes:

> [Nixon's] administration also inaugurated the new responsibility of government to manage the emerging crisis of life . . . the Nixon administration worked to defuse the more revolutionary potential of negative ecology by bending its insights away from assailing the material foundation of the

figures like Bruno Latour also promotes, nature is produced through its interaction with humans, who co-produce the world since they have developed technological instruments. By making the world socially produced, they can also socially engineer the natural world's ecological limits. According to Kohei Saito, this allows them to avoid the pitfall of crude Malthusians, which they correctly oppose, but, in doing so, they create a flat ontology that allows for the flourishing of a "Promethean" narrative of technological progress.

In response to the divide between a scientific foundation and a constructivist frame, Saito, John Bellamy Foster, and others propose the analysis of the "metabolic rift." The idea of the metabolic rift comes from Marx's ecological analysis of nineteenth-century agricultural science by Liebig's theory of replenishment. The metabolic rift by Marxian thinkers claims that capitalism, by creating zones of production and zones of consumption/waste, extracts nutrients from one location and piles them up in another, creating a metabolic imbalance. This imbalance serves as the basis for what Foster calls "Marx's ecology." To Saito, it is also central to Marx's overall analysis of *Capital*. However, critics of this approach highlight how it reinforces a dualism where humans and the earth are treated as existing in separate spheres. Saito counters this claim by highlighting that a complex claim is being made with the idea of metabolic rift and that while there is an assertion that humans and nature exist in separate spheres, such a claim is empirically valuable. In highlighting that nature functionally exists as a "substratum" that serves as the foundation for human life, not a sphere from which humans are removed, Saito contends that the metabolic rift is methodologically dualist but ontologically more nuanced and complicated. The metabolic rift approach allows for a combination of a particular form of social constructivism as our analysis and language of science is socially constructed, but the material foundation of life and its limits are not.

> American empire and towards a more accommodating science providing modest guardrails for uninterrupted consumption: the environment we recognize today. (Bond 2022: 50)

In other words, the concept of the environment is formed in response to a movement of opposition contesting the destructive capacity of industrial and military capitalism to toxify the world. This response was intended to pacify the growing revolutionary fervor of the 1960s and turn ecological analysis into a docile science that benefits the state, corporations, and the military. The concept of the environment that the US state constructed functions "As a shorthand for the resulting crisis of life, the environment became an insurgent field devoted to understanding disrupted life and taking responsibility for it" (Bond 2022: 6). The anxiety and fear of catastrophe and the analytic power of the concept of the environment allowed for state and nonstate agencies to construct a series of metrics and variable to observe, regulate, and manage toxic inputs and outputs to manage catastrophe. Bond highlights that the concept of ecological thresholds, embedded in our conception of the environment, authorizes pollution, shifts our attention to ruptures and not the everyday violence of industrial life, and erases the embodied and embedded experiences of toxicity.

The conception of the environment developed institutionalizes the logic of what Tim Luke calls eco-governmentality, or the application of administrative rationalism onto the nonhuman world. Under eco-governmentality, Tim Luke writes, "Nature is reduced to a system of systems that can be dismantled, redesigned, and assembled anew to produce its many 'resources' efficiently and inadequate amounts when and where needed in the modern marketplace" (Luke 1997: 79). To put this another way, the administrative concept of environment, and the environmental science that contests and supports it, comes to assert that "human health and industrial poisons can cooccur" (quoted in Bond 2022: 62). The state administration of the environment shifts the revolutionary ecological discussion, which criticized industrial progress and the entire apparatus of pollution, to an analysis that instead focuses on measuring and balancing toxicity in a way to allow for economic growth, state power, military expansion. It, in effect, justified the poisoning of the world via the language of "maximum allowable concentrations."

In addition, the legalized construction of the environment with the development of NEPA—the logic of which was globalized through the sustainable development programs developed at the Rio conference in 1992—shifted the power/knowledge hierarchy away from the embodied and lived experience of workers, down winders, and activists to that of the scientific establishment. Bond highlights that the creation of the EPA, much like the institutionalization of economics in the state via the Council on Economic Relations, institutionalized environmental science and provided it the authority and legitimation from the state. "The discourses . . . that rhetorically construct Nature, as suitable for governing contemporary society through particular knowledge," Tim Luke writes, "also must assign powers to new global governors and governments, who are granted writs of authority" (Luke 1997: 84). The construction of institutionalized science and policy procedures centered around toxic thresholds and environmental impact assessment neutralize and de-politicize the environment's politics. Rancière, in "Ten Thesis on Politics," contends that such a move—or any move that seeks to protect an institution from contentious politics and dissensus—is an act of "police" power. Rancière claims that "the police is not a social function but a symbolic constitution of the social. The essence of the police likes neither repression nor even control over the living. Its essence lies in a certain way of dividing the sensible" (Rancière and Corcoran 2016: 36). Police powers are inherently reactionary, institutionalizing the state's hostility to democracy and effectively shifting the terrain of politics to exclude anyone put the power elite. To police is to maintain the status quo, which exists in defense of material state structures and defends the representative logic and order that state institutions reify. The EPA, the IPCC, and the higher education institutions all work to reify the representative system we call the environment. The language of expertise and the focus on managerial and procedural processes are part of a broader project of policing the borders of politics, excluding the voice and agency of those impacted by the ecological crisis. This, of course, does not mean that there is no material foundation to what we call "the environment," simply that the categories and logics we use to construct the social arrangement that we call the environment are shaped by ideological and political lenses, distorting the material real by layering over it a hologram of industrial capitalist imperialism.

The Politics of Models: Administrative Rationalism and the State Regulation of Illusions

Baudrillard introduces the idea of hyperreality to make sense of postwar advertising and the media-dominated cognitive landscape we currently inhabit. The hyperreal, according to Baudrillard, forms when our simulated reality becomes entirely self-referential. In this self-referential world, there is no longer any attempt to link representations with what we experience emanating from the Real. He writes that the hyperreal is "the generation by models of a real without origin or reality" (Baudrillard 1994: 1). The focus on modeling is central to Baudrillard because the model takes fragmented aspects of the Real and, like digital photography, fills in the gaps in our knowledge with computer-generated data. The resulting concept of reality relies on a recursive cultural cycle of representation. Our experienced reality is merely a copy without an original, or a simulacra. Baudrillard has primarily been used in media and cultural studies projects, as the simulacra of life are seen in the absurdity of reality TV but there are more profound political implications of Baudrillard's analysis that are often ignored. For instance, in *In the Shadow of the Silent Majority*, Baudrillard uses the concept of the hyperreal to deconstruct how contemporary politics, through its use of statistics and media analysis, create, out of nothing, the concept of "the masses," which are then imbued with collective values, agency, and desires. In that work, Baudrillard contends that "the masses" do not exist but function as a haunting of statistical analysis—an asocial class constructed through that hyperreal fiction. He writes that "the term 'masses' is not a concept. It is a leitmotif of political demagogy, a soft, sticky, lumpenanlytical notion" (Baudrillard 1983: 4). Unlike the "working class," which can be understood logically as a relation to property, the masses stand in only as a shimmering nonexistent thing in relation to no material or social force. Unlike accounts of the multitude, either from Aristotle or from Hardt and Negri, which describe an undefinable group filled with unrepresentable differences, the mass is considered a unified subject with opinions, feelings, political hopes, and, most importantly, an apathetic attitude toward the political.

The liberal political order, unlike the sovereignty of the king, roots its supposed legitimacy on the direct will "of the people," itself an unrepresentable fiction. Since "will" is central to the legitimacy of the modern liberal state, one of the biggest dangers to the political institution is the spread of political apathy and disillusionment, which highlights the fraud of democratic representation and points to ways that violence and force are the real foundations of political legitimacy. If the people are the "good" subjects of modern political representation—the group that is supposed to be represented by the state—the masses are their other, the dangerous unrepresentable left over. The masses are "According to their imaginary representation, the masses drift somewhere between passivity and wild spontaneity, but always as potential energy, a reservoir of the social energy" (Baudrillard 1983: 2). In short, "the people" are a fiction that reinforces the logic of legitimation for liberal regimes, while the masses are the apathetic counter-fiction that represents an existential threat to liberalism. Politicians and political institutions shroud themselves in "the people," whom they defend and supposedly represent, and harangue "the masses," which always function like barbarians at the gate.

The masses are modeled populations whose data—gathered through public opinion polling—is their DNA. Baudrillard writes, "The whole constellation of the social revolves around that spongy referent, that opaque but equally translucent reality, that nothingness: the masses" (Baudrillard 1983: 1). The multitude, when transformed into a mass or the people, are a form of hyperobject, and much like the hyperobject that is the climate we cannot find "the masses" or "the people" in any one individual, nor can we trace the contours of the population through anything but modeling.[4] Nevertheless, polling also reifies and constructs the image it analyzes in our hyperreal world. For instance, the media reports on political polls, especially with the horse

[4]In many ways, the mass is also a figure that haunts the flip side of public opinion polling, that of advertising. According to the Pew Research Center, in explaining the difference between their work and consumer data, they write, "Market research explores opinions about products and services and measures your buying patterns, awareness of products and services or willingness to buy something. Our polls typically focus on public policy issues, mainly to inform the public." In short, polls function like market research, but instead of describing which soda company is more popular and analyzing how to shape and manipulate market share, polling focuses on which political positions people hold and how to manage and manipulate those feelings to alter market share.

race political analysis of twenty-four-hour new cycles, and as a result our conception of "the masses" becomes a tautology, in which the justification for its existence is found only as a statical mirage in the data that constructed the population in the first place.

However, like life under hyperreality, representation becomes the lived reality for those of us who inhabit a world shaped by the spectacle, and, in doing so, those who are lumped into "the masses" see themselves represented, albeit poorly, back at them in the form of polling and opinion data. The masses are "a black box of every referential, of every uncaptured meaning, of impossible history, of an untraceable system of representation, the mass is what remains when the social has been completely removed" (Baudrillard 1983: 6–7). We know that the representational category that supposedly represents us does not—the media landscape attempts to spoon-feed opinions and data to impose meaning and order onto the masses. However, as Baudrillard's entire project highlights, in hyperreal postmodernity we are not experiencing a lack of meaning but a glut of meaning. There has been a radical breakdown in consensus meaning and, with it, a multiplicity, a radical democratizing of meaning, to such a degree that meaning itself has been hollowed out and has become an open wound infecting the social. As a response, those who supposedly make up the masses reject the representation and the imposition of meaning and, with it, much of the logic of liberal politics. In rejecting the politics of imposed meaning and liberal representation, "the masses," according to Baudrillard, desire the comfort of the spectacle. So the political, in chasing its imaginary friend, turns politics into a spectacle, hoping to capture the masses in the process. The attempt to fill the concept of the masses with more and more meaning and identity makes them the black hole at the center of "the social," which is currently being torn apart and consumed as societies worldwide are fragmented and unraveling.

The modeling of climate change functions in many ways like the modeling of the masses. The climate is not a singular thing but a product of modeling, in which various ecological functions and cycles are combined to construct a representation, which becomes the target of state policy and regulation. In short, the idea of the climate is an abstract representation of an aspect of the natural world. Horkheimer and Adorno write:

> Abstraction, the instrument of enlightenment, stands in the same relationship to its objects as fate, whose concept it eradicates: as a liquidation. Under the leveling of abstraction, which makes everything in nature repeatable, and of industry, for which abstraction prepared the way, the liberated themselves finally become "the heard," which Hegel identified as the outcome of the Enlightenment. (Horkheimer, Adorno, and Schmid Noerr 2002: 9)

The abstraction of climate models, like the construction of the masses, is an attempt to make forces in the world repeatable and manageable by demystifying the world through the process of quantification. "Nature, before and after quantum theory, is what can be registered mathematically: even what cannot be assimilated, the insoluble and irrational is fenced in by mathematical theorems," Horkeheimer and Adorn write (Horkheimer, Adorno, and Schmid Noerr 2002: 18). In short, the climate is a fiction, like the masses, which exists simply as haunting of statistical analysis and complex tools of modeling. In making the model, a range of quantifiable aspects of the natural world is combined to show the outlines, and the contours, of the hyperobject. The climate, as a concept, is also imbued with meaning by the media and state apparatuses as scientists attempt to impose an identity on the nonidentity of nature.

Accepting the Nonidentity of Nature: Cthuhlu, Solaris, and the Masterless Object

This desire to find authenticity in the self and the world is part of a broader project of Western enlightenment that seeks to replace the "mystification" of nature with the logic of scientific domination and control. Instead, to borrow a phrase from William Conolly, we need to understand nature (and time) as existing as an "enigma of otherness" (Lem 2002: 64). To say that the material foundation of our world is shrouded in an enigma of otherness is to reinscribe the relationship of mystification over the world. This is not to say that there are no material limits to human (and nonhuman) development but merely that these foundations are inherently unknowable through the process of science or human cognition. The "climate" concept attempts to impose a universal and unified conception of identity onto a force with no such identity. The modeling itself, though, is rooted in the social and political world and is therefore shaped by those values. In a way, what we call the climate or the environment are merely mirrored representations of how we want to see the world's otherness without humans, to borrow a phrase from Eugene Thacker.

Stanisław Lem, in his masterpiece *Solaris (1961)*, provides one of the most compelling examples of how humans interact with an unknowable and unrepresentable other. This book follows the failed attempt by a team of scientists on a mission to explore a planet with an unknown form of intelligent life. Since finding the enigma of a planet, human scientists have spent decades trying to understand and uncover what sort of life and consciousness exists. Much like the simulacra of the climate, the best the scientists have been able to accomplish is collecting a disparate mix of seemingly unconnected facts and data, creating an entire discipline of science, "Solaristics," which attempted to model the data to create a unified picture of the other. Shortly before the book starts, the scientists bombard the planet with high-energy X-ray bombs, which leads to a reaction from the planet but not in a way that provides any insight into the inherent unknowability of the planet. The planet, which itself is a conscious ocean being, is unrepresentable, and the attempts by human scientists to engage with it or understand the being leads to disaster.

Philosophically, this book explores the complexity of human attempts to discover and unearth Truth through science and provides a profound critique of the logic of scientism. The process of discovery, for Lem, does not unearth the truth about the world but instead functions as a mirror to express what is inside of us. Lem writes, "We have no need of other worlds. We need mirrors. We don't know what to do with other worlds. A single world, our own, suffices us; but we can't accept it for what it is" (Lem 2002: 72). By understanding science not as a tool of external discovery, Lem also contends that the process of science functions as a form of colonization, in which we do not try to see the other as it is but instead impose the meaning we want to see on that other and force it to conform. "We have named all the stars and all the planets," Lem writes, "even though they might already have had names of their own. What a nerve (Lem 2002: 184)!" The humanness of the scientific process is a pitfall for Lem because we cannot conceive of thought or life outside of the bounds we experience. For instance, he asks, "Was it possible for thought to exist without consciousness?" (Lem 2002: 24). To the scientists studying Solaris, the answer they brought with them was "no," but in reality the planet provided that thought could exist in a way we cannot understand as consciousness.

Related to Lem, we can turn to the work of H .P. Lovecraft, whose weird fiction often focuses on how human consciousness fails to understand the thoughts and meaning of the elder gods. Lovecraftian monsters function as inherently unknowable, like the planet Solaris. For instance, in *Call of Cthulhu*, the story revolves around Francis Wayland Thurston as he investigates a mysterious cult he discovers through his great uncle's research journals. In this story, the horror of the unknown is hinted at through the mediation of science (academic research journals) and the dance of cults, but the intention and nature of the elder god Cthulhu are never uncovered. Lovecraft, an avowed racist, sexist, and antisemite fascist, understood how the enigma of otherness taps into a primordial fear of the unknown, or as Lovecraft stated: "The oldest and strongest emotion of mankind is fear, and the oldest and strongest kind of fear is fear of the unknown" (Herbert P. Lovecraft 1927).

Similarly Horkheimer and Adorno assert, "The gods cannot take away fear from human beings, the petrified cries of whom they bear as their names. Humans believe themselves free of fear when there is no longer anything unknown. . . .The enlightenment is mythical fear radicalized" (Horkheimer, Adorno, and Schmid Noerr 2002: 11). When combined, we can see the Enlightenment as a radicalization of our human desire to avoid fear, which requires conquering the unknown and, in doing so, trying to make everything visible and clearly defined. In a society rooted in industrialism and enlightenment rationality, Lovecraft's work highlights the undergirding anxiety that the entire edifice of modernity is rotten to the core and powers exist that are unknowable and predating humanity. Expressing this, he writes:

> The most merciful thing in the world, I think, is the inability of the human mind to correlate all its contents. We live on a placid island of ignorance in the midst of black seas of infinity, and it was not meant that we should voyage far. The sciences, each straining in its own direction, have hitherto harmed

> us little; but some day the piecing together of dissociated knowledge will open up such terrifying vistas of reality and of our frightful position therein that we shall either go mad from the revelation or flee from the deadly light into the peace and safety of a new dark age. (H. P. Lovecraft 2014: 381)

In Lovecraft's fictional world, the unknowable foundations of the cosmic peer from behind the imaginary visage we create of order and control. The existence of the unknown threatens enlightenment rationality as "nothing is allowed to remain outside, since the mere idea of the 'outside' is the real source of fear" (Horkheimer, Adorno, and Schmid Noerr 2002: 11).

Lovecraftian horror decenters humans and places us not as masters of the world but as insignificant beings living under the illusion of importance. Unable to embrace the nihilistic truth of a world that is indifferent toward us as a species, Lovecraft places the blame onto nonwhite populations, Jews, and women who are seen as coconspirators with the evil forces seeking to destroy the centrality of the white race in our world. Lovecraft's paranoia mirrors the conspiracy theories of neo-Nazi and the alt-right, who see behind everything a Jewish agenda, but that does not mean that he is not hinting at lived anxiety—the anxiety of the unknowable. Lovecraft, while pulling out a truth about the world, primarily projects his racial fears onto the nihilism he uncovers, and like all fascists he refuses to embrace and exist within nihilism but instead tries to fill the void of meaning with a mythical, authentic past.

Another way contemporary thinkers have tried to understand the nonidentity of the world beyond the human is through the hyperobject. According to Morton:

> the term hyperobjects refers to things that are massively distributed in time and space relative to humans. A hyperobject could be a black hole. A hyperobject could be the Lago Agrio oil field in Ecuador or the Florida Everglades. A hyperobject could be the biosphere or the Solar System. A hyperobject could be the sum total of all the nuclear materials on Earth, or just the plutonium or uranium. A hyperobject could be a very long-lasting product of direct human manufactures, such as Styrofoam or plastic bags, or the sum of all the whirring machinery of capitalism. Hyperobjects,

> then, are "hyper" in relation to some other entity, whether they are directly manufactured by humans or not. (Morton 2013: 1)

Hyperobjects are concepts that transcend the ability of humans to comprehend or understand. They are objects that, to Morton, have five different attributes. First, they are viscous, meaning that the object adheres to whatever it touches, leaving a trace of its existence, like ectoplasm. Second, they are molten, extending through time and space to such massive degrees that human sense and consciousness cannot fully grasp them. Third, they are nonlocal. This means that while we might see the traces and oozes of the hyperobject, we can never point to a single interaction between ourselves and the hyper object that illustrated or fully shows the hyper object. Fourth, hyperobjects exist in dimensions that we cannot explore and understand. Finally, hyperobjects are interobjective, meaning they do not exist as an entity in and of itself but as a multitude of relational links. This led Morton to correctly asserts that "An environment is precisely something one is unable to point to yet is strangely there nonetheless" (Morton 2016: 149).

Similarly, in William Connolly's book, *Facing the Planetary* (2017), we see an attempt to understand contemporary politics through the lens of the planetary. He defines the planetary as "a series of temporal force fields, such as climate patterns, drought zones, the ocean conveyor system, species evolution, glacier flows, and hurricanes that exhibit self-organizing capacities to varying degrees and that impinge upon each other and human life in numerous ways" (Connolly 2017: 4). The planetary in this conception attempts to do what Jordan Peterson accused climate modeling of doing, which is to try to create a theory of everything. In contrast to the planetary, he places the Anthropocene, the geologic order defined by the human capacity to shape and alter the world. With these two forces, we see a relational back-and-forth between the nonidentity of nature and the human attempt, or at least desire, to share and make the world in our image, to, in effect, impose our identity onto the planetary.

The work of Conolly moves toward decentering the enlightenment project of domination over nature but does not go far enough. The focus on scientific analysis to make clear the unknowable planetary, and with it, the rational conception of cause and effect haunts his work. We see an attempt to describe the complex planetary flows of the world through the creation of a more complicated model and not an exploration of the limits of imposing an identity, through computer modeling, on that which has no identity. Connolly understands the environment not through the traditional system of cause and effect but as a weatherman using complex modeling to make sense of atmospheric changes. The move to flows and blockages allows us to see politics as a planetary force and not the traditional politics of national state citizens, which is a significant move. However, the project still accepts the authority of climate modelings ontological and epistemological claims. It is in Sabu Kohso's work that the concept of the planetary is radicalized. Kohso contrasts the planetary—the natural flows and forces the Earth—with the World—human-constructed institutions like states, legal regimes, markets, and the like—and positions his politics as "anti-world." To Kohso, the Fukushima disaster and nuclear radiation, more general, functions as an antiworld force that transcends the institutions of the World in bypassing national borders and being beyond control by any human legal or policy regime. Radiation is a form of mushubutsu (無主物), or "masterless objects." After the massive disaster in Fukushima on 3/11, TEPCO, which owned the reactors in Fukushima, argued in court that radionuclides are masterless objects and are, therefore, not something that the corporation owns or can control and that it is the job of the state to enclose the masterless object and domesticate and control them. It asserted that "nuclear contaminants behave like a group of disowned workers roaming around society and posing a threat to its stability. These unleashed objects need to be renowned by the company and remastered by the state in a new way" (Kohso 2020: 104–5). To Kohso, these radionuclides, in conjunction with activists and inhabitants, refuse the dictates of state power, which "unveils the horizon of a new political ontology by reminding us of the situation we are thrown in, where everything in everyday life is interconnected via flows" (Kohso 2020: 11). This does not mean that the World or the state forms do not try to take advantage of the crisis of nuclear disasters; they, of course, do. The position of the state and capital is to use the uncontrollable nature of the mushubutsu to create a disaster economy in which they are tasked with continuously bordering and enclosing the mess they created. In short, the nuclear industry is doing what industrialism always does; it blackmails the populace to constantly fund them to clean up the mess that they created.

Kohso calls for more interesting politics, not of capture and control but of relationality and acceptance. He writes:

> Radiation is deadly and invincible for all vital activities. But it should not be considered transcendent or treated as a mere enemy. Instead, it must be dealt with through full passion, care, and rigor, both technopolitical and ontometaphysically, for us to live happy lives in the catastrophe. (Kohso 2020: 111)

Kohso rejects the idea that we must control or eliminate the masterless object. Instead, we must learn to live with it, not as an enemy, but as a part of the community that we also inhabit. He reminds us that "we are neither rulers nor saviors of the planet. We are just trying to live in a way comfortable for us and to die in a way that is suitable for us" (Kohso 2020: 165).

To end this section, I want to turn to the work of Gruppo di Nun, an anarchistic and nihilistic revolutionary occult group from Italy, and explore the unique way that they understand the destruction of the current order of things. Their collected book, *Revolutionary Demonology*, seeks to understand how an occult mindset, rooted in the destruction and disintegration of social institutions, can functionally counter the growing occult and irrationalism of the far right. The last few decades have seen an increase in occult-type practices, astrology, witch identification, Jungian archetypical thinking, and conspiracies. While there is a standard analysis of the growing irrationalism of this moment that primarily mocks such approaches or individualizes the process, there is a need to understand this phenomenon as a response to the crumbling social, semiotic, and ideological order. There was a similar rise in occultism, during the development of mass industrialism in Europe during the late nineteenth century and a second bump of irrationalism during the rise of fascism.[5]

---

[5]Eric Kurlander's *Hitlers Monsters* is a masterful historical analysis work detailing the relationship between Nazism and the occult. Kurlander contends that all national projects have an imaginary associated with them that serves as a way for the cult of the nation to operate. This imagination could be rooted in science fiction—such as early Soviet imaginaries—or in the supernatural—which

Gruppo di Nun is unique because while their analysis is influenced by certain mystical traditions—kabbalah and left-hand magic—their analysis is more nuanced and rarely seems to understand these mythical frameworks as giving them insight into truth or any comprehension of the real. For instance, they write that "the universe is by definition spontaneous; the spontaneity of things is independent of our will" (Gruppo di nun 2022: 19). As such, they do not view magic as allowing them a form of control over the world, nor do they believe it allows them to understand the universe. Both magic and specific aspects of science function as oracles and provide tools for uncovering the untruth of the contemporary world. In their ontology, there is, in fact, no eternal salvation or utopian revolutionary period. "We may easily understand that the future is a lie when we reflect that not only will our own life sputter one day," they write, "but also the sun, all the stars in the sky, and ultimately the entire universe. . . . If nothing is of any importance, if everything degenerates and crumbles, Man stands as an emperor of dust, because he knows no way of existing other than domination" (Gruppo di nun 2022: 25). Their ontological view understands the world as a deep and unknowable void, one that is indifferent to the wills or actions of humans. That we humans live and function in such a world opens up possibilities for new ways of living and political projects that allow for fleeting moments of joy, celebration, love, and excitement. While there may not be any 1000-year Reich or a stable period of endless joy, there are ways we can forge temporary autonomous zones in both space and time.

Their committed aims are to dismantle and destroy the institutions of contemporary life like the state, capitalism, systems of gender, white supremacy, and colonialism. In other words, an "antiworld politics." They write that "the world has already burned yet, at the same time, has not yet burned enough: our principle opponents are still standing . . . there is still much to be thrown into the flames, and there is still much to be said and done" (Gruppo di nun 2022: 131). Fusing their occultism with the work of Mark

---

was the case with fascism. With fascism, the supernatural was part of a broader project to project a form of deep authenticity, looking for long-held mythic truths, as well as an attempt to weaponize the enlightenment sciences to justify this mythical imaginary through "border" science, such as race science which included a fascination with Atlantis.

Fisher, the group sees their target as capitalist realism, which in their analysis fuels fascism and despair. Gruppo de Nun writes: "If a single message could be distilled from *Revolutionary Demonology*, it would be that there is always another world hidden in this one. A claim whose guarantee does not lie in the redemptive promise of a new dawn but in black incandescence of the long shadows of limitless modernity—darkness that reveals all the monsters that hide in the light" (Gruppo di nun 2022: 312). We must embrace the politics of the Underdark, and become partisans of the hidden city, saboteurs throwing our wooden shoes into the machinery of industrial production while offering playful and liberatory, though transient and temporary, situations of different ways of living.

Antiworld Politics and the Destruction of Enlightenment Order

Don't burn the Witch, burn, burn the rich.

—OI POLLOI, "DON'T BURN THE WITCH" (1999)

The planetary forces on Earth, like those on Solaris, are unknowable by the human mind. Religion and science both attempt to impose on the natural world a logic of identity so that we can use the same tools of agency, responsibility, and cause and effect to analyze human behavior. But nature is not a cohesive entity with a sense of identity, a knowable conscious purpose, or desires that can map onto the human cognitive frame. The anthropophorism of the world around us is not only an attempt to make the unknown familiar; it is part of a project to impose our domination on the world. Horkeimer and Adorno write:

> The spirit which practiced magic was not single or identical; it changed with the cult masks which represented the multiplicity of spirits. Magic is bloody untruth, but in it domination is not yet disclaimed by transforming itself into a pure truth underlying the world which it enslaves. The magician imitates demons; to frighten or placate them he makes intimidating or appeasing gestures. Although his task was impersonation he did not claim to be made in the image of the invisible power, as does civilized man, whose

> modest hunting ground then shrinks to the unified cosmos, in which nothing exists but prey. (Horkheimer, Adorno, and Schmid Noerr 2002: 6)

They here note that the logic of magic differs from that of enlightenment science. Both attempt to mediate and shape relationship with the world around us, but with magic the goal is not to dominate nature but to instead engage and play with the inherent unknowability of the planet. Such magical systems have more in common with art than they do with science. This, of course, does not mean that magic is "real" in a metaphysical sense but that magic can have profound social and material effects. David Abram, a former magician turned phenomonolgical philosopher, writes about his experience studying Balinese magic and notes that many of the rituals he witnessed expressed a playful engagement with the world around the human. As an example, Abram's noted that his host family put out an offering to the spirits around their house. Ants, daily, swarmed the offerings. He writes:

> It became apparent that the daily palm frond offerings served to preclude such an attack by the natural forces that surrounded (and underlay) the family's land. The daily gifts of rice kept the ant colonies occupied—and, presumably, satisfied. Placed in regular, repeated locations at the corners of various structures around the compound, the offerings seemed to establish certain boundaries between the human and ant communities; by honoring this boundary with gifts, the humans apparently hoped to persuade the insects to respect the boundary and not enter the buildings. (Abram 1996: 18)

Magic, or any spiritual practice though, can also become reified, and when that happens, identity is once again forced onto that which does not have one.[6] The imposition of a set and fixed identity marks the end of self-reflexivity

[6]We should also not just replace science with some preindustrial logic of magic. This is what we often see within the spiritualist community where magical rituals, practices, the runes are given fetishistic magical power based on the perceived "authenticity" of the tradition leading to either fights around cultural appropriation, or a potentially white supremacist project to regain pagan European magic. Magic, much like science, does not provide an access to Truth but is instead a way of mediating relationships and about descriptively accounting for material reality. Magic and science both need to learn from one another and reject desires to control the world on terms defined by human social and political relationships, while not slipping away from materialism into some primordial, presocial and pre-political, world of forms.

and marks the period when human systems attempt to control and dominate masterless objects.

The scientific approach to modeling the world around us seeks to make and remake the planet for our benefit, making us world watchers and active geoengineers. If populations of deer could be managed through statistical analysis and government regulation, so can we. What makes this even more ironic and sad is that the lack of action on the climate crisis has nothing to do with the lack of information or data. To bastardize Baudrillard, the problem is not that there is not enough data; there is too much data. The structural barriers to addressing the climate crisis are rooted in industrial economic impulses to continual growth, the states' desire for colonial expansion, and governmental desires to manage a stable and docile population. While often well-intentioned, the demand for more data, monitoring, and modeling is dangerous. We do not need to turn to abstract representation to be a part of the natural world; we need to feel and engage, without mediation, with the world around us. Instead of viewing the climate as a crisis to be controlled and regulated, we must view the climate as a dance partner, not as a beast to be held into submission.

During 2023, there have been many news stories about the rise of orcas' attacking and sinking yachts and other boats of the wealthy. In response, many on the left have correctly stated their solidarity with the orcas, viewing them as coconspirators in a class/species war against capitalism and the rich. There have been multiple attempts to make sense of why the orcas have begun attacking boats. Is it a result of increased underwater noise pollution? A result of the fiberglass bodies used in boat construction? Is it an intentional assault against invaders poisoning and despoiling their waterways? (Beddington 2023). Or is it, as Jacob Stern wrote in the Atlantic, in an absurdly serious piece in defense of yachts, that killer whales are "sadistic jerks"? (Stern 2023). Instead of looking to explain the purpose behind the orcas' assaults, is it not better to find a linkage of solidarity in the actions of the orcas? Does their purpose or intent even matter? Instead of seeking intentions or attempting to figure out the "cause and effect" that has led orcas to be collaborators against the wealthy, we must understand them as masterless objects, independent beings with a consciousness we cannot fully understand. This means not seeking to control their behavior but learning to dance with them, and to look them in the eyes, to feel their emotions, and to understand that they are our allies in the struggle against industrial destruction. Capitalism and the state are destroying the ocean ecosystem, and it is possible, within our lifetime, that we will witness a fisheries collapse that could lead to feedback cycles of extinction within the ocean that are unique in the planet's history. Regardless of whether we know why they are acting, we must support their actions and, in solidarity, also attack the yachts of the rich, the oil infrastructure that threatens the climate, and the sources of pollution poising the waters. We must learn to have solidarity without an understanding or an agreement on purpose, intentions, and the ability to coordinate and strategize. This applies to orcas, the climate, and our fellow human communities fighting oppression and violence.

4

A Rising Tide Sinks All Galleries

During the May 1968 uprising in Paris, René Viénet defaced a portrait of Cardinal Richelieu hanging in the Sorbonne. The militant drew a speech bubble on the portrait that said, "Humanity will not be happy until the day when the last bureaucrat has been hanged with the guts of the last capitalist" (Hemmens and Zacarias 2020: 99). On October 14, 2022, activists with the group Just Stop Oil threw tomato soup at Vincent van Gogh's "sunflowers." Two weeks later, climate activists glued their bodies to Johannes Vermeer's "Girl with A Pearl Earring" while Claude Monet's "Haystacks" had mashed potatoes thrown at it in Germany. The pieces of art, all of which were protected behind the glass, were not damaged, unlike the portrait of Richelieu. Even so, the outcry in the media and among the political and managerial classes has been vitriolic. The Atlantic's Robinson Meyer states, "So we don't know that the protests are effective, and we do know that they're likely to cause financial problems for many museums. Here I will add my own concern: The activists look so silly" (Meyer 2022). This critique of the "effectiveness" of the protest is found in every mainstream media discussion of the event, from Fox News and the *Washington Post* to Axios and Slate. The central question facing our culture, and which these acts bring up, is: What is the role of art on a burning planet?

Theodore Adorno, in 1949, wrote, "To write poetry after Auschwitz is barbarism" (Adorno 2003: 280), because that poetry after the horrors of the holocaust must engage with the ungraspable spectacle of modernity. Art in this moment is similar as it must either ignore the brutality of industrial society—which is a barbaric position—or actively engage with the horror of the holocaust—which is also a barbaric choice. Since the industrial revolution and the rise of industrialism, capitalist production systems have churned enough greenhouse gases to alter our atmosphere's chemical composition. Before industrialism, there were 280 ppm of carbon in our atmosphere. In 2022, there was 422 ppm. For the last thirty years, we have lived in an atmosphere in which climate change discussions have insisted that there are decades to act, and yet, even as the crisis gets worse and worse, that time frame never seems to change.[1] Especially since, on nearly every metric, the earlier models showed themselves to be too conservative. Ice has melted at unimaginable rates; the oceans have warmed quicker than expected; and in 2022, greenhouse gas emissions reached the highest level in human history. We live on a planet burning, and our cultural focus is not on the mass extinction, forced migration, or weather disasters of the climate crisis, because to do so would be unsettling and sad; in short, it would be barbaric.[2] The goal for art, at this moment, needs to center the horrors of the world and not shy away from being barbaric.

Art, the Economy, the State

Soulless pale monsters
Strip mined our futures
Our only birthright to suffocate, starve and die
—PUNITIVE DAMAGE, "THIS IS THE BLACKOUT"

[1]I use this data not to reify science as finding objective truth, but to show that there are descriptive aspects of science that are valuable to us. That said, the main desire that comes from the dominant approaches of climate management is to regulate and control the planetary for the perceived benefits of the World. This sort of management is a form of domination and as the domination of the planetary groups, so does the domination for those inhabitants of the planetary (i.e., us and all other life).

[2]We live in a spectacle of cruel optimism that seeks to distract from the horrors of the world. Most "art" functions as a spectacle; as a distraction from the horrific violence of the present. But even mainstream art and film is haunted by the horrors of the present and likely future. The barbarism worms its way through to even the most banal and escapist forms of art and culture.

Walter Benjamin (1986) states, "Mechanical reproduction of art changes the reaction of the masses toward art" (Benjamin, Arendt, and Zohn 1986: 234). The capitalist and industrial logic of mass production, combined with shifting technological innovations, alters the role and function of art in society. Art in the Lascaux cave paintings differs in its social function from the Van Gogh dipped in tomato soup like grilled cheese. To Benjamin, the cave paintings were tied to a conception of the cultic ritual, while the museum paintings exist through the logic of exhibition value. What is the role of exhibition value in relation to the modern system of capitalist accumulation? For wealthy collectors, the work of art functions primarily as a means of avoiding taxes, while the museums, through a façade of cultural importance, serve as laundering firms doing the dirty work for the ultra-wealthy. The focus on the value of the Van Gogh, $110 million according to a 2019 evaluation, is primarily related to the tax avoidance logic of modern art value. In 2008, the *LA Times* reported that over $1 billion were written off taxes due to donating art pieces for museum exhibitions. A quick search shows countless websites offering advice for wealthy clients who wish to lower their tax burden through the laundering mechanism of the museum (Felch and Smith 2008). The hyperinflation of art, as Baudrillard understood in *Critique of the Political Economy of the Sign*, is linked to a shift in the structure of value in the postmodern world. In Marxist theory, value was linked to labor, but in the postmodern era the sign itself has the ability to create its own inflated conception of value. This inflated value is linked to the logic of branding and identity, which allows for people to shift from use value, or even symbolic value, to the value of the sign. The shift to sign value marks a logical shift from that of capitalism—which is just about maximizing accumulation—with the consumption of art as a form of expressing one's social power and position. Baudrillard claims, "Museums play the role of banks in the political economy of paintings" (Baudrillard 2019: 122), which allows for art to maximize the accumulation of social and material capital by decreasing the economic cost of purchasing one's social importance.

Museums' existence are also linked to fossil fuel wealth, as anyone who walks into any of the Koch brothers-funded art and science museums can attest.[3] A Grist article from 2019 asks, "Oil money has fueled the arts for ages, and can museums survive without it?" This piece, which highlights the long legacy of oil wealth support for museums and cultural institutions provides a new meaning for the phrase "putting oil on canvas."[4] The study astutely states:

> Across the country, museums are working to protect their irreplaceable collections from the ravages of climate change: rising seas, more frequent flooding, and worsening wildfires. In an ironic twist, many of these institutions, through their boards, funding sources, and fortunes amassed by their founders, are closely tied to the fossil fuel companies that have contributed the most to the problem. (Yoder 2019)

Art Not Oil, a climate change nonprofit, highlighted how BP has funded and influenced the British art world. Their 2016 report illustrates how fossil fuel money shapes the curation of galleries throughout the country and how fossil fuel logic shapes the ideological apparatus of the museum. Because of this, to assert, as so much of the media coverage of the current climate protests in museums, that they are targeting the wrong institutions is flat-out wrong. The museum and the art they house as a tax break for oil corporations and the rich are complicit in, if not actively supporting, the expansion of the climate crisis. If oil is the lifeblood of the museum world, then the museum world is complicit in every death and extinction caused by the climate crisis. To engage in a détournement of a Raoul Vaneigem quote: museums have a corpse in their mouth, and if we only engage in half measures, we do too (Vaneigem 2012).

Negation as an Artistic Medium: Activism as Performance Art

Much like statues or any other curated use of space, museums provide ideological narratives that frame the world. George Maciounas, in his Fluxus manifesto (1963), understood this. This piece reads: "PROMOTE A

[3]Nearly everything stated here also applies to the universities and individual and corporate donations.

[4]A colleague and friend, Eyal Barr, made this joke, and I felt it was too good to not include.

REVOLUTIONARY FLOOD AND TIDE IN ART, Promote living art, anti-art, promote NON ART REALITY to be fully grasped by all peoples, and not only critics, dilettantes, and professionals" (Danchev 2011: 365). This anti-elitist and public conception of art are also found in the work of the situationists, CoBra, the letterists, dadaism, punk art, and other art movements. These projects attempted to shatter the divide between art and everyday, between the artist and the consumer, and between the world of play and creativity and the doldrums of everyday existence under capitalism.

As a historical example, the activist art collective Up Against the Wall Motherfucker/Black Mask embedded the anti-art praxis of Dada with the political militance of a "street gang with an ideology" (Grindon 2015). Like the punk movement, which was heavily influenced by the motherfuckers, "what was only hinted at, for example, in surrealism or Fluxus, was exaggerated or taken to (brutal) reality in punk, which resulted in a double effect of seemingly both admiring and mocking the paragons" (Skov 2023: 145). The first significant action organized by black mask was a protest against the Museum of Modern Art. In a pamphlet/manifesto, they wrote and distributed before the action; they wrote: "DESTROY THE MUSEUMS . . . our struggle cannot be hung on walls" (Hahne and Morea 2011: 5; ellipses in the original). The second significant action from the group had twenty-five members dressed in black masks carrying signs along Wall Street, declaring it War Street by changing the street signs. In defense of the action, they wrote, "If unemployment rises, you are given work, murderous work. If education is inferior, you are taught to kill. If the blacks get restless, they are sent to die. This is Wall streets' formula for the great society" (Hahne and Morea 2011: 22)! Their overall analysis fused art and radical activism, refusing to accept the boundaries and authorities of galleries or museums, and instead turned art into a revolutionary weapon to be wielded in the streets and opposition to the galleries. "The aesthetic revolution of today must be part of the total revolution," they wrote. "A revolution will be about a society where the arts will be an integral part of life, as in primitive society, and not an appendage to wealth" (Hahne and Morea 2011: 13). The art collective embraced a total liberation approach that centered the museums and the art world as being the handmaiden of liberal, imperialist, society. Their actions targeted these institutions in direct ways. For instance, in an action against the poet Kenneth Koch in 1967, group members pulled handguns and shot blanks at the poet during a reading before throwing radical pamphlets throughout the audience and running away. In the same year, they interrupted the opening night of an art gala by dumping uncollected garbage into the fountain in front of the Lincoln Center. Like the situationists, contemporaries they shared theoretical and interpersonal links with, Up Against the Wall attempted to shatter the line between art and life, often at gunpoint (Grindon 2015).

An example of a contemporary form of blurring the lines of art and everyday is Kevin Nguyen and T. J. Khayatan's piece "Glasses," where the two high school students played a prank by placing a pair of glasses on the ground in the San Francisco Art Museum (Hunt 2016). The impromptu piece "Glasses" highlights that the prank and the performance of art coexist in everyday acts. The prank becomes art as art becomes the joke. Flipping this discussion and showing that protest and everyday are also forms of performance art, the "Christopher Columbus Discovers the Sidewalk, circa 2022, colorized" is an appropriation of art logic by activists resisting the long legacy of white supremacy and colonization. The public debate and discussion of the role of monuments in this meme translates the act of resistance as a form of performance art, which is, in fact, an accurate assessment. If art is to be understood broadly and through a lens of social critique and resistance, then many aspects of the protests against the edifices of this destructive culture—white supremacy, fossil capital, consumer capitalism, patriarchy—need to be analyzed as both a form of protest and an example of performance art; likewise, art must not attempt to be neutral or reactionary, but embrace a radical politics that seeks to upend the world. As Guy Debord stated: "Art in the period of its dissolution, as a movement of negation in pursuit of its own transcendence in a historical society where history is not yet directly lived, is at once an art of change and a pure expression of the impossibility of change" (Debord 1994: 135).

The collapsing of protest and art is best theorized by the situationists with their conception of "constructed situations." In a constructed situation, the situations attempted to shatter the hold of the spectacle on everyday life and liberate people from the passivity that consumer capitalism created for them. In his "report on the construction of simulations," Debord writes, "Our central idea is the construction of situations, that is to say, the concrete construction of momentary ambiances of life and their transformation into a superior passional quality. . . . The construction of situations begins beyond the ruins of the modern spectacle" (Knabb 2006: 22). The situationists were unsettled by infusing artistic resistance into the everyday. This could include détournement, which is seen in the film *La Dialectique peut-elle casser des briques?* In this film, René Viénet re-subtitled the martial arts film *Crush* by Tu Guannqi, making the film into a radical critique of capitalism, colonialism, and the banality of everyday life. The hijacking of a movie and changing its meaning is an example of creating a situation in which the everyday experience of something, like watching a kung fu movie, is shattered, and revolutionary politics fills the ideological space that the situation opens (La Dialectique peut-elle casser des briques? 1973). The current climate protest in museums is a form of a constructed situation in which the activists are using the logic of the spectacle—as their acts are, without any question, a spectacle, and thus why these actions have garnered as much news as they have—to critique the political economy of modern fossil fuel capitalism. That said, they have failed to understand the work as a constructed situation which weakens the political impact of these actions. The climate protestors are aware of the power of the spectacle but do not provide critical politics in opposition to the spectacle.

One core way these protests differ from the situationist's examples is that the climate protestors are not enacting an assault on the banality of the everyday but are instead using the logic of the media spectacle to amplify a didactic political message. Didactic art and protest foreclose politics and debate and, as such, are a totalizing discourse. The climate protestors have shown how quickly such uncritical situation construction can be recuperated through media framing. This is because the protests seek to use the media's fascination with great works of Western art to shed light on the climate change crisis. They view the art as a protest location, not a source of the protest itself. By avoiding the direct linkage between museums and colonialism, extractive capitalism, and slavery, the protestors turn the art pieces into empty signifiers. When René Viénet targeted the portrait of Cardinal Richelieu, he centered the work of art as part of the broad cultural institutions of power that needed to be destroyed. He turned the art from reactionary propaganda to radical propaganda. The art's form was hijacked with the speech bubble, and its symbolic meaning was hijacked through the message added.

There is a long history of art being destroyed or defaced as a form of art. Guy Debord and Asger Jorn's book *Mémoires* (Jorn and Debord 1959) was bound with sandpaper and was designed to cause damage and destroy the books next to it and the shelf itself. In his 1953 "Erased de Kooning drawing," Rauschenberg used an eraser to remove the line art from a de Kooning work. This work by Rauschenberg, through negation, created a new piece of art. Gustav Metzger, in his manifesto on "auto-destruction" writes:

> Man In Regent Street is auto-destructive.
> Rockets and nuclear weapons are auto-destructive.
> Auto-destructive art.
> The drop drop dropping of H bombs.
> Not interested in ruins (the picturesque)
> Auto-destructive art re-enacts the obsession
> with destruction, the pummeling to which individuals and masses are subjected.
> Auto-destructive art mirrors the compulsive
> perfectionism of arms manufacture—polishing to destruction point.
> (Danchev 2011: 345)

Much like the nuclear arms race, the industrial logic of contemporary capitalism is an inherently auto-destructive form of expression. In response to the suicidal reason of our modern society, art needs to be destructive, and as a political tactic it needs to target all institutions of life, including the gallery and museums. Our society is on the pace toward destruction, and auto-destructive art and protest bring this reality to the fore. On a burning planet, the destruction of a Monet or a Van Gogh can serve as a form of artistic resistance to art's complicit role in the destruction of the world.

Mausoleums of Our Extinct Culture

Most things go unnoticed with your eyes gouged out.

—THE LOCUST, "KILL RODGER HEDGECOCK" (1997)

Now, we can hear the yelling crowds, outraged at the idea of great works of art being destroyed. Why would you ruin a Van Gogh simply as part of a political protest? All you get is attention, and that attention is negative. There are other ways to protest. You can vote. You can hold signs. You can, for a little bit, disrupt traffic. Why destroy Western culture? That is going too far. In response, we must scream, "What value does art have on a dying planet?" As sea levels rise, forests burn, crops die, species go extinct, and refugees are forced from their homes only to face xenophobic hatred of the industrial world, to center the importance of "great art" is obscene, and not in a fun or exciting way. When people are dying and species are going extinct, does a Monet or a Van Gogh, or the existence of any museum, matter? Art, at this moment, must be part of a broader resistance to the forces destroying the planet. The idea of art as comfort, a commodity, and a distraction (especially when that comfort is primarily provided to the political and economic elite) is a form of cruel indifference that is more distasteful than anything the climate protestors could do in a museum.[5]

The museum and curated collections that serve as reminders of colonialism and coconspirators of capitalist wealth accumulation need to become a target of this resistance. In his book *Ecocritique (*1994), Tim Luke decries the nature conservancy for trying to save nature, a term that has always been fraught with Western and colonial narratives of conquest, which had already died with the rise of the Anthropocene and globalization of the logic of capitalism. Luke highlights how the nature conservancy uses the tools and logic of property rights and ownership in order to protect the natural world. All they are doing is using the logic of private property to protect against the harm caused by private property. But, of course, this approach does not work, and Luke contends that the nature conservancy builds and maintains nature cemeteries

---

[5]I do want to highlight that there is, of course, value to joy and beauty regardless of its broader social value. The issue at odds here is the way that our current system excludes this joy from the majority of us, who are instead suffering under the social institutions that these wealthy art collectors use as a tax avoidance scheme. To enjoy hedonism and playful fun on a world on fire, is no vice; to get to do so only through exclusion or deep exploitation of those poorer than you is.

as mausoleums where we can preserve the memory of nature. He writes, "Because Nature has ended, material signs of its now-dead substance need to be conserved as pristine preserved parts, like pressed leaves in a book, dried animal pelts in a drawer, or a loved one's mortal remains in a tomb" (Luke 1997: 68). We are in a similar space with Western culture. It is dying, as the waters from raising sea's fill our collective lungs, and these museums, these pieces of "great art," are the dried animal pelts and pressed leaves we keep to remember some mythical great past; they are artifacts left for those who scavenge in the rubble of our modern civilization.

Besides the dangers of climate change, modern industrial capitalism has already devalued art. As Walter Benjamin noted, the mass production process of art diminishes the aura found within it. He writes that the aura results from "A peculiar web of space and time: the unique manifestation of a distance, however near it may be" (Benjamin, Arendt, and Zohn 1986: 238). The advances of industrial technologies around art—notably film—decay this aura, as the work is flattened into a mass commodity. It is not only film, though, that decays the aura. Benjamin, in describing the anti-art project of Dadaism, states, "what they intended and achieved was a relentless destruction of the aura's of their creations, which they branded as reproductions with the very means of production" (Benjamin, Arendt, and Zohn 1986: 237–8). The barbarism of Dada mirrored the barbarism of industrial technologies, and, in doing so, they auto-destructed the aura of their work. The early punk focused on Super 8 films and other detritus of crumbling Western society (like the current return to cassette tapes in the punk community). According to Skov, those early punk practices were radical because they used the disposed of technology of the past as a way to undermine the ability of the arts to be a mass commodity. Super 8 degrades with every playing, as do cassettes, meaning that the medium is, in a way, auto-destructing itself. Dirk Schaefer stated, "Every screening [of super eight] can be the last: indeed, every screen is the last in a certain sense because a little bit is eroded from the original every time" (Skov 2023: 76). Punk, as well as Dada before it, embraced the destruction of the aura of art because, with the rise of industrial mass production, it helped limit the arts from being coopted and turned into a commodity.

However, capitalism itself has done more to degrade the art than any anti-art activists ever could. For instance, a reproduction of Van Gogh's Sunflowers, the piece with tomato soup thrown at it, is available in many different forms with prices ranging from $8 for a used poster to $70 for a wall-mounted stretched canvas. The presence of millions of copies of this piece increases the value of the original in an exchange logic that mirrors that of the NFT market. Anyone can have and reproduce this piece of art in a digital form (or printed sense), but the collector owns the rights to the "authentic" real version. With each printing of this work, the aura decays, and, just like NFTs, the mass reproduction of a piece of art increases the exchange value of the "authentic" by draining the art of any actual aura. If a capitalist accumulates by sucking the dead labor of workers, then the political economy of the sign functions by sucking dry the aura from art. Every Banksy reproduction, hanging in a college dorm or a coffee shop, increases the original's exchange value while ensuring the radical message is pacified. This crisis of "aura" is only growing with the advent of AI art, which has led to various reactions within the art world. When AI can produce art, is there any aura to that work? The fact that AI art "produces" new pieces through the theft of artists' work is an expression of the algorithm viewing art and culture as a form of "readymade" that can be taken and repurposed. What makes this readymade so much more destructive than the readymade art of the Dada works is that the AI system attempts to replace artists, not so that they can engage in less-alienating labor, but to depress their wages and push them into even more alienating forms of labor. In short, the value of art has been altered by the expansion of industrial forms of production, and that value will decay more as the climate crisis worsens. The more the center of value hollows out, the more abstract financialization logic, rooted in tax avoidance schemes and investment logic, will create speculative bubbles. As sure as the seas will rise, that bubble will burst. Art cannot avoid the decaying of its aura under capitalism, and instead of giving art over to the logic of exchange and curation value, we need to recenter art's radical and utopian potentiality.

Art as Resistance and Resistance as Art

Rosa Luxemburg claimed that we had only two choices: Socialism or barbarism (Luxemburg and Le Blanc 2010). In the century since she made this declaration, the prospects for a future that resembles, in any way, the industrial logic of the present have disappeared. Barbarism is the only option. The forces of the status quo—media pundits, the art establishment, social movement, and political leaders—know that we must be made blind to the dangers on the horizon. They might give the abstract acceptance of "the science" but only in a way that keeps the attention to the present and away from the foreclosed future.

At this moment, the role of art is that of revolutionary resistance; it is no longer—if it ever was—purely aesthetic. Art that does not undermine the legitimacy of the institutions or industrial capitalism only facilitates the speculative economy of death. The climate protestors have shown the uncomfortableness our society has when the destructive effects of the climate catastrophe threaten not life but wealth and power. Instead of social pressure to make them stop these protests, the art community needs to push them to go further. There is a space for the logic of art to merge more with insurrectionary desires and dreams, as we saw with the protests to destroy and remove colonial and racist memorials. The divide between art and activism and between performance and insurrection must be blown to bits. This can only be done through direct actions to undermine the museum's role in constructing and maintaining the climate crisis and the spectacle more broadly. The climate protests against museums pieces are a solid start, but the critique needs to go much deeper, as do the targets of the attacks. The board of trustees of museums should be targeted, bringing back the class critique against high art. Projects to negate the financial value of art in the gallery through direct action, which may damage or destroy the pieces, are needed as, according to the tax ledger logic of the art world's, creative expression primary value is its use as financial tool of class oppression. The arts need to shift their projects away from the gallery and art world and embed their projects in the lived world of people. Looking at the history of punk—with its reliance on graffiti, performance, and lived experience—offers a glimpse into the actions that might be needed here. The museum must become a site of revolutionary resistance and the critique must be expanded beyond the white walls of the galleries to the social museums of life. Last, art needs to open up the space for insurrectionary potential by centering the creation of situations. Art projects should disrupt the banality of the everyday and, with that, either provide alternative ways of living and being in the world or illustrate the horrible violence and untruth of the spectacle. But they should also encourage or make people into accomplices against the spectacle. Performance art and activism should not embrace the spectator logic of the spectacle but offer a Molotov cocktail or brick to every man, woman, and child to throw at the walls of our crumbling civilization. Insurrectionary performance art must express solidarity with the ghosts that haunt the museums' hallways and the alleyways of our cities.

5

No Future, No Hope

There ain't no future and there ain't no hope
For humankind or change within the system
There ain't no future and there ain't no hope
In a fucked up system that takes your life away
There ain't no future and there ain't no hope
Rules and regulations getting in our way
There ain't no future and there ain't no hope
The only hope and dream I have is to watch it all destroyed

—DEFIANCE, "NO FUTURE, NO HOPE" (1996)

In *Combined and Uneven Apocalypse*, artist and philosopher Evan Calder Williams contends that the punk suffix in genres like cyberpunk and steampunk, as well as the ethos and philosophy of punk as a genre and subculture, overlaps with the assertion that there is "no future" (E. C. Williams 2011). The boyband branded radicals, The Sex Pistols, express this clearly in their 1977 hit "God Save the Queen." Johnny Rotten sang of there being no future for "you" or "me"—a vision that can be read as a form of existential defeatism. There is a truth to that, but it has a much more nuanced and complicated political vision. Claiming that there is no future is a form of refusal against the logic of capitalist realism. If, as Fisher claims, there is no outside logic of capitalism and, with it, no visions of a postcapitalist world, the only revolutionary practice is apocalyptic. Through an analysis of salvage punk films, like *Mad Max*, Williams contends, "We do not become post-apocalyptic because the plague swells, the bombs drop, or the earth cools. We become post-apocalyptic when we accept the present as rubbish, undead, and under attack" (Williams 2011: 9). This becoming postapocalyptic requires the rejection of a political future and a turn toward a politics of salvage. Echoing a similar feeling, Sabu Kohso in *Radiation and Revolution* calls for an apocalyptic communism that openly rejects the politics of the future. He writes:

> All in all, none of us are optimistic. We perceive signs of civilizational decline in all kinds of disasters. We know that our living conditions will change for the worse and possibly the worst: the apocalypse. We feel that our struggles may be losing the race against apocalyptic time. It is hard not to imagine the end of our living environment through apocalyptic imaginaries, scientific data, and increasing experiences of disasters. (Kohso 2020: 158)

The dominant ideological positions under industrialism all center a logic of the future. In liberalism, a continual present is projected forward, while fascism grabs a mythic past and makes "the future great again," and communism, through its dialectic historical materialism, imagines a future free of class conflict—an end of history but not a claim against the future. The punk ideological position against the future shatters the temporal logic of industrialism. The punk chant of "no future," of course, does not mean that there will not be a tomorrow, though, at some point, there will cease to be one; it is instead a rejection of the ideological project of time.

Michael Truscello's book *Infrastructural Brutalism*, following the punk ethos above, illustrates that the cultural discourse around ecological sustainability hides a violently necropolitical project. Truscello uses the phrase infrastructural brutalism to explain how infrastructural projects construct features into the landscape—such as dams and roads—which hide the massive suffering and death that these projects require. The capitalist and industrial realism of modern life, to Truscello, is leading to development that forecloses future possibilities. For instance, the political and economic forces are increasing their investment into fossil fuel infrastructural projects, which locks in fossil dependence for the next forty to fifty years (Truscello 2020). The scope of this development is never discussed in popular news or media, and, if anything, infrastructure is always championed as a positive that everyone can agree to. But the scope of building right now is jaw-dropping. China has used more concrete, one of the most carbon-intensive materials, in the last decade than the United States used in the entire twentieth century. China will only use more concrete as their Belt and Road Initiative really swings into full gear. With those sort of development, we are being railroaded into the death camps of fascism and ecological collapse. The analysis of *infrastructural brutalism* undercuts the industrial and growth logic used to justify every engineering solution: renewables, electric cars, bioengineering, and gene hacking. Truscello's analysis also elucidates the complex ways in which the popular conversations on the climate crisis and development ignore facts that undermine their ideological project. Instead, the industrial focus on building its way through the ecological crises we face is in reality just a form of collective accelerations toward societal collapse or fascism.

Temporal Nihilism

Space and time are interrelated socially constructed concepts. In other words, the ideological underpinning of how we understand space shapes how we conceive of time, and vice versa. Italian theorist Franco "Bifo" Berardi writes that "the future is not an obvious concept, but a cultural construction and a projection" (Berardi 2011: 17). While linear time is often naturalized, the concept is relatively new, emerging from the Enlightenment. Linear time and, most importantly, the vision of a future are part of the larger project of industrial society. According to Bifo, pre-enlightenment visions of time focused more on the past, with the narrative of the fall from the Garden of Eden, or cyclical visions of time related to the growing seasons. With European "discovery" and colonization of the Americas, books and maps had to be rewritten to include all the new information. By showing that the past was ignorant of the broader world, colonization created an optimistic sense that as time unfolded so would our general knowledge about the world—the future functions as telos providing a circular defense of industrial production. Since today is better than the past (a dubious ideological assertion), it is assumed that the future will be better than today. While we might be destroying the land, sea, and air, it is merely a collateral damage on a planned path into the future. Time is a psychological phenomenological experience and not a scientific one, and therefore our political, social, and economic realities shape our perceptions of time much more than any scientific theory. What we call the future is a complex social image manufactured by competing ideologies of industrial production.

All industrial ideological projects focus on and center the future, using the future as a place to transfer wish fulfillment through fantastical projections. Utah Philips, the American anarchist bard and folk singer, claimed that "there is pie in the sky when you die. That's a lie!" Philips was critiquing the Christian logic that justified present suffering for deferred gratification in heaven, but Christianity is not the only ideological system that does such a thing. According to Bifo, "liberalism and social democracy, nationalism and communism, and anarchism itself, all the different families of modern political theory share a common certainty: notwithstanding the darkness of the present, the future will be bright" (Berardi 2011: 18).[1] For those ideologies that embrace modernist assumptions, there is a universal focus on an optimistic account of the future. There is a crisis that emerges when the future is shrouded in catastrophism, since these ideologies need to project a telos. Not being able to forces a contradiction that leads to a suicidal and fascistic drive.

The language and topic of hope has been centralized in the majority of our political and intellectual discussions. The defenders of hope argue that we need hope to provide a light to guide our actions through the darkness and that pessimism is more likely to turn people toward apathy or conservative political projects. As James Davis writes, "From a rhetorical standpoint, catastrophism is a win/win for the right . . . fear and paranoid serve as rights political predisposition more than the left or liberal on" (Lilley 2012: 106). Similarly, Rebecca Solnit states that "Hope calls for action; action is impossible

---

[1]For anarchism, counter to Bifo's claim, there is a more complicated relationship with the idea of a future. There is an argument to be made that certain forms of "classical 19th century anarchism—with the exception of Stirner—does project a future oriented telos." But, there are many examples of anarchist theory that reject any future projection. For instance, Gustov Landauer argues that "for us, however, the moment alone exists; do not sacrifice reality to a phantom!" Similarly, Uri Gordon argues regularly for a present-tense focus for revolutionary or radical change. That said, these are strands of anarchism that tend to be critical of industrial production and workerism and are therefore also critical of most of the core assumptions of modernity.

without hope" (Solnit 2016: 4). This general logic that pessimism breeds conservatism and that liberal or left politics requires hope is at the core of the current tensions and problems we find with the current attempts to engage with the current limits of the World marked by climate change. The dominant approaches to communists, fascists, and liberals all project fantasies into the future, which allow them to justify and legitimate current sacrifices and suffering. In a World where their future claims seem increasingly unlikely, the violent focus on suffering and sacrifice gets turned inward, functionally creating a suicidal death drive.

The reification of linear time hides the void of representational failure within modernist ideologies, helping to form a capitalist-industrialist complex. Our current world is shaped by the postwar spectacle, which followed not the cyclical rhythm of the planet but the repetition of the workday: sleep, work, consume, continued ad nauseam. According to Fredric Jameson, postmodernism functions under a logic of a pure present-projected forward. Tomorrow will be the same as today. Even nostalgia, a longing focused on the past, is really about anxieties and tensions within the present. *Too Many Cooks (2014)*, an absurdist horror short produced by *Adult Swim* in 2014, is an excellent example of the horror of the collapsing of time during Covid. In *Too Many Cooks*, the stereotypical introduction to a TV sitcom—a sappy song playing over cut scenes of a family doing banal tasks such as cooking or sitting on a couch taking a photo—is repeated ad absurdum. However, when the theme song ends, instead of simple repetition the story gets more surreal as new neighbors and family members are introduced as characters in this ever-growing surreal sitcom intro. In the repetition, a secondary story emerges in which a serial killer hunts down and kills the family. Before that murder story can be solved, the narrative shifts again as the show shifts to different genres, from police procedurals to science fiction to medical drama. Even genre ceases to make sense as, toward the end, the actors and the embedded text shift place. Text becomes moving characters—sitting on a couch or making dinner—while the characters, screaming in existential dread, are transposed under the character forms of "text." The repetition of the TV sitcom, which is a perfect example of the Debordian and Baudrillardian critique of postmodern society, mirrors the postmodern structure of life. Though made before Covid, the collapse of time experienced by Covid is apparent in this short film. Covid, and its lockdowns, stretched the repetition of daily life at the core of liberal fantasies to a breaking point where death haunted our lives, much like the serial killer in the background of the video hunted and killed the family members. As we experienced the absurdity of telling a co-worker, "You are muted," and laughing while the news reported daily death totals in the tens of thousands globally, the horror of the present became projected forward, replacing the illusory sense of stability that was previously projected. At the same time that Covid collapsed time in on itself, time has also been stretched to a breaking point with the development of "deep," "geological," and "climatological" time scales. The John Web Space Telescope, which began taking photos in July 2021, has provided the deepest images of space to date. The oldest galaxy photo is JADES-GS-z13-0, the light of which showed a snapshot of this galaxy only 320 million years after the theorized creation of the universe 13.8 billion years ago. Meanwhile, on Earth, the development of nuclear technologies has led to the issue of nuclear waste, which, in the case of uranium 235, has a 700 million-year half-life. Creating waste byproducts require over 2,000 times more time to decay than humans have lived on the planet. The stretching of time functionally creates instability in our perceptions and conceptions of time. This instability threatens the stability of political conceptions of the future as well.

While liberalism projects an endless present forward, fascism looks toward a mythical past and projects that vision forward. Rodger Griffin, in his study of historical fascism, uses the term "palingenesis," a mixture of "birth" and "again," to define how fascism tries to birth a past vision into the future. Andreas Malm and the Zetkin collective write, "But whenever and wherever fascism appears, it will posit the sequence of past grandeur to present crisis to coming rebirth of an exalted and exclusive nation" (Malm 2021b: 291). But fascistic visions of the future are not just "backward-looking" as they fuse old values with a fetishistic embrace of industrial technologies. In the *Futurist* Manifesto (1909), Marinetti centers the automobile in his artistic imagination. He writes, "We declare that the world's splendor has been enriched by a new beauty: the beauty of speed. A racing automobile with its bonnet adorned with great tubes like a serpent with explosive breath . . . .a roaring motor car which seems to run on machine-gun fire, is more beautiful than the victory of Samothrace"

(Danchev 2011: 5). Futurism, which also had its Soviet variants, found an alliance with fascism over their shared love of industrial machines—primarily those of war and speed. In a later poem, Marinetti wrote, "Gasoline is divine. So is religious ecstasy inspired by 100 horsepower" (Malm 2021b: 504). The religious fetish for the automobile was embraced by both Mussolini and Hitler, who used state resources to build the first high-speed roadways such as the Autobahn in Germany. The fascists in both regimes saw in highways a fusion of the erotic desire for speed and machines. This technophilia still functions as an ideological underpinning the contemporary far-right's fascinated with gasoline-powered cars.

Fascist writer Ernst Junger defends machines as essential to fascistic politics since industrial machinery allowed for the perfection of war and the art of killing. He wrote, "the motion of machines is of a coercive character. It runs over whoever stands in its way, becoming a means of destruction. Any protests will crash against its steel shell, like the protest of English factory workers who revolted against the use of the first steam engines" (Malm 2021b: 516). In crushing opposition, a machine is a tool of war against the opposition—either internally in the form of communists, anarchists, and feminists or externally in the form of foreign nations that were to be colonized and conquered. Similarly, Marinetti writes in his manifesto, "We want to glorify war—the only cure for the world—militarism, patriotism, the destructive gesture of the anarchists, the beautiful ideas which kill, and contempt for women" (Danchev 2011: 5). The machine of industrialism, for fascism, functions as a symbol of power, control, and conquest, and while they might reject the values of enlightenment equality, they embrace the domination of industrial science. The expansion of machine power was the form of progress they supported. Junger writes, "There are such moments when we truly are proud of that, which is called progress. Let's remember the intoxicating joy that overwhelms the modern man at the sight of his own creations burning gigantic amounts of energy in the sky above the metropolises" (Malm 2021b: 516). This destructive power, and the feelings of power, control, and speed that come from it, shape the fascist imagination of the future.

The power of industrial technology to increase the speed of movement also flattens and shrinks the world. Bifo states, "As long as spatial colonization was underway, as long as the external machine headed towards new territories, a future was conceivable because the future is not only a dimension of time but also of space" (Berardi 2011: 24). This process of deterritorialization of space, according to the Zetkin collective, creates a shifting and unstable foundation for society, and the more unstable the situation is, the more that the fascistic appeal to a stable and mythical is appealing. They write:

> Fascism, then, was not for ordinary times. No masses would have found it attractive had they not felt the ground disappearing beneath their feet. No dominant classes would have called on its services had their dominance remained secure. As long as lives in advanced capitalist states proceeded in well-worn furrows, with only average levels of dislocation and disorder, as was the case for a long time before the First World War and again after the Second, politics could be managed with the normal procedures of a bourgeois democracy: peaceful party competition, regular elections, alternating governments, civil conversations, rule of law, at least some basic freedom of expression and other democratic rights. (Malm 2021b: 298)

In short, the appeal of fascism is stronger when the stability of the present is weakest. At these moments, the norms and institutions of liberal democracy are likely unable to function correctly. This is when the crisis of representation reappears, which allows for a fascistic figure to claim to represent all those who are unrepresentable under liberal politics. As industrial technology destroys the planet, it increases speed and shatters the temporal and spatial confines of liberal society. That any nation has ever been great is a myth, but one that many want to believe in order to provide order and meaning to their lives.

It is in similar moments of crisis that communism also has its most significant influence. Communism, an ideology that formed dialectically in response to the crisis of liberal political economy, has always focused on crisis moments built into the logic of linear progress. In *The Communist Manifesto*, Marx and Engels contend that as the industrial power of capitalist production grows, so does the potential for crises that can bring about revolutionary change. They write:

> Constant revolutionizing of production, uninterrupted disturbance of all social conditions, everlasting uncertainty, and agitation distinguish the bourgeois epoch from all earlier ones. All fixed, fast-frozen relations, with their train of ancient and venerable prejudices and opinions, are swept away, and all new-formed ones become antiquated before they can ossify. All that is solid melts into the air, all that is holy is profaned, and man is finally compelled to face with sober senses his real conditions of life and his relations with his kind. (Tucker, Marx, and Engels 1978: 476)

These constant revolutions in production, which are the foundation for the capitalist logic of growth and expansion, both increase the productive capacity of our economy, allowing us to transcend the limits of scarcity, and produce the class of people that will destroy the capitalist system. They write, "But not only has the bourgeoisie forged the weapons that bring death to itself; it has also called into existence the men who are to wield those weapons—the modern working class—the proletarians" (Tucker, Marx, and Engels 1978: 478). Like much of Marx's work, the descriptive critique of capitalist production is accurate. Capitalism does require constant growth, expansion, and technological revolutions. This requires the constant deterritorialization of space and time, creating a world of instability and crisis that requires constant change. But the logic of progress and growth here only becomes more developed in the Bolshevik political project, which reinforced a fetish for industrial production and capacity building.

In his sci-fi novel *Red Star* (1908), Alexander Bogdanov, the Russian cosmist and Bolshevik theorist, depicts a future communist utopia on Mars. The bodies of dead revolutionaries are sent to Mars and revived, and on this Planet, free from capitalist imperial violence, the worker can live in a utopian existence. The book read as an eco-Marxist narrative, correctly understands that the capitalist logic of exploitation is destroying the worker and the planet itself. "Colonization of Earth requires the utter annihilation of its population," Bogdanov writes (Bogdanov et al. 1984: 113). However, the overall eco-Marxist edge is blunted through a claim that Martian communism forms only through the collective labor of humans to colonize and control the Martian environment. The species of workers is forged through the logic of industrial control and domination and communism forms. Similarly, in *Fully Automated Luxury Communism*, Bastani argues that communist politics has to focus on colonizing the stars and expanding industrial production and automation. Looking, especially, to new technologies—such as AI, renewable and nuclear energy, and automation of work—Bastani finds a future in which scarcity can be erased via industrial production and in which alienation in labor can also be eliminated since machines will replace human labor for the work that no one wants to do. He writes:

> After the realm of speculation, we draw upon the world as it is or is becoming. Here we examine seemingly disparate technologies—in automation, energy, resources, health, and food—before concluding that the foundations are cohering for a society beyond scarcity and work. Nothing is certain about where these technologies will end, nor whose benefit they will serve. However, it is discernible that a disposition can be drawn from them—if only they are allied to a political project of collective solidarity and individual happiness. (Bastani 2019: 12)

Their vision, a future world defined by an industrial fixed post-scarcity society, links Bastani with Bogdanov and his vision of Martian communism. However, both require a conception of society intimately connected with industrial production and technological progress. Bastani asserts that without such productive power there is no solution to the crisis of alienation that Marx developed in the *Economic Manuscripts of 1844*. However, unlike Saito, who rejects Marx's industrial formation, Bastani accelerates these technologies to the point where they supposedly implode the concept of scarcity, replacing it with endless material luxury. But what is going to be the collateral damage of such an explosion? This focus on communism only existing through space colonization is a literal pie in the sky. There are other images of Soviet futurism, from Lenin's fascination with trains—a symbol of modernization and progress—to Mao's rhetoric of "a great leap forward." For those opposed to capitalist domination, liberation cannot be found in the annuls of the industrial past—where nothing but a history of violence and domination are documented—so liberation only occurs in a deferred future that is not yet written.

If liberalism projects an endless present, fascism a mythical past, and communism a liberatory future utopia, what happens when these visions of the future crash into the increasing anxiety and acceptance that the industrial world is dying? In centering a politics of "no future," the entire edifice of modernist ideological projects is dismantled. Industrialism, focusing on a continuing expansion of domination and control over the natural world, cannot abide by a logic of limits. In addition, the use of a future allows for sacrificial logic to be employed within politics, one that legitimates the structural violence of contemporary society as essential in moving humanity forward. But, if there is no logic of "forward" through time, the structural violence is instead seen for what it is—as part of a campaign to centralize the accumulation of wealth and power. For instance, under the economic logic of industrial production, the worker is sacrificed at the altar of the factory in order to ensure that wealth is concentrated in the hands of the capitalist, communist party, or fascist leader, while small crumbs fall to the multitude. Each sacrifice is justified because as the industrial economy grows, so does productive capacity, and at some point—always deferred into the future—the spoils will liberate the multitude of the horror of present life. The future is nothing but a fantasy constructed for the multitude to keep them pacified, while in reality the state, the capitalist, or the party are not putting society on a path toward liberation, but instead are simply churning the bodies of living beings into the further accumulation of their own wealth and power. When there is "no future," the spectacle ceases to function, forcing everyone to see the pools of blood on the altars of progress that the elite are lapping up.

Confronting Cruel Optimism with an Antiworld Politics

The logic of the future, of progress, and of the obsession with growth functions as a spectacle fantasy that legitimates violence. But the constant deferral of a future utopia and the growing realization that the present cannot continue endlessly forward opens up an even more immense chasm in politics—the apathy and social breakdown that emerges when collectively we confront the cruel optimism of industrial logic. Lauren Berlant (2011), in *Cruel Optimism*, writes:

> I described "cruel optimism" as a relation of attachment to compromised conditions of possibility whose realization is discovered either to be impossible, sheer fantasy, or too possible and toxic. What is cruel about these attachments, and not merely inconvenient or tragic, is that the subjects who have x in their lives might not well endure the loss of their object/scene of desire, even though its presence threatens their well-being, because whatever the content of the attachment is, the continuity of its form provides something of the continuity of the subject's sense of what it means to keep on living on and to look forward to being in the world. (Berlant 2011: 25)

In her book, she argues that the ideological commitment to optimism, which undergirds liberal political culture, has negative consequences. For instance, the myth of the "American dream" structures how we interact and engage with the world, but data increasingly shows the limited potential for class mobility. When the reality of lived material life confronts the internalized fantasy of the "dream," an insidious form of optimism emerges. The anger and frustration at failing to meet the American dream are pushed inward, personalizing the failure and increasingly disempowering those who refuse to accept that the dream is, in fact, a nightmare.

When it comes to the many overlapping ecological catastrophes, there are many examples of cruel optimism—from the claim that wearing a sweater, driving a Prius, or changing light bulbs can solve climate change to the much deeper optimism that liberal governmental reforms could ever work. The failure of political institutions when it comes to climate change means that "these moments of optimism, which mark a possibility that the habits of a history might not be reproduced, release an overwhelmingly negative force" (Berlant 2011: 45). Similarly with climate change the optimism that argues that we can solve this problem—either through personal changes or through technological innovation—leads to an overwhelmingly depressive force when experiences disproves this claim. The irony of cruel optimism is that, since it is ideological in its function, even when the optimistic perspective is shown to be false, we often refuse to accept what is possible at a systemic level and instead assume that we are personally to blame.

Those born after September 11, 2001, in the West have lived in a period in which there is almost no sense that their lives will be better than their parents. Instead, they were born into a world shaped by various stages of staggard collapse and are confronting a future on fire. In this situation, as philosopher Jonathan Gray argues, the myth of progress is ceasing to hold onto its onto-mythical foundations. Gray writes:

> For those who live inside a myth, it seems a self-evident fact. Human progress is a fact of this kind. If you accept it, you have a place in the grand march of humanity. Humankind is, of course, not marching anywhere. . . . But the myth of progress is extremely potent. When it loses its power, those who have lived by it are—as Conrad put it, describing Kayerts and Carlier—"like those lifelong prisoners who, liberated after many years, do not know what use to make of their freedoms." When faith in the future is taken from them, so is the image they have of themselves. If they then opt for death, it is because, without that faith, they can no longer make sense of living. (Gray 2013: 12)

What Gray is describing here is the actual violent horror of cruel optimism. As the dream of progress dies, the longer we hold onto the myth, the more harm it causes, and the less likely we will be actively engaged and living in a world that is falling apart. Instead of a politics of a future, we must embrace a politics of "willful sadness."

Nicolette Gable latches onto the phrase "willful sadness" from the writing of American Decadent writer Louise Imogen Guiney, to explain the late nineteenth-century American pessimists. As Gable argues, American culture is often defined for its optimism; therefore, there are few examples of widespread pessimism. The American Decadent movement, whose most well-known author, Edgar Saltus, attempted to promote a uniquely American version of pessimism that not only confronted the cruel optimism of American liberalism but also undermined the masculine gender norm that had developed in the late nineteenth century. In order to do this, the authors of this movement embraced a "willful sadness" in which the authors fixated on the darker and sadder aspects of life—death, despair, pain, suffering—and in this more gothic narrative found a politics of pleasure. As Gable described this process:

> Decadents are pictured as deliberate inversions of everything good and normal. The Decadents associated themselves with death and despair, not because they have to, but for fun. Pain, wounds, fevers, hangings, dyspepsia, and nerves were the words that Americans associated with the Decadents, not Chopin or Art or Beauty. Here we see the beginnings of the pleasure that Decadents took in their pessimism. (Gable 2017: 107)

Unlike the pessimism of Arthur Schopenhauer, in which he advocated for chastity and extreme aesthetic repression, the American Decadent movement found a politics of libertine pleasure. This was a pleasure in embracing, accepting, and enjoying the negative aspects of life and, with it, a withdrawal and refusal to engage with the optimism of American culture. It also rejected the actionism of American masculinity. At this time, American masculinity was being defined in relation to the colonial expansion of the American empire. This view tied masculinity with colonial power grabs. In response, willful sadness and the pessimism of Edgar Saltus argued against this view of masculinity by denying the liberal view of agency and empire. Gable, discussing this, writes, "In the worlds of Saltus, where no real historic action could take place, characters were left to amuse themselves in the glittering world of fashion, dinner parties, adultery and duels" (Gable 2017: 106). When combined with the rejection of American optimism, historical action, and of dominant norms of masculinity, the American decadence provided a hedonistic pessimistic politics that, unlike European pessimists of the nineteenth century, could appeal to large swathes of the American public. The American Decadent movement did not question or engage with issues of class, gender, or racial supremacy in the United States, and, as such, their politics of pessimism and withdrawal tended to be radical politics only open to wealthy, white Americans. But that does not mean there are no ways to mobilize and weaponize a form of willful sadness to agitate and motivate for active rejection of modernity.

The lesson from the decadent movement is that there is no way to engage with the negativity and darkness of the world other than to embrace it and, within the barriers to liberation, find joy. A playful and libertine form of pessimism is, in a world slowly destroyed by climatic catastrophe and rising fascism, much less cruel and destructive than a misplaced form of optimism. What needs to be addressed, and which will be the center piece of the next chapter, is that nihilism does not need to lead to a politics of inaction or of suffering and unhappiness. Through a nihilistic engagement with the political systems of the world, a joyful and playful politics of insurrection, refusal, and resentment can form, creating the basis for a unique revolutionary project. Even if the revolutionary is a doomed person, it does not mean that the revolutionary has to be crippled by ennui and inaction.

What the End of the World Means

Indigenous populations in the Americas have lived in a postapocalyptic world since 1492 when Columbus, the genocidal monster he was, upset their World and left it in ruins. Before colonization and the creation of the European global empire, humans lived on a polycentric planet shaped by many different, overlapping worlds. Walter Mignolo writes, "First, let's imagine the World around 1500. It was, in brief, a polycentric and noncapitalist world. There were several coexisting civilizations, some with long histories, others being formed around that time" (Mignolo 2011: 3). In the 1500s, and before, multiple civilizations existed throughout the planet, creating a patchwork of different Worlds. The process of European colonization and the expansion of global capitalism cannibalized these other Worlds. Western colonial history is a direct reminder that Worlds have ended in the past and that apocalypses occur at uneven paces around the planet. When this book discusses the end of the World, what is implied is not the literal end of the planet but the destruction of a shared cognitive frame for shaping our lives in the world.

Sabu Kohso contends that the World differs from the planetary. The planetary encompasses the flows and cycles of the planet Earth, while the World is the abstract institutions that humans constructed. The logic of nation-states, capitalist markets, imperial governance, and scientism shapes the modern World. These human-made institutional logics, as Mignolo claimed, have colonized the entire planet, erasing and destroying all other worlds as they grow. The concept of the World is related to the Marxian notion of "Second nature," which is the built human environment. Under capitalism, this second-built environment is shaped by the commodity form. The logic of exchange permeates the logic of human-constructed institutions and is part of the overall process of reification. We are embedded within the second nature of the capitalist exchange, and the logic of commodity fetishism obfuscates our collective capacity to experience and witness the logic of the first nature. Thus, the human world—with its border, legal regimes and markets—phenologically feels "natural."[2]

In *Nomos of the Earth*, Carl Schmitt provides a detailed theoretical exploration of how Western logics of nomos, or law, expanded and conquered the Earth, creating a unified univocal world shaped entirely by European logics (Schmitt 2006). By constructing juridical and political institutions to govern and regulate the entire planet, Europe has effectively constructed a massive world empire, a concept that Hardt and Negri famously take as the starting point of their critique of neoliberal capitalism (Hardt and Negri 2003). Schmitt, in another work, *Land and Sea*, highlights the world's constructed nature and how human ideology and knowledge shift and shape the contours of the earth. Schmitt contends that when there is spatial closure, politics between competing international powers come into conflict. The expansion of the World—in the European case, the colonization of the Americas—offers a pressure valve to allow competing empires to engage in politics without

[2]Of course, in the Marxian case, there is an assumption that through human knowledge and science, as a species, we can come to understand nature. The last chapter critiqued the assumption that human knowledge and science can impose an identity on nature's nonidentity, claiming that part of the problems with industrial and enlightenment science is rooted in that logic of control. Planetary foundations are neither completely knowable nor controllable via human science or technology, but that does not mean that the relationship between us and that unknowable material reality is not an essential part of living. Part of politics is the complex game, the dance between ourselves and the unknowable foundations of the planet. The current map of the World fails to represent and follow the contours of the planetary. Climate catastrophe, soil depletion, ocean acidification, and industrial pollution are the environmental symptoms of this disconnect. Worlds that are self-reflexive, fluid, nonrepresentational, and ontologically grounded in nondomination can flow and change according to the scream, regulation, and reactions of the planetary assemblages.

wars against each other (Schmitt, Berman, and Zeitlin 2015). The creep of the World led to the death of the polycentric world and the construction of a univocal world, what Walter Mignolo critiques as the zero-point epistemology of colonization. Because Europe was the starting point for the World, Europe and its history and philosophy are treated as universal. The European man stands in as a representative of humanity as a whole, and the logic of progress is defined in relation to how European societies developed and grew. The European world, with its industrialism, capitalism, and nation-states, appears to be radically disconnected from the planetary foundations of society as the logic expanded. As nations worldwide strive to live Western-type lives, the depth of the unsustainable nature of European modernity has been made clear.

When environmental activists and climate writers discuss the vital role of indigenous environmental activism and knowledge, they are tapping into the potentiality that previous worlds offer in living in a metabolic relationship with the natural world. There is a compelling logic to this argument. Humans have lived and thrived in relation to the planetary for countless millennia, and while there are many examples of localized failures—often leading to the collapse or complete disappearance of civilizations—the scope of the material disconnect has never been greater than it is today. We currently inhabit a world that has been toxified to such a degree that the past may no longer be anything but a prologue to the apocalypse to come. Until the structures of the current World are destroyed, or at least fragmented so that alternatives can grow and thrive in the shell of the old world, there is no space for alternative worlds to exist. In other words, we need antiworld politics if we want to even imagine a future in which Worlds exist.

As long as the world's institutions are in place, any attempts to create alternative conceptions of the world are doomed to the colonial violence of the World. The industrial world refuses to allow an outside to itself and will target any alternative way of living as either a threat or a new opportunity for capital recuperation. This is also why, while refusal plays an integral part in antiworld politics, it has to be combined with a defensive politics protecting from state violence and attacking the institutions of the World. To assume that alternative worlds can form, exist, and thrive in the world's cracks mistakenly ignores the industrial world's inherently colonial nature. To speak of the end of the World means the end of this world. There may or maybe not be other words that can form after the destruction of the present, but there is no space for imagining or creating a polyvocal world order while the colonial logic of industrial society exists.

6

Without the Gallows Humor, There Are Only the Gallows

A collective of French nihilists in 1883 published the "Manifesto of Nihilist Women." Their manifesto called on women to embrace their anger and resentment against the bourgeoisie. The short manifesto calls on housekeepers and cooks to poison the food and drink of the rich. In an almost-humorous homage to cookbook recipes, they wrote, "From hundreds of ingredients with incontestable results, we can cite: lead acetate, which you can get in a few days if you leave lead shot sitting around or leave a piece of lead in vinegar; pieces of rotten meat; hemlock, which is so often mistaken for parsley and which grows" (Anonymous 2018: 1). Like the witches of Macbeth, foreshadowing and mocking the king's demise, the nihilist women raged against the values and oppression of mass society. They turned the "eye of newt and toe of frog" into an elixir of arsenic and hemlock. They attempted to choke the elite of the world to death. What makes the political nihilists, who are rarely spoken of today as a movement, such a unique political force is that they did not necessarily have any sense that their resistance would lead to revolution. Whether it led to revolution or not was none of their concern; instead, they desired action. Action provided them with a purpose and allowed them to enact justice, even if it was individualized and temporary, against the forces that caused them so much harm. In the manifesto of Nihilist Women, they wrote, "At least we will give back to our despicable oppressors some of the evil they give us every day. . . . They want to be the masters! Let them suffer the consequences" (Anonymous 2018: 2).

Max Haiven, in his book *Revenge Capitalism*, claims that the era of neoliberal capitalism has centered on the sadistic violence inherent in capitalism. This shift often means that the elite cause suffering for those below them, not because the suffering is financially beneficial, but because the rich find joy in the suffering of the poor. While it might be reprehensible for the rich to enjoy the suffering of the poor, there is nothing wrong with revenge politics against the elite. The nihilist women of France and the meme spreaders mocking the suffering of billionaires are not the same as the fascist forces demanding that the poor and weak suffer. Haiven ends his introduction with the paragraph:

> The people destroying the earth and our future have names and addresses. They ought to be brought to justice. We know that, in the current system, they will not be, but also that any one of them is almost instantly replaceable, with so many already competing for places at the top. Without a revolutionary movement, their power will be undiminished, and capitalism will continue to wreak its vengeance. Yet I confess myself to be too full of the milk of human kindness to have a taste for revolutionary violence. My argument throughout this book, however, is that, whether we agree with it or not, revenge is here, and all our saccharine moralizing against it just stokes its flames. The debts of history will be paid, one way or another. (Haiven 2020: 15)

The more that revenge and resentment grow within society, the more there will be a moralistic argument for a politics of respectability in which "love trumps hate." The moral platitudes, though, will not be universally applied as the wealthy, who regularly sacrifice countless lives in their endless quest to make more profit, will be given a free pass. The structural violence of capitalism has, to these institutions, become reified and part of the natural order of things. Lost limbs in meat packing plants, children choking to death from asthma, and the poor starving as governments destroy food supplies to maintain high prices on goods are not seen as forms of violence. The dominant institutions will only condemn resentment and violence that punches up.

Social inequality, failed political systems, government and police oppression, and ecological destruction are all processes that spur resentment and anger. The right has understood this and has attempted to create enemy/friend relationships that direct and focus the anger of those who are suffering, not at those who are causing the suffering (i.e., the wealthy and elite) but at those with the least amount of political power. The rich and the powerful try to convince the multitude languishing on the gallows that their enemy is the other prisoners, not the well-dressed royals eating, drinking, and laughing during the public lynching. Without a class-consciousness gallows humor, all we have are the gallows.

Russian Political Nihilism and Clearing the Rubble of Social Collapse

> Eat the rich, eat the rich before they turn and eat your children
> England's ending, death's still pending, burn those fucking buildings
>
> —BOB VYLAN, "WICKED AND BAD"

As a political and philosophic movement, nihilism is shrouded in the shadow of Fredrick Nietzsche. Nietzsche's work provided a much-needed critique of the modernist and Enlightenment tradition, undermining the illusory foundations of Western thought and a critique of liberal logics of progress. Library wings have been written on the philosophy of Nietzsche and the bourgeois form of nihilism that formed following his death in 1900. This is what I will call "philosophic nihilism." But overall, I want to decenter Nietzsche in discussing nihilism and instead focus on the forgotten and under-discussed nihilist political movement of the late nineteenth and early twentieth century, which I will refer to as "political nihilism." This movement has received minimal academic analysis, surviving and thriving primarily within the writings of anarchists and other fringe radicals. The Nietzschean tradition provides a bourgeois conception of nihilism, founded on the logic of the "master morality," while the political nihilists represent the anger and rage of the lumpen proletariat and their bohemian allies. The politics of political nihilism, unlike philosophic nihilism, does not reject resentment but instead centers resentment as a positive aspect of their politics. In addition, instead of focusing on philosophic and psychological strategies of enacting a "will to power," they coordinated and engaged in revolutionary political action that desired the destruction of political and social institutions. In the most ideal situation, theoretically such destruction would clear the debris of modern social institutions so that others may have a chance to build a bridge into a new world.

The Russian nihilist political movements formed in the 1850s, the decade leading to the reforms that freed the serfs from the land. The movement was formed, according to Kristian Petrov, by the children of those radicals that lived and dreamed during the 1848 period of revolt. The 1848 movement strove to transform Europe's political systems and failed. The movement of 1848 were focused mainly on rational reforms and certain forms of political liberalization. The nihilists was less interested in reforming the state or pushing for liberal democratic reforms but instead wanted to see the wholesale destruction of the Russian Czarist system. The critique of the political reality of Czarism extended to a broader critique of the entire Russian social and political system. One memoirist of the time wrote that "[. . .] everything that had existed traditionally and had formerly been accepted without criticism came up for rearrangement. Everything—beginning with theoretical peaks, religious views, the basis of the state, and the organization of society, all the way to quotidian customs, clothing, and to hairstyles" (Paperno 1988: 5). Similarly, a young Peter Kropotkin, the anarchist prince, wrote that the nihilists expressed "the Highest Revoltees against the conventional life in all its aspects" (Kinna 2016: 83). As the Russian state repressed the nihilist movement it morphed into a terroristic movement that weaponized anger against the state, and its apparatchiks, culminating in the assassination of Czar Alexander the Second on March 13, 1881, by the nihilist revolutionary group Narodnaya Volya, or People's Will.

According to Victoria Thorstennson, nihilist men and women wore their politics sewn onto their sleeves, using fashion as a cultural strategy of rejection of traditional gender values and norms. She writes, "Russian nihilist women became 'fashion guerillas,' who rejected the enslaving frills and charms of conventional femininity and used their bodies as the new site of signification for their political ideals" (Thorstensson 2016: 268). It was common for nihilist men to wear their hair long and dress in plaids, while nihilist women wore their hair short and dressed in more gender-neutral clothing. Kristina Petrov mirrors Thorstennson's work, writing:

> young nihilist men dressed in ill-fitting dark coats, aspiring to look like unpolished workers, let their hair grow bushy and often wore blue-tinted glasses. Correspondingly the young women cut their hair shorter, wore large plain dresses, and could be seen with a shawl or a big hat, together with the characteristic glasses. Such a nihilist could, however, above all be identified by a reversal of official etiquette. (Petrov 2019: 77)

These were a form of revolt against the gender norms of dress within conservative Russian society, and the association of nihilism with revolutionary fervor and beliefs even led the police to target people dressed as nihilists.

However, forms of dress were not the limits of the nihilist revolt against traditional values; their main social target was the institution of marriage. In reflecting on the nihilist movement that influenced him, Kropotkin writes, "Marriage without love and familiarity without friendship was repudiated. The nihilist girl, compelled by her parents to be a doll in a doll's house, and to marry for property's sake, preferred to abandon her house and her silk dresses" (Kinna 2016: 84). Overall, the Russian nihilists, a social and cultural youth movement—like that of punk—opposed the entirety of contemporary Russian society at a time when major state reforms were being pushed through by the czar, including the ending of serfdom.

Politically, the Russian nihilist movement first focused on refusal and the creation of alternative communes in an attempt to build solidarity and links with the newly "liberated" Russian serfs. In 1874, many Russian nihilists joined the Going to the People movement. Inspired by Bakunin, between 2,000 and 4,000 young revolutionaries moved from Moscow and Saint Petersburg to the rural areas of Russia to work on farms and in towns and to spread revolutionary fervor and values. The radically decentralized movement, which Kropotkon called the "mad summer of 1874," failed. The radical students found little support among the younger rural peasants, while older generations were politically more in-line with the nihilist they were put off by generational and class divides. In addition, the movement faced significant oppression and violence from the Russian state, who viewed the open and public campaign as a threat against their order—which it was. The failure of this movement shaped the nihilist political movement and is partially responsible for the move away from open political organizing to coordinating through small cadre-type cells and underground organizations.

While students and youth rejected social norms, and many nihilists moved to rural communes, nihilism developed and grew in the literary world, where Ivan Turgenev's book *Fathers and Sons* and Chernyshevsky's book *What Is to Be Done?* influenced Lenin's book of the same title. Turgenev's *Fathers and Sons* is a story of generational clashes, where the main character, Kirsanov, travels home with his friend, Bazarov, after graduating from university. The two are both nihilists, which leads to tensions with the older generation at the manor. In the book, Turgenev writes, "A nihilist is a man who doesn't acknowledge any authorities, who doesn't accept a single principle on faith, no matter how much that principle may be surrounded by respect," while Bazarov decries, "We act by virtue of what we recognize as beneficial. At the present time, negation is the most beneficial of all—and we deny it" (Turgenev and Freeborn 2008: 16). Bazarov became a literary hero for the burgeoning nihilist movement, and influenced Dostevesky's caricature of nihilist political activists in his *The Demon*.

Chernyshevsky's 1863 book *What Is to Be Done?* follows Vera Rozalsky, a young woman living with a very controlling mother, who meets and falls in love with a nihilist student. Vera flees the oppressive home life, and the two attempt to forge and form antiauthoritarian and feminist ways of life in small communes. *Vera* became an important literary figure in Russian life and directly influenced nihilist activism. Vera declared:

> You call me a dreamer and ask what I want out of life. I prefer neither to dominate nor to submit. I wish neither to deceive nor to dissemble. I don't want to be concerned about other peoples' opinions or strive for what others advise. . . . .I don't want to submit to anyone. I want to be free. I don't want to be obligated to anyone for anything. I don't want ever to say, "You're

> obligated to do this for me!" I want to do only what I desire, and I want others to do likewise. (Chernyshevsky and Katz 1989: 172)

Taken in tandem, *Fathers and Sons* and *What Is to Be Done*? opened up a literary and philosophic discussion around nihilism within the Russian intellectual world.

Other than Dimitry Pisarev, few academics and philosophers at the time embraced political nihilism, as the trend was more commonly to criticize and mock the youthful political movement. Dimitry Pisarav, a communist and nihilist philosopher who was arrested in 1862 for radical writing and released in 1866, contended that nihilism focused on the role of destruction and negation. He wrote, "The Romanov dynasty and the Petersburg bureaucracy must perish . . . that which is dead and rotten will crumble down into the grave of its own; our task is merely to give it the final thrust and bury their stinking corpses in the mud" (Edie, Scanlan, and Zeldin 1976: 126). This focus on destruction was part of a positive political project to clear the rubble and the wreckage of the czardom, opening a potential bridge for a new revolutionary era to emerge. In expressing the political role of the nihilist, he writes, "In short, here is the ultimatum of our camp: what may be smashed must be smashed: whatever will stand the blow will do, what flies into smithereens is rubbish; in any case, strike out right and left, no harm will be or can come of it" (Edie, Scanlan, and Zeldin 1976: 135). The politics of clearing the rubble are central to the political nihilist movement and is increasingly relevant in an era in which the future possibility of life in the world as it currently exists is nearly impossible.

In the West today, and Russia during the Czardom, for instance, there are no paths through official state channels for any significant political reforms. In such a situation, before any possibility of imagining or creating an alternative world, the old world has to be dismantled and destroyed. "The idea that one could clear the impediments of the emergence of the future by destroying the remnants of the past in the present could also be seen as a radical interpretation of the methods of modernity," write to Pisarav (Edie, Scanlan, and Zeldin 1976: 93). The act of clearing the rubble is, thus, a philosophically valuable way of understanding the goal of what is needed in politics today. According to the Russian nihilists, the focus on negation and destruction could not happen only through refusal or communes but required direct political violence. According to the nihilist argument, state institutions must be destroyed before alternative communes and spaces can flourish. Refusal, without destruction, is not politically viable. This does not mean that every state institution was the same. Petrov writes,

> Russian nihilism did not comply, as one might expect from a purely semantic viewpoint, a universal "negation" of ethical normativity, the foundations of knowledge or the meaningfulness of human existence. Its negation was aimed at a particular political, social, and aesthetic regime equivalent to Tsarist autocracy, religious orthodoxy, fine arts, and, most notably, the ideas, attitudes, and customs of an older generation. (Edie, Scanlan, and Zeldin 1976: 74)

Certain institutions needed to be destroyed immediately—like that of the police, military, or capital—while others were less important. In today's political environment, we might need to distinguish between those institutions that are, in small part, providing support for people—that which provides access no matter how limited, to food, health care, environmental protection—and those that are protecting the overall system—like the police, military, and security apparatus. This distinction illustrates the difference between a political nihilist project and a reactionary right-wing accelerationist politics.

Following a failed assassination plot against the czar in 1862, the Russian state cracked down on the nihilists. The result was a hardening of the nihilist political project and a further turn toward terroristic action as members of the movement began a strategy of killing political leaders. In this era, Sergey Necheyev wrote his "Catechism of a Revolutionist." In this work, which the anarchist Bakunin initially supported, Necheyev put together a political platform that zealously promotes violence as both a means and an end. He writes, "The revolutionary enters the world of the State, of the privileged classes, of the so-called civilization, and he lives in this world only for the purpose of bringing about its speedy and total destruction" (Nechayev 1869). In bringing about this revolution, Necheyev calls for rejecting all forms of morality, allowing the revolutionary to infiltrate any institutions he needs and to lie in wait, ready to pounce and destroy when needed. He also calls on using violence to target large segments of society. He breaks society down into different classes. The first class comprises of the people "who must be condemned to death without delay" (Nechayev 1869). This includes those whose presence makes revolution impossible, such as the higher-ups of political institutions, military leaders, and capitalists. The second class are those "who will be spared for the time being in order that, by a series of monstrous acts, they may drive the people into inevitable revolt" (Nechayev 1869). The third are the lower-level bureaucrats and officials, who will be pressured to give in to the revolutionaries' demands. Finally, we have the liberals, who will be pushed to choose a side in the revolt, and the non-nihilist revolutionaries, who will be considered friends until the current order is destroyed. While there are many reasons to criticize the fantastical stance of Necheyev, it is worth exploring how Joel Olson understood fanatical politics.

In "the freshness of Fantasticism," Joel Olson looks to the abolitionist tradition in the United States to provide a unique defense of fanaticism. Olson centers the American abolitionists, like John Brown, and contends that their fanatical and zealous politics opened up space for more liberator and democratic forms of engagement. This analysis, which runs counter to the general narrative of fanaticism being antithetical to liberation, focuses on the strategic use of fanaticism in politics. He writes, "Accordingly, zealotry is political activity, driven by an ardent devotion to a cause, which seeks to draw clear lines along afriends/enemies dichotomy in order to mobilize friends and moderates in the service of that cause" (Olson 2007: 688). Looking to Schmitt, Olson explores how the abolitionist strategically used fanatical politics to divide the nation into enemies/friends based on the political line of slavery. Since you could not compromise with slavery, without, in effect, defending the institution, this Manichean politics led to an inevitable conflict between the two sides. In his analysis of zealousness, Olson claims that fanatical politics divides the political world into three camps—enemy, friends, and the middle—and targets the middle, forcing them to pick a side. In an anecdotal example of fanatical strategy, he mentions how John Brown's organization would provide addresses of moderate abolitionists to runaway slaves and have them knock on the door of these moderates and demand that they help hide them from the slave patrols. If the moderates refused, they were enemies of abolition;

if they agreed, they were made more militant and radical as they had now become accomplices.

In general, Necheyev and the Russian nihilists represent a form of zealous militant radical politics. Unlike most other radical movements, though, there was little focus on what the future would look like or even if a future would or would not exist. Instead of focusing on debates and discussions around the future utopian society, the Russian nihilists put their effort into the project of destruction, seeing their role as clearing out the rubble of modern Russian political and social institutions in order to, ideally, bring about an opening for new alternatives to form. But their action was not predicated on a liberatory future. Instead, the focus was actively confronting and destroying the current institutions and making the wealthy and the powerful quake in fear. And quake they did. During the "small deeds" period, as era of Russian nihilist terror was called, countless government officials were affected by revolutionary violence. According to historian Anna Geifman, between 1894 and the beginning of the Russian Revolution in 1917, approximately 17,000 government officials were killed via revolutionary terrorism. While not all of these assassinations were committed by the nihilists, the nihilists and their militant fanaticism during the 1860s to the early twentieth century helped set the stage for the rest of the revolutionary violence. She writes:

> Whereas in the nineteenth century, every act of revolutionary violence was a sensation, after 1905, terror became so widespread that many of the country's newspapers no longer bothered to publish detailed reports on every attack. Instead, they introduced special new sections dedicated exclusively to chronicling violent acts, in which they printed daily lists of political assassinations and expropriations throughout the empire. After 1905, these terrorist enterprises indeed became part of everyday life in Russia, and, as some radical admitted, a mass psychosis developed, a true "epidemic of combat activity." (Geifman 1995: 69)

While many condemn the effectiveness of political violence, the Russian nihilists are an example, as are the American abolitionists, for how, in certain spaces, political violence can actually jump-start a broader social dialectical conflict.

The role of violence in the discussion requires a detour into debates around political violence. Within the liberal political tradition and many of the left and progressive world, nonviolence has become sacrosanct due partly to the martyrdom of figures like Gandhi and Martin Luther King, Jr. According to Martin Luther King, Jr., the argument for nonviolence rests on the claim that "First and foremost in the philosophy of non-violence is the affirmation that means must be as pure as the end. Means and ends are convertible terms" (Martin Luther King Jr 1960). With this, King contends that the moral strength of nonviolence relates to its unwillingness to cause harm and injury to anyone. Instead of looking to use physical force and violence, using love and "moral right" means that "Means must be as pure as the end" (Martin Luther King Jr 1960). In understanding violence as an ethical or moral relationship, King can maintain the Buber-esque argument that one should never turn an I into an object. In short, this allows for a Kantian shortcut, in which any politics which treats any subject as a means to an end is discounted as against a categorical imperative.

This moral and ethical argument makes a handful of assumptions. Most importantly, there is a sense of shared humanity between the oppressed and the oppressors. According to Fanon's analysis of Hegel's master/slave dialectic in *Black Skin White Mask*, we can see that in a racial/colonial system there are no grounds for shared humanity in the relations. Fanon writes:

> Locked in this suffocating reification, I appealed to the Other so that his liberating gaze, gliding over my body suddenly smoothed of rough edges, would give me back the lightness of being I thought I had lost. But just as I get to the other slope, I stumble, and the Other fixes me with his gaze, his gestures and attitude. . . . I lose my temper and demand an explanation. . . . Nothing doing, I explode. Here are the fragments put together by another me in. (Fanon 2008: 150)

In his article "The Dialectic of Standing One's Ground," George Maher uses Fanon's analysis to analyze the lynching of Trayvon Martin by George Zimmerman. Maher contends that "In his critique of Hegel's master-slave dialectic, Fanon thereby draws back the curtain to reveal what lies beneath the ostensible universality of Ground, diagnosing a sub-ontological realm, a 'zone of nonbeing' to which certain subjects are condemned" (Ciccariello-Maher 2012). This zone of nonbeing shatters any prospects for an ethical, political relationship between the oppressed and the oppressor. Since one side of the relationship already has transformed the other into a "thing" to be manipulated and used, there is no requirement for the slave to treat the master as a human being. Instead, the oppressed have to equalize the relationship between the master and the slave, which can only be done through violence. Violence shatters the divide between the two and shows their shared humanity through vulnerability. The moral argument for nonviolence, on the other hand, assumes that shared humanity already exists. As such, violence by the oppressed is a morally unjustifiable position since it transforms the oppressor into a thing instead of respecting their humanity.

Second, King's definition does not distinguish between structural and interpersonal violence and, as such, moves the debate around violence to an individualized ethical framework. But violence does not only exist interpersonally as structural and institutional forms of violence are the most pervasive and destructive. Approximately nine million people worldwide die from air pollution every year. Another nine million die from starvation, and at least eight million from lack of access to health care. This does not include the monumental and unthinkable industrial violence to nonhuman life, as nearly ninety-two billion land animals are killed in industrial agricultural operations worldwide. The millions of humans, and billions of nonhumans, who die every year are victims of structural forms of violence. These structural forms of violence greatly exceed the number of people killed by interpersonal violence. These structural violence are less spectacular and often happen over long periods—hence why Rob Nixon calls it "slow violence"—and do not generate the same levels of outrage or concern (Nixon 2013). If anything, the reification of capitalist economics has transformed these deaths into nothing but a form of background rates of death. In such a situation, revolutionary violence can be understood as a form of collective self-defense. Expressing this argument, anarchist Malatesta wrote that "the slave is always in a state of legitimate defense and consequently, his violence against the boss, against the oppressor, is always morally justifiable. [It] must be controlled only by such considerations as that the best and most economical use is being made of human effort and human sufferings" (Errico Malatesta 2015: 51). If the slave or the worker is always threatened with violence, then any violence directed up the hierarchy is justified as self-defense.

Similarly, but inverting the focus, Emma Goldman wrote, "It is organized violence on top which creates individual violence at the bottom. It is the accumulated indignation against organized wrong, organized crime, organized injustice, which drives the political offender to act" (Emma Goldman 1917). Here we see Goldman contending that violence from below is always a response to violence from above, and as such, the violence from below is not the source of the problem; it is the violence from the top that needs remedying. There is, of course, an evident truth that the violence of capital and the state is invariably disproportionate to the violence from below. However, the more significant issue with the concept of structural violence and revolutionary resistance has to do with the legitimacy of the state and the way that the state claims a monopoly on the legitimate use of violence. If state violence is no longer accepted as inherently legitimate, police murder, state-sanctioned terrorism via war, and kidnapping and confinement of imprisoned individuals loses its reified luster. Alexander Berkman wrote,

> You don't question the right of the government to kill, to confiscate and imprison. If a private person should be guilty of the things the government is doing all the time, you'd brand him a murderer, thief and scoundrel. But as long as the violence committed is "lawful," you approve of it and submit to it. So it is not really violence that you object to but to people using violence "unlawfully." (Berkman 2003: 143)

If the state is understood for what it is, a form of coercive violence that legitimates itself through the threat of violence and social control over institutions, revolutionary violence is instead placed into a different category. Violence ceases to be understood in the traditional frames of the morality of good and bad.

In his book *Anarchy Alive*, Uri Gordon provides one of the more valuable engagements with the complexity of violence. Gordon defines *violence* thus: "an act is violent if its recipient experiences it as an attack or as deliberate endangerment" (Gordon 2008: 93). Gordon's definition rejects the narrative that property destruction, for instance, is not violent and also rejects the lazy framing of violence = bad and nonviolence = good. Instead of such simple framing, he argues that we need to understand violence through different axis: the source of the violence and the political goals of the violence. When these axis are used, and not just the frame of good and bad, we can differentiate between the fascistic and reactionary violence of January 6 in the United States and the insurrectionary resistance and violence we found in the Black Lives Matter (BLM) protests of 2020 and the French anti-police riots of 2023. On January 6, 2020, right-wing violence, orchestrated and funded by well-funded far-right-wing groups with corporate connections, funded middle-class and upper-class violence against an election in an attempted coup to keep their strongman in office after losing an election. First, there is nothing morally wrong with any tactics used by the January 6 groups—from the occupation of the capital to skirmishes with the police to attempts to shut down and block the results of a liberal election. The problem was not the tactics but the political location of the group protesting—in relation to hierarchies of power—and the goal of the group—which was not for the expansion of liberties and equality but to impose a more reactionary hierarchal social formation. On the other hand, violence from below is directed against the state apparatus, seeking to shatter social hierarchies. The revolutionary violence of the Russian nihilists and BLM fit within this category of violence. Such violence is focused not on expanding oppressive state powers but in dismantling them. As such, like the fanaticism of the abolitionists, which was about expanding freedom and liberty, violence from below functions similarly.

Focusing on political nihilism and the following debates on violence, the conversation is moved away from the bourgeois philosophy of Nietzschean nihilism. What we see here is not a defense of the "master morality" over that of the slave, nor is it a focus on an "ubermensch" who can, through their force of will, overcome the herd mentality of society. Instead, nihilism becomes a political project to undermine and destroy the institutions of society that cause suffering and harm. This is a politics of mobilizing the losers in society against the elite. The following section will explore the politics of Kaneko Fumiko and will serve as a clear example of a political nihilist theory of the loser.

"The Goal of My Activities Is the Destruction of All Living Things": The Revolutionary Nihilism of Kaneko Fumiko

The anarchist, nihilist, feminist Kaneko Fumiko wrote poems while sitting in her prison cell awaiting death. In one of her prison poems, she wrote, "*Is it the soul of those perished/under the guillotine/the crimson of azaleas in the garden.*" Waiting out her death sentence, her poems addressed the horrors of state violence, which she had seen firsthand during her time living in Japanese-occupied Korea. The Japanese state, which claims it has a two thousand-year-long history of an unbroken emperor system from Emperor Jimmu in 660 BCE to the current emperor of Japan, Naruhito, who took the throne in 2019, is in reality a relatively modern creation. The modern Japanese state formed in 1868. In 1853 Commodore Mathew Perry of the US Navy brought warships into Tokyo Bay and coerced the shogunate to open up trade with the United States. This imperial project by the United States shocked the Japanese elite, who understood that if they did not modernize and industrialize, they would be colonized by Western forces, in much the way that Hong Kong in 1841 was colonized by the British. The elite of Japan passed the Oath Charter, formally ending the Tokugawa shogunate, which dominated the island chain politics from 1616 to 1868 and started the Meiji Restoration. It was during the restoration that much of what we understand of modern Japan formed.

This period of nation-building and centralization led to the formation of a centralized Japanese language, the creation of national mythos, and the development of modern techniques of schooling, bureaucracy, industrial capitalism, and military system. By the 1870s, unions and labor organizing had already started and struggles for liberalization of government and worker protections shortly followed. In the late nineteenth century, both anarchism and Marxism were introduced to the Japanese populace and quickly spread among the oppressed of the new Japanese state, especially among women. Women had no rights under the Meiji Constitution. Japanese women were barred from voting and even being involved in political organizations until 1922. That said, women were forced into factory and industrial labor at wages much lower than their male counterparts. Oppressed at home, excluded from public and political life, and exploited at industrial work, women made up a significant influence within the radical movement of Japan.[1]

Kaneko Fumiko was born in 1903 to a poor family in Yokohama. Her father—a drunk and abusive man who ran away with his sister-in-law—refused to register Kaneko with the state, making her an undocumented person. Without documentation, she was not allowed to attend public schools and was marginalized from mainstream Japanese life. Kaneko grew up so poor that she regularly went hungry, and her mother attempted to sell her to a brothel, but the brothel was unable to provide the agreed-upon yen. Shortly after, her mother sent Kaneko to live with her paternal grandmother in the newly colonized Korean Peninsula. According to Mikiso Hane, the translator of Kaneko's memoir and prison interrogations:

> The trauma of being abandoned by her father and mother profoundly affected Keneko. She remarks in her memoirs, "I want to cry out to the father and the mothers of the world. Do you really love your children? Your love really lasts only as long as your primitive parental instincts. After that, you pretend to love your children so long as they serve your interest" (Hane 1993: 77)

This early relationship of abuse and neglect from her parents, as well as her ostracism from Japanese society, shaped her political and social analysis.

Life in Korea was no better for Kaneko. Lacking refinement and embarrassed by the classist and racist values of her grandmother, she was not adopted and instead lived as her grandmother's maid. Kaneko was regularly mistreated by her grandmother, for instance being beaten for befriending someone below their station, and forced to work long hours for no pay and often for little food. While in Korea, she also witnessed firsthand the oppression of the Korean people by the Japanese state and Japanese settlers like her grandmother. She

[1]Figures like Fukuda Hideko (an early feminist and pro-democracy activist who was arrested during the 1885 Osaka incident), Ito Noe (an anarchist and feminist editor and writer who was murdered along with her anarchist partner Osugi Sakea during the Amukasu incident), and Kanno Sugao (anarchist feminist author and activist who was executed by the state in 1911 for the "high treason incident") serve as precursors to Fumiko and are also inspirations for the politics of this project.

built close friendships and relationships with her Grandmother's Korean help, who were the first to treat her kindly. During this period of her life, Kaneko planned to commit suicide but decided against it due to the overwhelming beauty of nature and decided to dedicate her life to radical politics instead. In her memoir, she wrote, "I mustn't die; I must join hands with others who are being tormented like me, and get even with those who are oppressing us" (Kaneko 1991: 104).

After returning to Japan, Kaneko spent time with her father, who tried to marry her to an uncle, and ultimately she left for Tokyo at the age of seventeen. In Tokyo, she worked odd jobs to make money and work her way through school, became involved and then disillusioned with Christian reformism and socialism, before finally finding a kindred spirit, Pak Yŏl, a Korean anarchist and nihilist. The two formed the "Society of Malcontents," a two-person anarchist collective, and linked up with revolutionary Koreans fighting against the Japanese state. The two were arrested, with other radicals and Koreans, following the Tokyo Earthquake of 1923. Kaneko, who was twenty, was charged with treason and sentenced to death. In prison, she wrote a memoir detailing her life's horrors and tragedies; in her prison interrogations, she laid out her anarcho-nihilist political doctrine and philosophy. Pak and Fumiko had their death sentence commuted by the emperor, but Kaneko refused and tore the emperor's decree. The information about her refusal to accept the emperor's decree was kept a secret until 1959. On July 23, 1926, at twenty-three, Fumiko hung herself in her cell. A final act of resistance against the emperor.

Mikiso Hane highlights what a unique individual Fumiko was. She writes:

> The views held by Kaneko Fumiko are remarkable for a young with of her day. She was hardly twenty, had a limited education, and grew up in an atmosphere in which patriotism and loyalty to the Emperor were the sine qua non of Japanese life. Not only is it remarkable that she formulated such a heretical political philosophy, but her refusal to grovel before authority is even more extraordinary. She refused to be mealy-mouth and cower before her persecutors. (Hane 1993: 79)

The heretical and radical politics that Fumiko promoted can be broken down into three broad, but overlapping, topics: power and oppression, morality, and the Japanese imperial state. Her understanding and analysis of these three broad categories are the foundation of her nihilist political project and, combined with her long-time association with the downtrodden and oppressed, are part of her politics of revolutionary resentment.

Central to Kaneko's nihilism is her analysis of power and oppression. Unlike more traditional Marxist or even communist anarchists, she does not have faith in humans to construct or create a nonoppressive social system. She fears that civilized humans will inevitably be waged in a Hobbesian war of all against all. She told her interrogator in prison, "Having observed social reality that all living things on earth are incessantly engaged in a struggle for survival, that they kill each other to survive, I concluded that if there is an absolute, universal law on earth, it's the reality that the strong eat the weak" (Hane 1993: 122–3). Kaneko seems to understand politics as a tension between the powerful and the weak. Like the famous bird of prey analog in *Geneology of Morals*, Kaneko understands humans in a relationship of predation, in which the powerful attempt to consume and exploit the weak. She contends, "As long as all living things do not disappear from the earth, the power relations based on this principle [of the strong crushing the weak] will persist." This nihilistic view of human nature undergirds her general hostility to utopian politics, "Now that I see the truth about the struggle for survival and the fact that the strong win and the weak lose, I cannot join the ranks of the idealists and adopt an optimistic mode of thinking which dreams of the construction of a society that is without authority and control" (Hane 1993: 122). What makes Kaneko unique is that her politics do not devolve here into apathy and inaction, nor does she attempt to invert the hierarchy and make herself a powerful exploiter of others. This is because she, at the core of her being, contends, "By nature, human beings should be equal. And yet human beings who are equal by nature have been made unequal because of the presence of an entity called the Emperor" (Hane 1993: 123). Thus, we get an interesting political philosophy that first understands humans as naturally equal but contends that under any form of social relationship hierarchies of power form that lead to a system where the powerful always oppress the weak. The social arrangements of humans and the hierarchies they put in place are the enemies that must be destroyed. For instance, she writes, "Ah nature! In nature there are no lies. Nature is open-hearted and free. It does not warp humanity as humans [themselves] do" (Raddeker 2016: 166), showing that inequalities and authority are not a product of nature but of human social construction. The emperor system, during her life, was the institution that enacted violence and coercion but Kaneko did not believe that removing the emperor would lead to total liberation. She felt that any political system would oppress the weak and that there will always need to be figures, like her, who revolt against power. Expressing this, in part, she wrote, "Because the wielders of power continue to defend their authority in the usual manner and oppress the weak—and because my past existence has been a story of oppression by all sources of authority—I decided to deny the right of all authority, rebel against them, and stake not only my own life but that of all humanity on this endeavor" (Hane 1993: 121–2).

Her experience with Christian reformers, rural peasants, and socialists helped shape her critique of utopian projects. In her experience, Christians, who claimed to oppose oppression, just reinscribed gender norms into their behavior and, as such, were just as concerned with conformity of values as the monarchists. Likewise, the rural peasants she saw as unable to shed their chains, and that even if "liberated, they are likely to go to the wielders of political and economic power with their chains and beg them to chain them up again" (Hane 1993: 121). Her most brutal critiques were reserved for the socialists, whom she joined for a short period before being disillusioned by the performative activities of the leaders, who seemed to want to generate and wield social power and not bring about revolutionary change. She wrote:

> I had imagined that socialists were people who rose above the meaningless costumes and morality of society . . . however, even though they denounce the irrational and hypocritical aspects of society, and pretend that they are indifferent to social criticisms and fame and reputation, they, in fact, are governed by and concerned about the standards of the mundane society. They seek to adorn themselves with conventional ornaments and take upon themselves conventional values. (Hane 1993: 121)

This frustration against socialism does not mean that her values where antithetical to the logic of defending the oppressed or the working people. She stated, "I began to realize that socialism had its validity" (Hane 1993: 111). If anything, her understanding of socialism and political power embraced the anarchist critique of the Marxist tradition. "Socialism will trigger social upheavel for the 'sake of the masses,' and the masses will probably rise up in rebellion with those who act on their behalf, even put their lives on the line with them," She writes. But she was critical that socialist politics would do anything to actually liberate the masses, because, at the end of the day, socialists did not seek to destroy power but to instead use power for their own benefit. This meant, to Kaneko, that socialism "simply means replacing one authority for another" (Hane 1993: 111). In short, we have an expression of an anarchist nihilism that, while uniquely developed by Kaneko, has sympathy with Stirner's critique of social arrangement and collective coercion.[2] Stirner contended that any structural grouping of humans by state, economic, or moral communities imposed a form of control on the individual, denying their ability to express themselves and develop their self via egoism (Dolinšek 2022). Kaneko rejects any form of social arrangement as another form of coercive political institution building that reinscribes oppressive hierarchal relationships. She wrote, "I used to believe that those who adhered to certain isms were a special kind of people, that they were outstanding. Now I feel that I had been a fool to indulge in such fantasy. I felt disillusioned, as if I had just awakened from a beautiful dream to find myself in a sewer" (Hane 1993: 106). In rejecting all ideological political projects as phantasmic to maintain power and control over others, her stance was to reject all social arrangements and resist all forms of institutional power when put into practice. This forms a constant struggle between the oppressed and the logic of society, marking an antisocial and individualist version of anarchist nihilism.

---

[2]Kaneko Fumiko and Park Yŏl both were heavily influenced by Stirner, whose work was translated into Japanese by Jun Tsuji, a Dadaist poet, egoistic anarchist, and former husband of the anarchist feminist martyr Ito Noe, who was executed by the Japanese paramilitary forces during the Tokyo earthquake (which was used as a cause to arrest Kaneko as well). Kaneko was introduced to Stirner, as well as Nietzsche, Bergan, Hegel, and Marx, via her good friend Hatsuyo, who would loan her the books and talk with her about the ideas and the implications. Her connection to Stirner grew more after her partnership with Pak.

This nihilism is always grounded not in ideological purity but instead in an emotional solidarity of anger, rage, love, and connection with those oppressed by the system. She writes in her memoir:

> I was poor. Even now, I am poor. For this reason, I have been pushed around, tormented, and oppressed, my freedom plundered. I have been exploited and controlled by people with money. Thus in the depth of my soul, there has been nourished an antipathy for people with this sort of power. And together with this, I developed a heartfelt sympathy for those in the circumstances like my own. (Hane 1993: 98)

This sympathy and solidarity was rooted in her own experience, where family, employers, lovers, and the state all exploited and used her. The more she lived and learned, the more she began to link her own identity with that of the oppressed. This meant not only siding with the oppressed, but in rejecting the logic and value of becoming "great." She wrote, "I feel it's pointless to try and become a success in the kind of society we are living in" and "I'd come to realize that there was no one as worthless as the 'so-called' successful, great people" (Hane 1993: 110). Instead of ideological linkages being the foundation for her solidarity and support, she focused on the relationship of power between the oppressed and the oppressor, the weak and the powerful, the loser and the great.

Kaneko's political project can be seen as an inversion of the Nietzschean ubermensch, or superman. While Nietzsche lionized the "master," who understood his power and greatness and acted without resentment, only to impose his "will to power." Kaneko embraced the politics of the untermensch, or subhuman, a term and phrased used by Nazi propagandist and theorists to define and justify the genocide of Jews, Roma, homosexuals, and other dissidents. In inverting the superman, the untermensch rejects any logic of domination and focuses on the losers and weak in society. In addition, this is an attempt to counter the logic of Nazism, which used racial hierarchies as part of a larger genocidal and biopolitical project of control. The racial logic of Nazism is not unique to the German experience under fascism but is, at the core, of liberal political orders throughout the world.[3] In the United States, a racial hierarchy centered on anti-Blackness constructs the Black body as an "untermensch," which justifies and allows state and parastate to use violence. To use this phrase, and center the untermensch, the goal is to also highlight the ways that hierarchies, fascist and liberal underlie modern political institutions which hide behind a veneer of "meritocracy" and individual "greatness." Last, by focusing on the untermensch, I am embracing and building on the anti-humanism found within the work of Max Stirner, who often associated his political project with that of the criminal, the loser, the monster. Stirner, for instance, argues, that under humanism the phantasm of humanity serves as a category that links people together. But the category does not allow actual solidarity, since it is a hollow concept; instead, it simply is used to constrain people and contrast the docile and domesticated populations with the monster "anti-humans" who rebel against the social and political order. In centering the loser and subhuman, I am embracing our inner monsterousness and nonhumanness and building a politics of solidarity around exclusions to the categories of humanness, not in order to expand the category of "humanness" but to destroy the category of humanity entirely.[4]

[3]Hitler and other Nazi thinkers looked to the racial apartheid of the United States—from the south's Jim Crow laws, to anti-immigration laws and US nativism, and the indigenous reservation system—as an influence for developing their own racial order. But, even deeper, the entire colonial experience was rooted in a racial hierarchy and order that constructed the colonized other as a subhuman. Read Aimee Cesear and Franz Fanon's work to get a clear account of how that racial subhuman othering functioned.

[4]Similarly, the punk subcultural movement can also be seen as a politics of the untermensch. Skov, for instance, argues that "there is a hunger for failure in punk." A wide range of punk bands embraced the loser mystique in their names (such as the misfits, the vandals, the weirdos, the subhumans, the dirty rotten imbeciles, the exploited, the marginal man, the bad brains, and countless others) and their politics, which often centers on lower-class resistance and dropout culture. Skov, again, highlights, "we can view these strategies of glorified imperfection as a protection against pressure, against the (capitalist) ideology of success. We can also view imperfection as a part of the punks' depiction of the world, as they say it: as a place full of failures, flaws, and faults" (Skov 2023: 256–66). The centering of squatter culture, especially in early punk and street life, with the genres of crustpunk and street punk, as well as tattoo culture is all part of a broader politics that links the punk with the underclass. The band His Hero Is Gone, for instance, in their song "Anthem of the undesirable" scream, "I fight everyday through rocks pelted in haunting memories/ Thoughts scarred by what was taught/ Ruptured hearts try to unlearn bouts of despair and the blatant lies/ Through years and years of held back tears, beauty was defined/The ugly confined and the mirror reminds" (from their album Fifteen Counts of Arson). In this song, His Hero Is Gone, like Kaneko, centers their politics in the rage experienced out of oppression. Similarly, the band G.L.O.S.S. (Girls living Outside of Societies Shit) express their

Kaneko claimed that the emperor system is both rooted in and is co-constructive with the Japanese morality system, which, just like all social and political arrangements, served as a mechanism of control. She writes, "Under the emperor system, education, laws, and moral principles were all devised to protect imperial authority." Morality, for Kaneko, functions solely to maintain the hierarchy and is primarily a value that is imposed, and internalized, by the nonelite in Japanese society. She wrote:

> Under the emperor system, education, laws, and moral principles were all devised to protect imperial authority. The notion that the emporer is sacred and august is a fantasy. The people have been led to believe that the emperor and the crown prince represent authorities that are sacred and inviolate. But they are simply vacuous puppets. The concepts of loyalty to the emperor and love of nation are simply rhetorical notions that are being manipulated by the tiny group of privileged classes to fulfill their own greed and interests. (Hane 1993: 124)

The elite, from politicians to the emperor, are not beholden to the same moral precepts as are the rest of the population. This includes not only workers and capitalists but radical as well. Moralism, like the striving for power more generally, highlights the deep radical change needed in society to liberate people from oppression. If a revolt only called for a shift in the system of power, the system of morality would be left in place and the oppressed would still be controlled. She writes:

> The so-called morality is based on the relationship between the strong and the weak. That morality is always manipulated to serve the convenience of the strong. That is, the strong insist on preserving their freedom of action while demanding the submission of the weak. . . . The primary aim of those in power is to preserve this moral principle as long as possible. The

---

solidarity and rage in the song "The Outcast Stomp" by declaring, "This is for the outcasts, rejects, girls and the queers/For the downtrodden women who have shed their last tears/ Fighters, psychos, freaks, and the femmes/For all the transgender ladies in constant transition, cast out," before finishing the song by repeating "The freaks are coming/The freaks are coming/The freaks are cumming, oh." This is all to say that Kaneko Fumiko's nihilistic political analysis are a precursor to punk politics.

> relationship between parent and child is also based on this principle. It is only coated over the attractive-sounding term familial piety. (Hane 1993: 119)

Morality, according to Kaneko, has similarities to Thrasymachus, the antagonist in Plato's Republic who claimed that justice is "nothing other than the advantage of the stronger." Thus, moralism, as well as the political and economic institutions of society, all needed to be destroyed if there was any possibility for lasting liberation. For those radicals that moralized—be they Christian, socialist, or communists—all they wanted to do was place themselves at the top of the hierarchy and use morality, and the state, to create a new class which would oppress the others.

While Kaneko provides an abstract political theory analysis, the full range of her politics is best seen in her analysis of the Japanese state. She defined the Japanese society as having three broad classes: the royal clan members, the government ministers and wielders of political power, and the masses. Of these three, she claimed that the "second class, the wielders of power, are the ones who have the real power to persecute the weak, like myself. For that reason I feel nothing but bitter hatred towards this class" (Hane 1993: 122), while the first class, the royals, primarily served a symbolic role. The symbolic provided cover for the practical application of power—creating a coalition between the first and the second class—which, due to ideological manipulation and the logic of morality, pacified the masses. The symbolic role of the emperors, since it was the ideological justification used to legitimate the Japanese state, was the primary focus of Kaneko's attention. She contends that the state is grounded in the myth of inherent Japanese greatness, which is connected to the godlike importance of the Japanese emperor. The planned assassination was meant to, as a form of propaganda by the deed, show that emperor was not a God but was just as frail as any other human. A bomb would rip his flesh and end his life, like it would anyone else. She told her interrogators, "We wanted to show the people that the emperor is an ordinary human being just like us. So we thought of throwing a bomb at him to show that he too will die. Like any other human" (Hane 1993: 124). This claim is similar to the reference Fanon and George Maher made about violence as a tactical project to force equality through the creation of shared logics of vulnerability.

The idea of the symbolic emperor system is still a pressing debate in Japanese political theory. The modern Japanese state constitution, which is a relic of the US occupation of the archipelago after the Second World War, enshrines the emperor as a symbolic representation of the people. According to Takahashi Tetsuya, the contemporary debates around the symbolic emperor during the 1999 policy proposal of formalizing the Hinomaru (Japanese flag) and Kimigayo (national anthem). According to Takahashi Tetsuya, "The Hinomaru-Kimigayo issue is not simply an issue of the national flag and national anthem. It is an issue of the symbolic emperor system, one that questions the very framework of the 'nation-state' Japan" (Calichman 2005: 223). Tetsuya contends that the symbolic emperor justifies and hides the colonial/imperial violence of the Japanese state, both historically and contemporarily, and constructs an artificially "we" via a symbolic representative. Kaneko, in the 1920s, created a similar analysis contending that while the Taisho-era ultranationalist state claimed the emperor as an absolute source of sovereignty, in reality the emperor was a symbolic position which obfuscated the mechanism of coercion and violence that was the actual foundation of the Japanese states sovereignty. In much the way that Schmitt understood the secularization of politics as merely a form of political theology, Kaneko claims the emperor has always been nothing but a symbolic and representational role and that at the core of all systems and isms is coercion, violence, and oppression of the weak by the strong.

Since she rejected utopian politics, all forms of ideological and social formation, and viewed politics as a constant and endless struggle against oppression until all life was destroyed, she had a unique understanding of her political agency. She told the interrogators, "I did not care whether this act would start off a revolution or not. I am perfectly content to satisfy my own desires. I do not wish to create a new society based on a new authority in a different form" (Hane 1993: 122). Even though her desired action, the assassination of the crown prince and as many members of the royal family as possible, was not designed to lead to a revolution, this did not mean she felt it was any less reason for action. She mentions many times that anger, rage, and disdain for the powerful, more than a commitment to any specific revolution, shaped her behavior. The rejection of expecting, or even believing that change would happen from her agency, never stopped her from acting. What mattered for her political agency was that it be would a form of retribution for the injustice and violence that the elite had enacted on the powerful and weak. Just because her focus was not on revolution, or the future, it does not mean that she did not have a strong commitment to radical politics. On July 18, 1925, during a police interrogation, when asked about her job before being convicted of treason, she said, "My job is tearing down everything that currently exists" (Hane 1993: 123). In a previous interrogation, on November 22, 1925, she had said:

> The government officials have finally thrown me in prison. But let me give you some sound advice if you wish to prevent the current incident from bearing fruit, you must kill me. You may hold me in prison for years, but as soon as I am released, I will try the same thing. I will destroy my body and save you the trouble. (Hane 1993: 123)

Her militant politics actually seems to have strengthened, and not limited, by her rejecting linking political activism to the likelihood of political outcomes. In a moment when the dialectic is frozen and politics seems impossible, when you link action to expected results, action becomes muted and politic becomes domesticated.

Overall, what I want to pull out of Fumiko's nihilist politics is her analysis and critique of all isms and systems, her solidaristic politics of the untermensch, and her rejection of revolutionary potential as a limitation of her behavior. These values and concepts are increasingly important today, as the reality of climate catastrophe and the growing power of fascism throughout the West has foreclosed the possibilities of reformism—if reformism was ever a long-term strategy. But, it has also limited the space for liberatory revolutionary change and left revolutionary politics. If there are no outlets for such rage among the left, the transference of class rage and antagonism will be shaped by fascistic forces and directed toward immigrants, queer folks, and racial minorities. Sadly, the left has instead, feeling the powerlessness of the current moment, a hyperfixation on identity politics and performative posturing. In response, Kaneko's politics highlights that action can happen even outside of the potentiality of revolt, and, as the Russian nihilist highlights, that action can clear the rubble of the present. By focusing on destroying and resisting the dominant system of power—from capitalism, the state, and also white supremacy and patriarchy—political nihilism can block fascistic desires from calcifying. My claim here is that centering the untermensch, that is, the subhuman, offers a way to embrace a militant politics of resistance without the fascistic drive toward greatness. Last, her analysis highlights how the symbolic nature of sovereignty reinforces the institutional and material structure of violence and state power. Kaneko planned to assassinate the emperor, not because it would lead to a revolution but simply because the powerful and the oppressors deserve to experience the same levels of vulnerability and suffering that their actions cause on the weak and oppressed. Her desire for revenge and her resentment are not faults in her thinking but are instead part of what we need to start cultivating. The seeds of resentment against the rich do not need to be cast since the soil is already filled with them. We need to water, cultivate, and harvest what the capitalist class has already sown, that is, their own destruction.

"We All Die in a Yellow Submarine": Resentment and the Tragicomedy of Dead Billionaires

On June 18, 2023, a group of billionaires squeezed their way into a small five-person submersible owned by Oceangate to see the debris and remnants of the Titanic, which sunk following a collision with an iceberg in 1914. The three inhabitants of the excursion—Shahzada and Suleman Dawood (a billionaire Pakistani businessman and his son) and Hamish Harding (a businessman and long-time adventure tourist)—paid a quarter of a million each for the experience. Two hours into what was supposed to be an eight-hour trip, the submarine imploded killing them all instantly. It was not till June 22 before those of us above the sea learned the details of the billionaires' demise. During these four days of unknown, the international media covered the submarine, while pundits and commentators filled hours of air time pontificating on the whereabouts and status of the disappeared billionaires. A week before, on June 12 and 13, an overfilled fishing vessel ferrying refugees and migrants from Libya to Europe had capsized off the coast of Greece. Judith Sutherland of Europe's human rights watch told NBC News, "The willingness to allow certain people to die while every effort is made to save others . . . it's a, you know, really dark reflection on humanity" (Chantal Da Silva 2023). While, thankfully, more than a hundred of the refugees and migrants were rescued, well over 100 died in the disaster. Even though many more people died off the coast of Greece, a significantly disproportionate amount of world media and search and rescue resources were dedicated to covering and attempting to rescue the billionaire adventure tourists.

While the media and state resources were directed at billionaires, leaving hundreds of poor refugees to die in silence, throughout Western social media trolls, meme pages, and leftist accounts posted meme after meme mocking the death of the billionaires, often relishing the potential suffering they had likely experienced. Most of the memes mocked the fact that these billionaires spent so much money on a poorly made submarine to enjoy death tourism, and laughed at the death of the billionaires in general. When asked about the memes, David Pogue, a CBS news journalist, said, "Obviously, when it comes to what we know now, joking is inappropriate and a little bit sick. Five people died. They had spouses; they had families. It's really sad" (Saba Hamedy 2023). Pogue was not unique in his take as the *Washington Post, New York Times, Forbes,* and countless other news sources posted articles or op-eds condemning the memes as signs of a sick and sad culture. They, of course, are right; the memes are a result of a sick and sad culture, the culture of a world on the brink of collapse in which stories abound of the ultra-wealthy mocking the poor and even betting on which worker would die next from Covid. While the social media and meme world mocked and laughed at the dead billionaires, many reports and commentators complained about the decorum of the conversations, asking for civility and respect.

Instead of focusing on the disaster, which would quickly be forgotten, I want to use this story as a quick way of exploring the politics of resentment. In *Geneology of Morals,* Nietzsche contends that resentment is a core aspect of slave morality. He writes, "the slave revolt in morals begins when resentment itself becomes creative and ordains values: the resentment of creatures to whom the real reaction that of the deed is denied and who finds compensation in an imaginary revenge" (Nietzsche and Smith 2008: 22). For Nietzsche, previous eras were defined by the dominance of the master morality, which defined the self internally, focusing on the traits that the master and powerful loved about themselves. So what the master did was beautiful and what the slave did was ugly. The master's identity comes from oneself and represents links to an internalized will to power. For the slave, the concepts are defined in opposition to that which they view as their oppressor. So if the master is rich, then the rich must be evil; if the master is strong, then strength must be rejected. "While the noble man lives for himself in trust and openness," Nietzsche writes, "the man of resentment is neither upright nor naïve in his dealings with others, nor is he honest with himself" (Nietzsche and Smith 2008: 24). In short, the master finds his power within himself, and therefore his identity is not linked to that of the weak, while the weak only define themselves in contrast to the powerful, meaning that they must domesticate and control the powerful. The slave cannot abolish the master since their identity requires their existence. The slave, while clever and smart, cannot create the world in this way and instead can only function by taming and controlling the powerful, turning their powerfulness against them through a complicated game of guilt and shame.

Wendy Brown, in *States of Injury*, uses the Nietzschean analysis of resentment in order to develop a critique of a specific strand of liberal identity politics. Brown contends that liberal politics, especially around addressing historical wrongs and current oppression, often embraces a politics of revenge and resentment. This forces liberal politics into a trap, where they weaponize morality as a political tool and make politics out of endless victimization. She writes:

> In its emergence as a protest against marginalization and subordination, politicized identity thus becomes attached to its own exclusion both because it is premised on this exclusion for its very existence as identity and because the formation of identity at the site of exclusion, as exclusion, augments or "alters the direction of the suffering" entailed in subordination or marginalization by finding a site of the blame for it. But in doing, it instills

its pain over its unredeemed history in the very foundation of its political claim, in its demand for recognition as identity. (Brown 1995: 73–4)

Brown, here, correctly critiques strands of liberal identity politics and posits how such identities lead to a politics of moralization, which can reinscribe Christian logic of patriarchy and empower the liberal state while also creating a false image of the state as a neutral arbiter of justice. But such criticism should be focusing not on resentment but on the logic of liberal individualism and the politics of recognition it promotes. In providing a powerful anti-colonial critique of recognition politics, Glen Coulthard writes, "Left as it is, it would appear that recognition inevitably leads to the subjugation" (Coulthard 2014: 42). While he agrees with Brown that recognition politics creates problematic and moralistic politics that can never heal the trauma of colonialism, unlike her he does not place this as a problem with resentment. If anything, he argues that resentment can be a valuable and powerful tool to mobilize radical politics. He writes, "One could argue, then, that resentment, unlike anger, has an in-built political component to it, given that it is often expressed in response to an alleged slight, instance of maltreatment, or injustice. Seen from this angle, resentment can be understood as a particularly virulent expression of politicized anger" (Coulthard 2014: 110). In his analysis, Coulthard critiques Nietzsche's claim that resentment is tied to an inability to forget one's past. What if ones past is not worth forgetting? What if the wounds of the past are still open?

"By way of consolation to the more delicate, perhaps in those days, the pain did not hurt as much as it does today," wrote Nietzsche (Nietzsche and Smith 2008: 49). James Marion Sims, the modern father of gynecology, developed his techniques and scientific knowledge through medical experimentation, without anesthesia, on enslaved Black women in the South. Their bodies were ripped and cut, and the pain and bruises, as much as Nietzsche might have claimed, hurt no less than they would today. The same is true of the 1,500 sets of twins that the Nazi Doctor Josef Mengele experimented on in Auschwitz or the beagles vivisected for the development of Viagra. Every case of violence is not made better because it happened in the past. The critique of resentment offered by Nietzsche attempts to erase and reify the violence the powerful have enacted on the weak through a politics of forgetting. In counter to this, resentment is not a problem to be avoided but a political topic that needs to be engaged with, by maintaining the anger and rage at the violence committed throughout the past (and that occurs in the present) and directing counterviolence at those who enacted or benefited from the violence. Doing so does not construct a liberal form of recognition and identity politics, which Brown and Nietzsche see as the outcome of a resentment politics, but that of militant and revolutionary anarchism. Of course, Nietzsche knew this was the reality of the situation, as he reserved his most ardent and feverous criticism toward anarchists of his time. According to Saul Newman:

> Of all the nineteenth-century political movements that Nietzsche decries—from socialism to liberalism—he reserves his most venomous words for the anarchists. He calls them the "anarchist dogs" that are roaming the streets of European culture, the epitome of the "herd-animal morality" that characterizes modern democratic politics. (Newman 2000)

Nietzsche's hostility toward anarchism is not due to the resentment at the core of the anarchist politics, but that the anger and violence is being directed at the powerful, the figures that Nietzsche links his own sense of self with. In fact, a stance against revolutionary violence and militancy directed at the powerful is part of, as much as Nietzsche would hate this claim, a politics of liberal domestication. Nietzsche, himself a vocal critic of domestication and a believer that all progress happens through blood and pain, by rejecting resentment, neuters the untermensch, the weak, from a politics of solidarity and struggle and removes the possibility of a collective formed will to power. But, of course, that is his desire. The aristocratic Nietzsche is interested in maintaining power hierarchies as long as the master, or the lost great man of history, or the tortured artist is placed at the top of that hierarchy. The anarchist politics of resentment differ from his in an attempt to mobilize and agitate the weak into collectively confronting the powerful, a form of collective will to power emanating from below. And most terrifying, the goal of a revolutionary political of untermensch resentment is the negation and abolition of hierarchies of power.

This does not mean that there is only space for a politics of revenge. Revenge has limitations. The insurrectionary anarchist Alfredo Bonanno in

Armed Joy, a book that was banned by the Italian state in 1977 and for which the author spent eighteen months in person, notes, "when we first become conscious of the process of exploitation, the first thing we feel is a sense of revenge, the last is joy. . . . Everything must come down, So we arm ourselves and strike the adversary to them pay for their responsibility" (Bonanno 2022: 127). This early phase of revolutionary insurrection is founded on rage and anger directed at those who have caused us pain. However, he buttresses this claim by highlighting that "anyone who desires to live does not produce death. A transitory acceptance of the guillotine leads to its institutionalization. But at the same time, anyone who loves life does not embrace their exploiter. To do so would signify that they are against life in favor of sacrifice, self-punishment, work, and death" (Bonanno 2022: 128–9). What is important in Bonanno's claim here is that he does not position rage and revenge and love as opposites. To Bonanno, there are times in which love and community require a politics of anger and revenge against those who hurt those you love.

The way that Bonanno balances this tension is to center the politics of joy. Joy here is not defanged and removed from political militancy or political violence, but linked with it. He notes that joy and play are inherently collective processes and that the process of play allows for forming categories of friends. It is through these bonds of connection and links that joy can emerge, even if it is still rooted in resentment against the elite and the powerful. "Joy emerges from the play of destructive action, from the recognition of the profound tragedy that this implies and an awareness of the strength of enthusiasm that is capable of slaying the cobwebs of death," he argues. However, "It is not a question of opposing horror with horror, tragedy with tragedy, death with death. It is a confrontation between joy and horror, joy and tragedy, and joy and death" (Bonanno 2022: 139). Resentment in this analysis is part of a broader political project of militant and armed joy, but only when that resentment is collective and playful. This is, in fact, the logic of the anti-billionaire memes spread in the wake of the billionaires' trip to their watery graves. In these memes, a collective spirit of joy and humor is fueled while at the same time refusing to empathize with or mourn those who oppress us and are killing the world. Is there anger and rage? Of course. Nevertheless, is there joy and humor in such resentful mocking of the rich? You bet your ass!

Cabin in the Woods and the Politics of Armed Joy

As a quick and cursory exploration of these concepts, I am ending this chapter with a critical engagement with the 2012 horror film *Cabin in the Woods*. This film has been read by the academics either as representing the conflict and struggle between urban and rural communities in the globalized World (Murphy 2013) or as a modern adaptation of a Lovecraftian cosmic horror story for the twenty-first century (Lockett 2015). However, the political and social dynamic of the film has not been fully explored. Here, I want to argue that the protagonists' actions in the film are an expression of nihilistic political action in the face of impending doom. In this film, a group of college students go on a vacation to a cabin in the woods. The cabin is not a place for respite or rest but is a sacrificial altar on which an ancient cult, using modern technology and techniques, sacrifices youth to satiate an elder god to keep them from destroying the earth. Central to the sacrifice is that the victims have to choose the path of their demise, and the cults manipulate the environment to ensure that the campers make a choice. The person in charge of the cult's game states:

> No, they have to make the choice of their own free will. Otherwise, the system doesn't work. It's like like the Harbinger. It's this creepy old fuck, who practically wears a sign, "You will die." Why do we put him there? The system. They have to choose to ignore him, and they have to choose what happens in the cellar. Yeah, we rig the game as much as we need to, but in the end, they don't transgress. (Cabin in the Woods 2012)

This focus on choice, like the structure of modern spectacle democracy, is an illusion that allows for the system to reify its violence via the guise of "individual choice." In addition, much like our world system, where millions are sacrificed each year to maintain the global order, the cult requires sacrifices to maintain the continuation of the world. In the movie, the group "decides" to be sacrificed by a crazy undead family of hillbillies.

The undead family proceeds to kill all but two of the college students—Dana Polk (Kristen Connolly), the "virgin," and Marty Mikalski (Fran Kranz), the stoner and joker. These two escape the cabin enclosure and enter the cult's underground bunker. In the bunker, the college students release the menagerie of "horror cliché" monsters that the cult has imprisoned, like a zoo of the macabre. These imprisoned monsters, much like those who are sacrificed, are victims of the cult and the structure of the World that requires their imprisonment. After being released, the monsters turn on their captors, slaughtering the members of the cult in a fury for revenge. Our two main characters work their way to the main room of the bunker and are confronted by the cult director (played by Sigourney Weaver), who tells them:

> This is all most unpleasant. I know you can hear me. I hope you'll listen. You won't get out of this complex alive. What I want you to try to understand is that you mustn't. Your deaths will avert countless others. You've seen horrible things: an army of nightmare creatures. And they are real. But they are nothing compared to what lies beneath us. There is a greater good, and for that, you must be sacrificed. Forgive us . . . and let us end it quickly. (Cabin in the Woods 2012)

Weaver offers them a choice of martyred sacrifice or the destruction of the world. Like Fumiko, who demands the destruction of the world, they refuse martyrdom. In a world where countless lives are sacrificed to maintain the hierarchies of inequality, martyrdom would make them complicit in the violence of the system by defending and protecting it. Deciding to watch the world burn, they shoot and kill the cult director and patiently await the end of the World. Marty and Dana share a joint and a laugh, and state:

> Marty: [*incredulous*] Giant evil gods.
> Dana: I wish I could've seen them.
> Marty: I know. That would have been a fun weekend. (Cabin in the Woods 2012)

Dana and Marty are emblematic of political nihilism. They, as victims of the systems of violence that maintain the world, reject the hierarchy and order that is imposed on them and seek to destroy that which has caused them suffering. In this film, the protagonists, instead of being forced into passivity by fear and apathy by a lack of hope, decide to act, and through their action, as futile as it might be in the end, they find joy and comradery. It is only after Dana and

Marty's path to survival is blocked that they shift their focus from running and hiding to a politics of attack. It is essential to highlight the extreme joy that Dara and Marty experience once their death is guaranteed. The two, who had previously not had much connection with each other, form a strong bond. They finish each other's sentences, act in coordination, and are seen smiling and laughing, even while all around them are walls coated in splattered viscera and the only background noise is of screams of pain from the dying cult members. For instance, toward the end of the movie, they have this short exchange:

> Dana: I'm so sorry I almost shot you. . . . I probably wouldn't have.
> Marty: Hey. Hey, no, shh, no. I totally get it. [*pauses to light a reefer*] I'm sorry I let you get attacked by a werewolf and then ended the world. (Cabin in the Woods 2012)

Ultimately, the two cannot liberate themselves or the world, but maybe the world did not deserve to continue? What they did find was a politics of solidarity and joy in resistance and revenge. In a movie that centers on constrained choices, they grasp power, for the first time, by refusing the logic of the game. Refusal of the game, mixed with a resentment-fueled politics of attack, provides them the experience of freedom and liberation, albeit for a few minutes. But maybe a world is structured and built on the endless sacrifice of human and nonhuman; as Fumiko claimed in her interrogation, "The goal of my activities is the destruction of all living things."

7

Toward a Nihilistic Politics of Attack

In the critically acclaimed bestseller *Ministry for the Future*, science fiction author Kim Stanley Robinson provides an optimistic imagining of a future in which the world finds a path to survive the climatic crisis. His near-future novel focuses on pragmatic bureaucratic applications of policy by the "Ministry of the Future," a Zurich-based international agency formed after the failure of the Paris Accords. The ministry is tasked with the mission "to advocate for the world's future generations of citizens, whose rights, as defined in the Universal Declaration of Human Rights, are as valid as our own" (K. S. Robinson 2020). The centering of future focuses attention away from current political and economic limitation of climate politics and allows for a bypassing of the nation-state power struggle of the present. Unlike the long-termism that has captured the hearts, minds, and massive Bitcoin wallets of silicon valley, Robinson's version has more in common with the indigenous logic of "seven generations," where choices and behavior need to be evaluated on their impact on the sustainability of the future and not on wealth accumulation.

In his book review, Bill Gates writes, "Some of these ideas are really intriguing, like the idea of the Ministry for the future itself. If we want to address climate change, our political institutions will have to start doing what the Ministry does: acting on behalf of future generations" (Gates 2022). However, Gates, ever the capitalist neoliberal, is concerned that Robinson does not provide a market-based solution such as Gate's proposed carbon currency, which allows people to make money by removing carbon from the air. Gates laments:

> I wish Robinson had spent more time on broad solutions that enable us to get to zero emissions while helping people escape poverty: Better seeds that don't require as much fertilizer and can withstand changing weather or ways to create cement and steel without emitting carbon. (Gates 2022)

Not surprisingly, Gates, a well-known advocate for neoliberal technocratic solutions, wishes that Robinson would have doubled down even more on technological innovation and accumulation-based market solutions.

The book primarily focuses on bureaucratic solutions to the crisis. However, to enact these policy proposals, a political revolutionary and insurrectionary act was needed to jump-start the desire for structural changes. While Robinson, and most of the reviews of the text, gloss over the need for such militant action, it is central to the beginning of the book. In the story, a heat wave ravages the subcontinent of India. Extreme temperatures and high humidity lead to the deaths of twenty million people. While the tragedy shakes the world, a group of Indian survivors form an eco-terrorist network, the Children of Kali, named after the Hindu goddess of destruction. This group launches a wave of terrorist attacks against fossil fuel infrastructure and the networks of global trade. The group, on "crash day," bombs commercial airliners, killing thousands, and scaring the economic and political elite from flying. They also use drones to sink cargo ships, turning the machines of industrial death into makeshift coral reefs for threatened ocean life. Robinson glosses over the terror acts, as the events are described primarily through news stories and character conversations, and he does not engage with the political, personal, and revolutionary impulse of the eco-radicals who, in his novel, are essential in "clearing the rubble" through insurrectionary and revolutionary terrorism. Because these terrorists acted following the death of millions of their family, friends, and neighbors, they were likely acting with at least some sort of resentment and desire for revenge. In this regard, they have more in common with the figures in the last chapter—the Russian nihilists, Fumik Kaneda, and even the main characters of *Cabin in the Woods*—than with any bureaucratic European international agency.

This chapter takes inspiration not from the *Ministry of the Future*, a problematic form of technocratic eco-reformism, but from the Children of Kali. It is worth remembering that, as Marcuse (Marcuse 1969) wrote in his essay on liberation, "Technocracy, no matter how 'pure,' sustains and streamlines the continuum of domination," and, as such, the *Ministry of the Future*, which technocrats and liberal figures have latched onto, is nothing but a justification and manual for liberal domination. The Children of Kali, on the other hand, models the insurrectionary and revolutionary political action that embraces the sort of revolution de-acceleration that the planet needs. Walter Benjamin wrote, "Marx says that revolutions are the locomotives of world history. But the situation may be quite different. Perhaps revolutions are not the train ride, but the human race grabbing for the emergency brake." This chapter takes Benjamin's claim seriously, focusing on revolutionary action as a form of emergency brake. Linking to the last chapter, revolutionary change cannot be rooted in utopian conceptions of the future but in stopping the destructive process. This means constructing a conception of radical action that fuses an anarchistic conception of destitute power with Benjamin's handbrake theory.

"The Revolutionary Handbrake": Walter Benjamin on Revolution and the Future

According to Walter Benjamin, history, materialism, and revolution are all intertwined with messianic desires. In his famous "Theses on the Philosophy of History," he lays out one of the most profound and unique critiques of linear progress. Narratives of progress are inevitably bound with certain traits of human domination and mastery of nature and to turn the duration of time into a quasi-religious search for truth. The quasi-religious nature of historical thinking, even when secularized through modernist logic, transmogrifies world histories into a universal theory of history that erases the distinctions between place and time. As this book has already highlighted, the logic of the Enlightenment, and with it the scientism and industrial logic of modernity, shapes much of what we think is possible and distorts and constrains the past into a tool of contemporary propaganda. If history has a telos—either toward revolution or toward the colonization of star systems—then all of history is consolidated into a singular narrative, a narrative that always provides empirical evidence for an ideological position. Progress forms a sort of zero-point epistemology in which, more often than not, the Western tradition is placed at the pinnacle, and alternative ways of living are treated as retrograde. Such a conception of history is a phantasm that limits our abilities to imagine and enact unique ways of being in this world and which binds people to ideological political projects. James Martel, in his book *Anarchist Prophets*, contends that politics is shaped by two forces, that of the archists, who wish to project order onto the world, and of the anarchists, who reject such ordering projects and instead center life. In a beautiful read of Benjamin, Martel claims that there is no such things as a future, it has yet to happen, and that archism requires a projection of order onto the future to maintain the perception of authority. By constructing a future, Martel and with him Benjamin argue that top-down authority imposes restriction and limitations on action—often enforced through the state—in a violent attempt to make their prognostication true (Martel 2022). In addition, *if* there is a universally shared human history, then, much like the concepts of humanism, there has to be those peoples that exist outside the bounds of history. These communities and groups must be pulled into human history's orbit or extinguished. Assimilation and eradication are the only paths of universalized values and claims. Messianic history is like the horse blinders, forcing our vision forward and potentially directing us off a cliff.

Benjamin famously contrasted this messianic vision of progress with his angel of history, which was based on a 1920 painting by Paul Klee titled "Angelus Novus." Benjamin notes that the figure in the painting has his face turned toward the past. Benjamin writes, "Where we perceive a chain of events, he sees one single catastrophe which keeps piling wreckage upon wreckage and hurls it in from of his feet." This long line of catastrophe is the legacy and history of barbarism, violence, suffering, and destruction that the civilizational logic of progress has brought to the world. "This storm irresistibly propels him into the future to which his back is turned while the pile of debris before him grows skyward. This storm is what we call progress" (Benjamin 1986: 257–

8). As a constant and unfolding series of disasters pulling history forward recklessly and dangerously, this narrative of progress contrasts beautifully with the teleological or evolutionary conceptions of progress that tend to circulate in left and liberal narratives. Hegel, for example, provided a claim of universalized history in which conflicts around values, such as freedom, are the motor force that drags humanity toward more and more progress. Marx inverted the idealism of Hegel and instead argued that shifts in the material conditions of society are the force that pulls us through history. Unlike Hegel, whose owl of Minerva could only look backward, Marx contended that through the scientific logic of socialism, the trajectory of history could be analyzed and directed. At the same time, liberal thinkers like John Stuart Mill and Bentham all contended that through science and enlightenment we will progress forward.

In all these accounts of progress and universal human history, Western colonialism is strongly defended. For instance, in his horrific piece "on colonization in India," Marx writes:

> England, it is true, in causing a social revolution in Hindostan, was actuated only by the vilest interests, and was stupid in her way of enforcing them. But that is not the question. The question is, can mankind fulfill its destiny without a fundamental revolution in the social state of Asia? If not, whatever may have been the crimes of England she was the unconscious tool of history in bringing about that revolution. (Marx 1853)

While Marx does correctly highlight the horrific violence of the British rule in India, and before that, the Dutch, he still saw a need to pull Asia out of its primitive political and economic reality and make them apart of the broader project of modernity. Similarly, in many ways, John Stuart Mill actively supported the British colonization of India, seeing it as a tool that could benefit the Indian people. Mill wrote, "as legitimate as any other if it is the one which in the existing state of civilization of the subject people most facilitates their transition to a higher state of improvement" (David Williams 2021: 413). According to David Williams, Mill's defense of colonization rested on two arguments. First, "was that there were civilizational hierarchies. Mill linked the idea of 'civilization' to progress, identifying such things as population density, level of economic development, extent of social cooperation, and the rule of law as key defining features of a 'civilized' society" (David Williams 2021: 415). This sort of civilizational racial hierarchy is, sadly, not unique to Mill but can also be found in the work of Immanuel Kant and most, if not all, major Western enlightenment thinkers. The second defense for colonization in India was that "that progress toward 'civilization' was not imminent. Mill did not employ the kind of teleology we find in the more optimistic enlightenment thinkers, and progress for Mill was not a matter of simply clearing away a few obstacles and then letting the course of progress unfold 'naturally'" (David Williams 2021: 416). For India to progress forward, Mill believed the British needed to govern in a specific way.

In his piece, Benjamin shatters these logics of progress by rejecting the imposition of a narrative of times and progress from above. Benjamin contends that any analysis centered on a universal historical narrative is merely telling a story of progress and redemption. Time is thus always political. As an expression to this, Benjamin critiqued top-down calendar building. "The notion of a universal history is bound up with the notion of progress and the notion of culture," he writes. "In order for all the moments in the history of humanity to be incorporated in the chain of history, they must be reduced to a common denominator—'culture,' 'enlightenment,' the 'objective spirit,' or whatever one wishes to call it" (Benjamin, Eiland, and Jennings 2006: 403). In other words, the need for a universal history requires the colonization of difference. This is why he also focused on the way that the calendar itself functions. He writes, "Thus, the calendars do not measure time as clocks do; they are monuments of a historical consciousness of which not the slightest trace has been apparent in Europe in the past hundred years" (Benjamin 1986: 262). These monuments to historical time, when imposed from above, serve as reactionary edifices that limit and restrict; they shape and narrow the logic of the working classes. Benjamin writes that "no man or men but the struggling, oppressed class itself is the depository of historical knowledge" (Benjamin 1986: 260). A concept of time that emerges from the lived experience of the oppressed differs from this top-down calendar-making in that it creates an unreified and unmediated conception of time, a vision of time rooted in shared oppression, suffering, and liberation.[12]

How does the politics of this time relate to political narratives of the past and future? Linear conceptions of time link all the past into a unified theory of history that led directly to the present. In viewing all the past as a prologue to the present, a simplified account of the past is created, one that inevitably erases most human and lived experiences and mono-crop experiences into a plantation logic of human dominance of the world. Benjamin writes, "A historical materialist cannot do without the notion of a present which is not a transition, but in which time stands still and has come to a stop. For this notion defines the present in which he is writing history. Historicism gives the 'eternal' image of the past; historical materialism supplies a unique experience with the past" (Benjamin 1986: 262). In creating that eternal image of the past, a simplified story can form that shapes how we imagine possibility, human nature, and the like. For instance, David Graeber and David Wengrow's *The Dawn of Everything: A New History of Humanity* critiques the simplified

---

[1]This should be placed in marked distinction with the attempts by the Soviets to impose their calendar, the continuous production week. On September 24, 1929, the Soviet Union created a five-day calendar. One-fifth of the population would have each day off, while 80 percent would work. The idea here was to maximize production and gut or cut the sabbath days from the calendar to abolish religious practice further. Similarly, after the French Revolution when the new revolutionary state, in an attempt to destroy the ancient regimes, transformed the calendar from seven days to ten-day weeks. The issue here is not that they changed the calendar, since time is an illusion and our framework of it is inevitably an arbitrary decision, but the top-down means of doing so. During the Paris commune, the communards also changed the calendar to a ten-day one, but that calendar decision happened organically from below. Humans, awash in the feeling of time, often construct ways and means to order the chaos of time, but how that time is imposed and the logic of its functioning matters. In many indigenous calendars, the weeks or months (or the equivalent) followed the natural cycles and flows of the planet around them. The calendar became a way to link and ground oneself into their place. However, the Soviet calendar was not about links to nature but the need for industrial efficiency. That value imposition of workerism is the horror of their calendar logic. An organic and nonmediated social construction of time differs from the logic of industrial time.

[2]Benjamin's concept of the calendar has links to Guy Debord's understanding of historical time in the society of the spectacle. Bunyard, in a piece on Debord's concept of time, writes that "[Debord's view of time] is a self-constitutive process, for Debord; history is not governed or steered by anything other than human action" (Bunyard 2023: 37). This vision of history contrasts the effects of the spectacle, which is commodified all aspects of our lives, and totalizes our entire lifeways. The tyranny of the clock structures our days and their relationship to work, and our free time is conditioned to consumptive activities, which are also rooted in the economic models of life. We live, under capitalism, in the form of pseudo-cyclical time.

narratives of human history by highlighting the many complex and unique ways humans have historically structured their social, political, and economic lives. They write:

> If something did go terribly wrong in human history—and given the current state of the world, it's hard to deny something did—then perhaps it began to go wrong precisely when people started losing that freedom to imagine and enact other forms of social existence, to such a degree that some now feel this particular type of freedom hardly even existed or was barely exercised, for the greater part of human history. (Graeber and Wengrow 2021)

Graeber and Wengrow's narrative leaves us with a story of human experiences that embraces the creative multiplicity of experiences and histories, and not a general grand narrative of history.[3] To have a vision of a future that we are moving toward, first, we have to colonize the histories of the past into a set and straightforward narrative.

One of the targets of Benjamin's attack is the Marxian logic of historical materialism, a topic that Saito also confronts in his work on degrowth communism. Benjamin writes, "A conception of history that has liberated itself from the schema of progression within an empty and homogeneous time would finally unleash the destructive energies of historical materialism which have been held back for so long" (Benjamin, Eiland, and Jennings 2006: 406). This does not mean a rejection of materialist understanding the world, but a rejection of the colonizing universal narrative that often accompanies such an approach. Benjamin's analysis here does not limit the radical potential of Marxism, if anything it liberates it from some of the baggage of the Western enlightenment. Instead of one universal history, a polyvocal narrative of history emerges. With it many different Worlds become possible.

If progress is not part of historical march toward liberation but instead a chaotic chain of disaster, we need to imagine a different form of revolutionary

[3]Similarly, but more forgotten, the anarchist theorist Freddy Perlman, in his book *Against Leviathan* (1983), argues that the leviathan monsters of the state colonized and conquered human societies worldwide under a massive logic of conformity and domestication. As more peoples were consumed by the Leviathan, their unique histories were lost, and they were instead assimilated into the historical narratives and logic of the state.

politics. Under most of the guiding logics of modernity, and post-enlightenment European thought, progress was seen as teleological end. Many Marxists used the image of the train, which served as a powerful metaphor for scientific growth progress. For Lenin, we even see the mythical production of his own journey in the "sealed-train," as part of the myth-making of the Russian revolution. Trains became a symbol of collective progress and development, as the laying of train tracks opened up travel for the masses while also allowing for expansion and industrialization. In the United States, the train was a tool of manifest destiny as US settlers first colonized the west with horses, then with missionaries, and lastly with trains. In Russia, a massive country, trains linked the landscape into a constellation of interconnection and communication. The communist writer China Mielville even uses train metaphors in his work as a stand in for revolutionary movement. In his book *The Iron Council*, an autonomous communist revolt by workers, slaves, criminals, and sex workers is directed back toward Bas Lag, the industrial capital of his fantastical world. The time for revolution, though, is not seen as ripe, and Judah, one of the main characters of the novel, creates a time golem which stops the train in a bubble of time. No one knows when the bubble will burst, bringing about the revolutionary force of the train, but the threat of it puts pressure on the political elites of the city and also inspires further revolt from the masses and oppressed (Miéville 2004).

Walter Benjamin argued against this logic of revolution as scientific progress. His idea of revolution as an emergency brake to stop the destruction and devastation that progress and industrial production have wrought on this planet opens up a conception of revolution that is neither teleological nor Eurocentric. In fact, this sort of revolutionary practice has been the centerpiece for the vast majority of radical indigenous forms of activism throughout the world. In April of 2016, tens of thousands of indigenous community members and their collaborators throughout the Americas joined together on the Standing Rock reservation in South Dakota to stop the building of an oil pipeline through the indigenous reservation, which not only continued a long history of resource colonialism but also put at risk a massive watershed, which, if polluted, could have severe negative health effects on hundreds of thousands of people.

Similar types of struggles against industrial devastation, resource extraction, and colonization dot the planetary landscape. Sabu Kohso calls these struggles "inhabitants movements," borrowing the term from Japanese political scientist Nakata Norihito. Kohso states, "This conceptualization connects various existing struggles, from antipollution to antidevelopment to anti—military base, whose constituencies are no longer limited to nationals and citizens but include minorities, indigenous, and refugees—the planetary crowd" (Kohso 2020: 133). Inhabitants's movements differ from citizen movements, or traditional logics of social movements, in a handful of ways. First, inhabitants movements include all those who inhabit an area threatened by industrial devastation and economic imperialism—from human animals (documented or undocumented) to nonhuman animals and even to the landscape itself. Second, inhabitants movements reject most of the logic of social movement politics, since they are not about capturing the state but about stopping destruction and opening spaces for autonomous form of political life. Kohso writes, "inhabitants' struggles against developmental power are not those of bipolar opposition (A versus B) but instead of host against parasite or receptacle against filler—as seen historically in the guerrilla warfare waged by a sea of people against the regular army of the state. Therefore, inhabitants' struggle is, on one level, beyond victory and defeat in an immediate sense." Standing Rock, the Zapatista's resistance to oil extraction in the Niger Delta, Palestinian resistance to Israeli Apartheid are all examples of these sorts of movement. Each of these movements resists the state and the capital, not in a direct relationship of conflict but through asymmettrical struggles. They use their numbers, flexibility, and connection to the land as tools to slow down and gum up the processes of destruction. Andrew Culp, in *The Guerrilla Guide to Refusal*, provides a theoretical account to a form of anti-state power guerrilla politics that overlaps with and helps expand the logic of the inhabitants' movements. He writes:

> There is nothing more important today than negotiating a release from all the intolerable things about this world—a process that will not occur in any legislature or town hall. The underground instead plants an explosive 'nothing' behind the police lines waging annihilation against Blackness.

> Subtraction offers an alternative to simply multiplying the long chains of capital, the gender binary, and white lines of filiation. (Culp 2022: 27)

He argues that using the camouflage and flexibilities we have to move and resist quietly, hidden in the shadows, and allows for an active resistance to the state by using "a politics of asymmetry that locates material vulnerabilities through the digital concepts of contingency, density, and clutter" (Culp 2022: 27). What Culp develops in this book—a queer, insurrectionary, and anarchistic conception of a guerrilla struggle—provides a way to imagine asymmetrical strategies of resistance to capitalism and the state that blur the line between individual, or affinity group-based, actions and mass strategies of refusal.

A third trait of inhabitants movements is that they are not durable and are actually unable to, on their own, destroy industrial system of violence. Kohso, again, writes:

> For that matter, every inhabitants' movement is doomed to lose at some point in time to the overwhelming force of totalizing development; none of them are able to abolish the root cause of their problems—apocalyptic capitalism itself. But their victories exist in different dimensions: the lives in agony of inhabitants can achieve ethical victory over state and corporation; they can critically reveal what makes the substance of authorities and being public in the nation; their heritages can be handed down to future struggles; and finally, their struggles can connect themselves on a planetary horizon by sending vibrations of the eros effect among themselves. (Kohso 2020: 134)

That these inhabitants' struggles are not capable of bringing down the system of domination on this planet is not unique to them as mass-based movements and elections have also been doomed to fail at addressing and fixing the massive crisis that we experience. Inhabitants movement's unwillingness to engage with state power has to do with their focus on negation. They engage in a form of destituent, and not constituant, power. The idea of destituent power was theorized by the Argentinian group Colectivo Situatciones from 2011. According to Idis Robinson, "the collective advanced the notion as a theoretical rendering of the revolt's most popular demand, ! *Que se vayan todos!* 'all of them must go! . . . in other words Colectivo Situaciones posited the notion of destituent power to capture the Argentinian mass's insatiable drive to repeatedly topple and overthrow without seeking to replace the unseated authorities" (Idris. Robinson 2023: 137–8). The idea of destituent power is the counter to the constitutive power, which is about the collective and generative ability to build new institutions and governing logics, that Negri and others champion. Instead of generating or creating new loci of power, destituent power is about negating and undermining institutions that allow power to centralize and develop in the first place.

The logic of the Colectivo is also found in Walter Benjamin's "critical reflection on violence" with his analysis of the anarchistic general strike. Benjamin, in using the work of Sorel, distinguishes between the political strike and the general strike. With the political strike the goal is to coerce the state to intervene in the union's behalf and to use contract and law. Benjamin writes, "the question makes it obligatory, above all, to establish that a fully nonviolent resolution of conflicts can never amount to a legal contract. A legal contract, however peacefully the parties entire into it, leads ultimately to potential violence" (Benjamin 2021: 49). Because the state exists based on its supposed legitimate use of violence, any form of political mediation organized and run through the state—such as contracts or acts of law—is by definition rooted in violence, or the threat of violence. As such, the political strike, as with any and all activities that center the state as a mediator of conflict, is inherently violent. The only possible form of long-term nonviolent political action then must focus on a politics that seeks to abolish state power. This is why the general strike differs from the political strike, in that the general strike "sets itself the sole task of annihilating state power" (Benjamin 2021: 32). In seeking to destroy state power, and not claim or mediate through it, anarchistic action opens up possibilities for nonviolent social arrangements. This runs counter to the narrative promoted by state and state officials that anarchism is inherently violent because of its desire to destroy the state; in reality, the inverse is true. The lesson we should take from Benjamin on the strike, and on violence more generally, is his overall critique of "law-positing" or "law-defending" forms of politics which are always rooted in violence. Destituent forms of power serve then as a tool and strategy to organize political action in a way that may open spaces for liberation and nonviolent, nonmediated forms of political life. A path that is foreclosed as long as we pray and sacrifice at the altar of the state.

A Strategy of Attack: Against Accelerationism and Withdrawal

Burning bright, burn it down till I burn out.

—PETROL GIRLS, "FEED MY FIRE" (2022)

I want to put into contrast the destituent forms of collective inhabitants struggle—a coordinated network of guerrilla resistance against the machinery of industrial destruction, imperialism, and the state that understands itself as a handbrake against industrial society—with the logics of accelerationism, an influential strategy of developing a postcapitalist world. The reason for contrasting these approaches is twofold. First, this book has argued that the revolutionary struggle at this moment needs to be about dismantling and stopping destructive institutions and not take control of them or accelerating their logic to the point of crisis. Second, illustrating the difference between these two approaches illuminates how a destituent form of politics is actually a strategy of attack and not withdrawal or refusal, as accelerationism often argues.

In 2013, Alex Williams and Nick Srnicek published *#Accelerate: Manifesto for an Accelerationist Politics,* which linked a Promethean Marxist analysis with the postcapitalist work of Mark Fisher and the crypto-right-wing politics of Nick Land. In this manifesto, the authors position the debate as between "those that hold to a folk politics of localism, direct action, and relentless horizontalism, and those that outline what must become called an accelerationships politics at ease with a modernity of abstraction, complexity, globality, and technology" (Mackay and Avanessian 2019: 354). They position themselves in the latter camp and argue that we must see capitalism as a stage of human technological development and that left politics needs to capture socialist ends. They use a traditional Marxist argument around the material capacity of capitalism and the revolutionary desire for a world of luxury as a justification for such a position. Instead of rejecting the logic of industrialism or modernity, they want to free these structures from the capitalist logic. In freeing these institutions, they can heighten the efficiency of technology and, through centralized planning and infomatics, cybernetics, and AI, create a world of endless surplus while drastically limiting the working day. They argue that "the material platform of neoliberalism does not need to be destroyed. It needs to be repurposed towards common ends" (Mackay and Avanessian 2019: 355). As an example of what this looks like, we can look to Leigh Phillip and Michael Rozworski's *The People's Republic of Walmart*. Philips and Rozworski write:

> So when we ask whether another world is possible, we are also asking: Is there an alternate method to allocate things? How would we distribute things differently? And who would decide how they are distributed? Could the plans that capitalists use every day to get goods and services into the hands of those who can pay for them be transformed to instead ensure that what we produce gets to those who need it most? And in transforming the way we distribute stuff, could we also start to transform everything else about the economy—from what stuff we make and how, to who works and for how long? (Phillips and Rozworski 2019: 15)

In response, they contend that Walmart's technological and cybernetic techniques efficiently distribute goods and services and can be a model of distribution in a postcapitalist society. While Philips and Rozworski are not themselves accelerationists, the concept of using Walmart's technological and managerial techniques fits well within the politics that Williams and Srnicek promote.

If anything, the accelerationist project is about reclaiming the possibility of a future from the destructive qualities of postmodern economic and ecological crisis. They, of course, find no fault with the enlightenment projects of domination and instead view technology, reason, and science as neutral forces that are only self-destructive because of their current link with capitalism. They claim that "this is a project that must align with the legacy of the Enlightenment, to the extent through harnessing our ability to understand ourselves and our world better (our social, technical, economic, psychological worlds) that we can come to rule ourselves" (Mackay and

Avanessian 2019: 358). Theirs is a project of industrial production as they claim that capitalism has put blockages in place to limit the advancement of industrial society and that human civilization can be saved only by removing those blockages and directing them to human ends. In their book *Inventing the Future: Postcapitalism and a World without Work,* they rearticulate their Promethean project, calling for the development of a "left modernity" in which the vestiges of the old (the mythical, religious, and traditional) are displaced for a politics of modernity that links technological advancement and growth with the abolition of work. The creation of a post-work world requires our societies "To unleash technological advancement, we must move beyond capitalism and liberate creativity from its current strictures" (Srnicek and Williams 2016: 371), and when combined with institutional democratic managerial control, we can see the elimination of work and the liberation of all humanity. While better than the horrifically dystopian hellscape imagined by figures like Elon Musk, this analysis still falls into many of the same traps that this entire book has been criticizing. First, they do not seem to have a coherent theory of environmental destruction other than linking it entirely to capitalism. This is a common argument from those on the political left—that capitalism is the source of unsustainable practices. One of the theoretical insights of eco-Marxism is the idea of the metabolic rift, which states that environmental destruction and pollution are a result of industrial capitalist forms of production. Since industrial production centralizes the locations of resource extraction, production, and waste in different geographical spaces, certain locations are inundated with excess nutrients and pollutants while other areas are denuded of needed nutrients. The metabolic rift highlights that this is the source of ecological destruction and pollution, and while capitalist economics exacerbates this crisis, the source of the destruction is linked to the industrial mode of production. The accelerationist theory erases any analysis of industrial production. By ignoring the critiques of industrialism—from the inherent pollution and disasters of industrial production to the logic of control domination embedded in industrial systems—the accelerationist position develops a form of uncritical Marxism.

Saito eviscerates this Promethean read of Marx, showing that ecological issues and precapitalist nonindustrial history dominate the writing in the notebooks of the late Marx. Saito argues that the late Marx came to critique his stance on productivism and that his earlier fascination with industrial technology was wrongheaded, as was his Eurocentric teleological analysis of the development of history. The industrial systems inherently break the metabolic rift between humans and the natural world, inevitably leading to ecological crisis. While capitalism might heighten the metabolic rift, an uncritical communism that embraces, or as we see here accelerates, industrial production cannot solve our ecological crisis. Saito, in a powerful critique of the accelerationist Marxist position,[4] writes:

> Technology functions as an ideology that mystifies this irrationality. In otherwords, technology suppresses and eliminates the possibilities of imagining a completely different lifestyle and as are and just society in the face of the economic and ecological crisis. Crisis is supposed to be a catalyst for critical self reflection on our irrational behavior and four envisioning a different future that is more democratic, egalitarian and sustainable. However, locking technologies deprive us of the imaginaries and creativities needed to go beyond capitalism. The ideology of technology is one of the reasons for the poverty of imagination that pervades contemporary capitalism. Automation utopia is one manifestation of this problem. (Saitō 2022: 162)

The accelerationist position, ecologically, is inherently unsustainable and will inevitably expand the tools of domination that capitalism has put in place. By not openly having an analysis of ecological devastation, accelerationists tend to ignore ecological question. Centering the ecological undermines their theoretical position, as it forces them to engage with the way that technology and science functions as nonneutral tools. Instead of dipping their toe into such critiques, they displace the issue by simply assuming capitalism is the cause.[5] Much like liberals, the Marxist accelerationism is a form of slow suicide.

---

[4]In my opinion, even this criticism does not go far enough since Saito does not link this desire for industrial technology to the system of domination and control that Horkheimer and Adorno noted in *Dialectic of Enlightenment.*

[5]This is very similar to how class reductionist Marxists ignore racial and gendered issues in society since, in their analysis, white supremacy and patriarchy are byproducts of capitalism. That analysis is

Second, their critique does not consider the inherent problems with representational political systems. In their critique of anarchist localism, they even argue that horizontal and eco-anarchist approaches to the ecological crisis "argue for what amounts to a left-wing survivalism: civilization is in catastrophe, and we should therefore become invisible, retreat to small communes, and learn how to grow food, hunt, heal and defend ourselves" (Srnicek and Williams 2016: 86). They contend that anarchists are wrong to critique and reject large-scale and complex political, economic, and social systems. But the accelerationist critique only holds if we accept their desired goal—a planetary-governed system regulated by algorithmic networks and systems of regulation and control—and do so uncritically. One of the lessons Lewis Mumford made is that complex systems, or megamachines, increasingly became autonomous from democratic control. In his analysis of the megamachine in his voluminous series *The Myth of the Machine Vol 1 and 2*, Mumford contends that megamachines, or the construction of massive society-wide techniques for managing and controlling populations, are inherently unstable and destructive. He claims that the more complexity a system has, the more efficient it might be in its ability to shape and alter the world, and also the more sacrifices (human and nonhuman) it requires to maintain the system. In addition, maximizing complexity and efficiency always requires balancing between crisis and expansion. Complex societies thus have a dialectic back-and-forth always happening: between destruction and creation and between collapse and growth. The more a system is on the verge of collapse, the more it has to require conformity from the world around it as discord and lack of coordination is now potentially catastrophic. He writes:

> Not merely does technology claim priority in human affairs, it places the demand for constant technological change above any considerations of its own efficiency, its own continuity, or even, ironically enough, its own capacity to survive. To maintain such a system, whose postulates contradict those that underlie all living organisms, it requires for self-protection absolute conformity by the human community; and to achieve that

just as wrong and lazy as is the Marxian tendency to avoid the ecological.

> conformity it proposes to institute a system of total control, starting with the human organism itself, even before conception has taken place. The means for establishing this control is the ultimate gift of the megamachine; and without submergence in the subjective "myth of the machine," as omnipotent. Omniscient, and omnicompetent, it would not already have advanced to the point it has now reached. (Mumford 1974: 283)

Life becomes a resource for the machine to consume, and life needs to be structured to maintain the machine. The accelerationist position of expanding industrial production and the complex networks of automated distribution are anti-autonomous projects that require the sacrifices of life and the structuring of our behavior to maintain the complexity that they think is needed for survival. In such politics, there is no path for liberation and no prospects for autonomy and liberty.

While Williams and Srnicek fetishize industrial production, seeing it as a path forward to a post-work world, they ignore that we have, and many still do, live in a post-work world. Sahlins in *Stone Age Economics* highlights that hunter-gatherer societies minimize the amount of work needed for day-to-day survival and that hunter-gatherer societies are more egalitarian and that their lives are more filled with leisure and play. Even feudal Europe saw the average person working significantly less than modern humans. The average European serf, due to the seasonal nature of their labor and the large amount of religious holidays on the calendar, in the late fourteenth century, worked at most 150 days a year, while modern Americans work much closer to 260 days. This is not to say that the past was utopian and that we must return to hunter-gatherer or feudal life, but merely that these are real examples of post-work or minimal-work existence and that one does not need fantasies of technological liberation. If anything, the more industrial production expands, the more work we are needed to do to avoid catastrophe. There is no reason to imagine that future industrial production developments will magically change that history either.

One aspect they did get right, though partly, is their critique of withdrawal as an effective political tactic. That said, they wrongly link withdrawal with a politics of refusal and with horizontal and localized forms of anarchist resistance. This is not to discount that there are anarchistic projects that are about mere "survivalism" and building small collective resilience while hoping to weather the storm of ecological and political collapse, but that does not mean that such a position is inherent. If anything, most of the political work that centers on refusal understands that withdrawal cannot dismantle and destroy capitalism or the state. Often, what is included in a politics of refusal is a rejection of working within organized and accepted political, social, and economic channels. This means a refusal to vote and lobby politicians, a DIY economic ethos, communal living, permacultural community projects, and the like. In *Envisioning Real Utopias*, Eric Olin Wright (2010) classifies this political and social activism as interstitial. "Interstitial transformations seek to build new forms of social empowerment in the niches, spaces and margins of capitalist society, often where they do not seem to pose any immediate threat to dominant classes and elites," Wright claims. "This is the strategy of building institutions of social empowerment that is most deeply embedded in civil society and often falls below the radar screen of radical critics of capitalism. To devolve authority and power to local and direct democratic means, under" (Wright 2010: 211). In theory, though, these sorts of refusal and autonomous politics are being misrepresented by Wright, who claims that ruptural political change only happens through a coordinated a "frontal attack on the state," misunderstand that there are other ways to attack the state (212). Culp, for instance, claims that refusal and anarchist politics can link a politics of refusal with guerrilla strategies and tactics against the state. Such an approach multiplies the strategies of attack by creating an alternative that takes advantage of the sluggishness of the state and the concealment of resistance movements in the clouded masses of cities to chip away at the armor of the state through asymmetrical insurrections, guerrilla sabotaging of supply and resource lines, and the creation of temporary autonomous zones where the utopian world of communism is not deferred (Culp 2022).

Part of the reason that these politics of refusal are not seen as effective forms of political action by many within the Marxian tradition has to do with the fact that such politics employs destituent, and not constitutive, power.[6] The goal of refusal is not to replace the location of power—politically or economically—or to forge new state institutions but to undermine the ability for such institutionalized power to form and exist in the first place. Much like Benjamin understood the general strike as potentially nonviolent since it refused to engage with the state and demand any enforcement, it simply wished to negate the state. That said, the modern state megamachine structures have spread like the cancerous mutant Kaneda in the seminal film *Akira*, incorporating more and more aspects of our political, social, and economic lives. Resistance to such a bulbous leviathan of death and decay requires active tactics of resistance against the state form. This is where inhabitants' struggles, which attempt to stop the spread of state destruction, work in tandem with refusal and the creation of nonstate autonomous spaces and guerrilla strikes against the state. This last part, the strikes against the state, are hinted at by Malm in *How to Blow Up a Pipeline* but are also found in insurrectionary riots against the police and the state, such as the burning down of Minneapolis third precinct building during the George Flyod uprising in 2020 and the toppling of statues and other symbols of white supremacy and colonialism. Unlike the reactionary violence of January 6 in the United States, the insurrection following Floyd's lynching did not seek to replace those in power but to burn down and destroy. It was a politics of destituent power.

"The Misplaced Optimism of the Doomed": *Snowpiercer* (2013) as Destituent Power

To finish this chapter, I want to turn to the 2013 Bong Joon Ho film *Snowpiercer*. *Snowpiercer*, a film that theorists Frank Lee and Steven Maniscastri describe as "political theory in the cinematic mode," (3) provides an example of the politics and strategies this chapter is trying to put together. Art regularly portrays

---

[6]Constitutive power always requires mass politics and can be easily managed and coordinated by a central representational institution. Destituent power, on the other hand, cannot be managed and coordinated by representational structures and does not require any form of mass politics. A small affinity group can topple a statue, dismantle a pipeline, or burn down a police precinct.

political logic clearer than any theorists. *Snowpiercer* is, in my reading, a film rooted in insurrectionary and autonomous politics of refusal and destituent power. The critically acclaimed film, based on the French graphic novel of the same name, uses the train as a metaphor for the political "World" that modernity and capitalism have built. The film takes place in a world ravaged by a climate catastrophe caused when wealthy nations pumped an experimental chemical, CW7, into the atmosphere to stop global warming. CW7 drastically cools the climate, leading to a global ice age so cold that life outside the train goes extinct. The train was designed by billionaire engineering tycoon Wilfred (Ed Harris), who feared that CW7 would have this effect. Wilfred developed an eternal motor that could run forever without additional energy sources and built a train-shaped biosphere filled with greenhouses, industrial animal agriculture, and aquaculture. The front of the train sucks in the snow and ice, like an elephant trunk, and also uses that fresh water to maintain life. As long as the train is running, humanity's extinction is delayed. Like industrialism, the train blackmails the surviving humans into maintaining the hierarchal system, which is structured around the status of the original ticket a passenger held. Snowpiercer has a three-tiered hierarchy: first-class ticket holders at the top, followed by economy ticket holders (working class), and then the unwashed masses of squatters and train hoppers who got on without a ticket and live in the tail. The tail of the train, where the lumpenproletariat survives, is an overcrowded concentration camp in which military officers do head counts (to maintain population numbers), break up families by kidnapping individuals who are needed by those in power, and provide protein blocks made of crushed insects as daily gruel meals. The hierarchy of the train is maintained by force and ideological control, as we see a group of children singing a song in praise of Wilfred, their god in human form. Mason (Tilda Swinton), the sniveling and selfish middle bureaucratic enforcer of the colonial regime, clearly explains the train's logic when she says, "Order is the barrier that holds back the flood of death."

The story follows Curtis (Chris Evans) and Gilliam (John Hurt) as they launch a rebellion from the tail section to take control of the engine room and replace Wilfred. As Curtis says, "Everything in one stroke. We control the engine, we control the World. Without that, we have nothing. All past revolutions have failed because they couldn't take the engine." With the coordinated and unified help of the entire tail section, the lumpen army, wielding sticks and clubs, push their way from the tail section into the prison section in order to release and coerce Namgoong Minsoo (Song Kang-ho), a security expert that is able to unlocks the gates that block their path. Namgoong and his daughter, Yona, are imprisoned for their addiction to kronole, an explosive industrial waste chemical that people use to hallucinate. We find out later that neither of them are addicts but are collecting kronole as fuel for an improved bomb to destroy the train. As the rebellion advances from car to car, we see the life of the middle classes and the rich, who eat real foods—including sushi—and have educational spaces for the kids and even disco raves for the wealthy idol rich. The picture of the World that Bong Joon Ho depicts is one of a multiracial and multinational hierarchy, in which the rich are not uniformly white, as the children of Africans and Asians exist in every single car of the train, though the closer we get to the engine, we see fewer nonwhite passengers. The same is true with the lumpenproletariat in the tail. We see a multiracial and multinational collection of discarded humans from various backgrounds, including at least two classically trained former professional violin players. In an interview he did for his Academy Award-winning film *Parasite*, Bong Joon Ho said, "there is no borderline between countries now because we all live in the same country, it's called capitalism." The train in *Snowpiercer* shows this same reality.

While the rebellion lurches forward, the lumpenproletariat experiences a high death toll, as according to Wilfred later in the film, 74 percent of the tail population is systematically killed, including Gilliam, the old wizened leader of the revolt. Though most of the tail section dies, Curtis, Namgoong, and his daughter Yona make it to the engine room. Before they confront Wilfred, Namgoong shares a cigarette with Curtis, the last-existing cigarette in the World, and attempts to convince him not to replace Wilfred but to escape with him and his daughter. Namgoong was close friends with an Inuit woman who led an earlier revolt (the Revolt of the Seven) and who taught him how to listen to and understand the snow; he had noticed that over the decade the climate has warmed. With evidence of melting snow and ice, Namgoong believes that human and nonhuman life could survive on the planet outside the train. Shocked by Namgoong's plan, Curtis asks, "What if you don't survive," to which Namgoong responds, "But what if we do?" Namgoong, whom Lee and Maniscastri highlight, is named after Vietnam, the colonial and imperialist war orchestrated by the United States that killed millions. Unlike the rest of the train, Nam and his daughter Yona are not interested in the struggles for power on a machine that requires death to maintain itself. Instead, they seek a path to liberation by destroying the World, the manufactured institutions that structure our lives, and returning to the planetary environment. Their struggle for refusal is rooted in the long history of anti-colonial struggles—from Vietnam and Korea to Inuit resistance to colonial power—and, as such, is a destituent decolonial project. In this story, the decolonial fuses with the lumpenproletariat classes to confront the logic of ecomodernism and ecofascism and uses the tools of the underclass—drugs—to destroy the train.

Nam and Yona are guerrillas against the train who refuse to play the game of domination and control. Culp writes, "The point is not to understand the world but to destroy it" (Culp 2022: 155). Unsurprisingly, Nam and Yona, both prisoners, represent the strongest desire to escape. "The politics of fugitive," Culp writes, "carries with it a vision of intensive escape" (Culp 2022: 160). It is important to note that their act of refusal and escape requires a politics of attack, not one of withdrawal or accelerationism because their exodus requires the entire destruction of the train. Like capitalism and industrialism, the train is a totalizing system in which there are not enough cracks to survive without a confrontation with the state. However, unlike Curtis and Gilliam, who desire a direct attack on the state, Namgoong and Yona use guerrilla tactics and seek to attack while hidden or while the elite is distracted.

Unpersuaded by Nam, Curtis confronts Wilfred and learns three important facts. First, he learns that Wilfred and Gilliam were coordinating to use revolts and riots to suppress the tail and kill excess populations. Wilfred engages in eco-governmentality, where human and nonhuman populations are regulated and controlled to maintain a specific social, political, and ecological world. In managing these populations, the hierarchies of power maintain themselves through ecomodernization and sustainability. Wilfred is a crasser version of the Ministry of the Future, a technocratic organization that attempts to manipulate and control the World for supposedly good reasons—sustainability and humanity—but, in doing so, expands the tools of domination, exploitation, and control over the planet. The ecogovernmental logic uses the tool of domination and control to regulate the delicate ecosystem of the train and maintain the class hierarchy built into the system (Luke 1997). Also, similarly to the Ministry of the Future, we learn that the elite—Wilfred—is coordinating the revolt from below to impose policies that would otherwise not be accepted by the population. In Kim Stanley Robinson's book, the Ministry of the Future does the same, manipulating and using the Children of Kali to push their eco-managerial policies. Robinson, frustratingly, does not criticize this form of manipulation or explore the pitfalls of eco-governmentality. Snowpiercer does.

Second, Curtis learns that Wilfred and Gilliam have been training him to become the engineer of the train. They both saw in Curtis a born leader who, coming from the tail, would offer a unique perspective as the engineer, since he is the only person who has ever walked the entire train length. Wilfred's assistant brings them a steak dinner, and Curtis stands in the engine's heart, experiencing silence for the first time in seventeen years. These are symbols of the gifts and privileges that come with being the person in charge and are meant to be tools of persuasion. It seems that Curtis will accept the offer before Yona breaks into the room in search of the last match and notices a hidden space under the floor where a child is imprisoned as part of the engine. The engine for the train does not require inputs of energy, but many parts are no longer made. For the engine to run, Wilfred needs a child's small hands to unclog the machine. This is the reason that at the beginning of the movie Wilfred's guards kidnap two five-year-old boys from the tail section. Curtis sees one of these boys, Tim (Marcanthones Reis), the black child of Curtis's friend Tanya (Octavia Spencer), manually removing the black muck and dirt the engine produces. They are turned into a cog in the machine. Like Benjamin's account of the cult of capitalism and Mumford's understanding of the megamachine, the train requires sacrifices to maintain itself.[7]

Seeing the use of Tim as a sacrifice highlights to Curtis the inherent violence and horror that is required to maintain the system. He reaches his

[7]Interestingly, the other child kidnapped by the guards, Andy, is unwilling or unable to hear Curtis and refuses to leave the machine. Andy, a white child, might be standing in for how whiteness and racial hierarchies blind workers to their oppression and allow them to forge a cross-class alliance with the elite to maintain the system.

arm into the machine in order to slow the gears and allow Tim to escape. Curtis does not just reject Wilfred's offer. He allies with Namgoong, Yona, and Tim and becomes an accomplice in the destruction of the World. The bomb he helps light blows out the door and results in a massive avalanche that derails the entire train, seemingly killing off the majority of humanity. When the crashed train settles, we see Yona and Tim, both wrapped in parkas and cold weather gear, leaving the train and stepping onto the snow before looking up and seeing a polar bear, a symbol to show the scope of climate devastation, traversing the landscape.

Tilda Swinton's character in the film decries the underclass revolt by yelling that they "have the misplaced optimism of the doomed." This is the only sort of optimism that is not cruel. We are doomed. The World—the colonial and imperial European project of nation-states, modernity, industrialism, and capitalism—falters and fails. Every year, we experience a warmer and warmer planet, with the summer of 2025 being the warmest ever, and as that heat increases, the prospects for an industrial, capitalist, and liberal future seem all but blocked. It is not just the ecological crisis—as this book has not even explored the impact of soil depletion, marine ecosystem collapse, or the increasing likelihood of future nuclear disasters—but the structures of the liberal order, from representative democracy to trade as a tool of diplomacy, that are failing to confront the growing threat of neo-reactionary fascism. Trump (the United States), Bolsanaro (Brazil), Meloni (Italy), Orban (Hungry), the Alternative for Germany, The National Front (France), Vox (Spain), Sweden Democrats, The Finns Party (Finland), and The Spartan Party (Greece) are examples of a growing wave of reactionary political parties and politicians taking advantage of the inherent failures of liberal democratic systems. Youth throughout the World feel the burning rage as they refuse to engage in political and economic life like their parents did. Many of the millennials and Gen Z in the United States are imagining a World where, at best, their life is noticeably worse than their parents, and, at worst, nearly apocalyptic. In Japan, the number of people identified as hikikomori (T. Saitō and Angles 2013), or having fully withdrawn from society, is growing, with Saito Tamaki, the scholar who popularized the term, claiming that the number could reach ten million shortly (which would be around 8 percent of the entire Japanese population) (T. Saitō 2019). The same phenomenon is also exploding in South Korea and China, where the Laying Flat Movement (tangping) has youth refusing to accept low-paying jobs and instead embrace a life of simplicity and nonmaterialism (Davidovic 2022).

Raoul Vaneigem claimed that the youth in the postwar West was experiencing the alienation of "survival sickness," a social disease in which the banality of life had filled them with nothing but despair and sadness. Today, we dream of experiencing the banality that existed during the 1960s boom, at least in the West. The sicknesses we experience today are more fundamental to the global order than when *The Revolution of Everyday Life* was first published in 1968 and are more universalized throughout the planet. In the 1960s, the hope of revolutionary change was still alive and well, no matter how flawed that hope was. Today, even that hope does not exist. Increasingly, it is clear that the World, the experiment of European modernity, has failed, and the only path of liberation will be found in destroying that system. As long as we, on the left, work to maintain the liberal order and resuscitate the corpse of modernity, we are simply holding the door open for fascism. Antonio Gramsci said, "The old world is dying, and the new world struggles to be born: now is the time of monsters." That was a simple moniker for a different time. Today, the World is dying, but too many of us refuse to let it; the only path is for us to become the monsters that the liberals and the right fear we are.

Conclusion

A Requiem for Our World

> A future like a guillotine for a dark world on its knees.
>
> —SEVERED HEAD OF STATE, "A FUTURE LIKE A GUILLOTINE" (2007)

Conclusions are often the worst chapters of any books. The reasons for the letdown are myriad, but one of the primary reasons is that conclusions are an attempt at closure, and closure, while desired, is often disappointing. After hundreds of pages of critical engagement with complex ideas, imagining an ending that can tie ideas into a cohesive argument is a Herculean task at best and a Sisyphean one at the worst. Like Camus, laughing at his Greek myths, we must, too, imagine our conclusions satisfied. In the case of this book, the conclusion is put into an even more difficult position. By starting with an anti-introduction that deconstructed the neoliberal turn toward personalized narratives and the commercial and spectacular logic of the introduction, it is nearly impossible to end with a traditional conclusion where it lays out four or five key takeaways from the text, like a BuzzFeed listicle or a TED talk. When the book is about the end of the world, its hard to conclude with a banal and shallow calls to action or a list of policy proposals. The World is in crisis and is hopefully going to rupture. The hope, if hope is worth having in these dark times, is that with the demise of industrialism, nationalism, capitalism, colonialism, and all the other systems of structural violence that shape and maintain the current World, the planet will be free of the universalizing and oppressive global order that formed during the period of European colonization. With the end of the World, there is a chance, but definitely no guarantee, that a polyvocal and complex mishmash of different ways of living and inhabiting the planet can form in the ruins. However, this is only a hope, and you know the cliché: shit in one hand and hope in the other and see which fills up first.

It is at least as likely that the World continues, like the Rolling Stones limping onto a stage to sing their greatest hits and bore crowds with their newer innovation. In such a case, liberalism will be replaced with more openly authoritarian regimes of power, either neo-feudal or a retrenched nationalist-oriented fascism. If this happens, we will see the fragmentation of our World in a slow-moving process of staggard collapse but the motors of industrial production and enlightenment rationality will be fueled in blood and will crap out genocide. Walled nations will be on a constant quest to invent new enemies, internally and externally, to serve as sacrifices to purify the sins of "the people." The more the crises grow, showing the inherent failure of industrialism, the more states will need to sacrifice at the altars of progress to distract and persuade populations that progress is possible. This is, of course, why our current World is a death cult. At some point, though, even this fascistic World will collapse. "Today's empires, tomorrow's ashes," Propagndhi contends, and due to the inherent unsustainable logic of industrialism and the intensive energy and violence needed to maintain increasingly complex social arrangements, fascism will crumble. The longer the World limps along, though, the less likely there will be any possibility of future worlds. As climatic feedback loops kick in and temperature feedbacks shift the World into the "doom" spiral that some climate scientists fear, Earth will follow Venus's path, and we will not only need a requiem for our World but a requiem for life on the planet.

Much of this book has focused on analyzing the representational and ecological crises that are directing us toward fascism and collapse. The rest of the book centered on the need for a politics of attack, a strategic and militant assault on the domineering social, economic, political, and psychological institutions of modern industrial capitalism. We act, though not because we know we will be successful or even because we can make the planet a better place, but because this world is horrific. The masters deserve to be dethroned simply because they are masters; and systems built on death deserve to be burned to ashes. Since left melancholia, capitalist realism, and leftist obsessions with industrialism has frozen dialectical conflicts, a lot of this book has forwarded insurrectionary and individualist projects and mindsets. However, the individual does not exist. The majority of the cells that make up each and every one of us are more nonhuman (from bacteria and virus cells to fungus and the like) than human. We are an assemblage of many forms of life, each individual an interspecies parliament. Similarly, this book has regularly confronted the way we reify and naturalize meaning, making meaning appear pre-political. Meaning is a social process. Meaning cannot be disembedded from collectives of people who contribute to and maintain a shared system of signs and codes. And we humans are meaning-making machines. And, likely, so are most other sentient species on this planet. Murders of crows, pods of orcas, and a homeowners' association of Karens all produce meaning collectively. And while these systems of meaning are not inherent, and pre-political, they do structure the ways in which each group engages and inhabits this planet. Since meaning is social and collective, alienation and isolation are massive threats to our ability to maintain communities of resistance. Many books have been written that explore the many ways that radical activists, peasant communities, subcultural resisters, and poets dream of new and inspiring forms of social arrangement. These projects and experiments are important, as are the books that detail and theorize about them. There is a need and impulse to imagine and experiment in alternative ways of living. That impulse is a creative and powerful one. This book, though, intentionally focused on the flip side of that coin, the impulse and need to negate, abolish, and destroy. This impulse is also creative. Life requires death; creation requires destruction.

In a book he wrote while dying from cancer, Ivan Illich stated, "In every society, the dominant image of death determines the prevalent concept of health" (Illich 2016: 213). In our current World, the cultural values of life and death are deeply troubling. As this book has regularly highlighted, many modern systems are built on an endless cycle of sacrifice. Human bodies and animal flesh are torn asunder to feed the machines of capitalism and industrialism. The scope of industrial thinking has made all life abstract in nature, and because of this life has likely never been less valued. On a planet with over eight billion humans, the fact that millions die every year due to the system itself is either hidden or uninteresting to those surviving within the system. This is the necropolitics of our World. The logic of industrialism is that of necropolitics, since once life becomes viewed as a population to be managed, regulated, and controlled for the benefit of the broader society, it becomes just another piece of data to manipulate. Like everyone within the industrial system, the more dangerous the system becomes, the more the privileged can purchase their protection. Musk and the other billionaires desire this with their technological attempts to skirt death. Their desire for eternal life is rooted in and linked to the spread of death we see elsewhere. The more we fear death, the more we sacrifice others to elongate our lives. In a sense, the poor and marginalized in our World are nothing but blood boys for the industrial system.[1] Regarding environmental issues, every government decision increases the likelihood that certain people will die while protecting or benefiting others. This is a sad reality of the World we currently inhabit. If necropolitics are an essential component of industrial life, we need to begin imagining a form of anarchistic, communistic, and democratic necropolitics. If not, the inequalities of the present—class, race, gender, sexuality, coloniality, species—will continue to uncritically shape necropolitics. Those who are always the victims will continue to be so. While we might hope to contrast the industrial system of death with a peaceful and life-affirming form of a revolutionary alternative, the people and species will die due to the crises we are facing. This is a reality that we cannot run from. But can we imagine or develop a form of necropolitics that targets those responsible for the horrors of the current World? In addition, can we create an insurrectionary necropolitics that destroys, like Benjamin understands the general strike, the capability for a necropolitical order to return?

---

[1]Many in Silicon Valley, for instance, desire to eradicate death and are looking to prolong their lives, or at least their consciousness, as long as they can. Musk, for instance, has already uploaded his consciousness to the cloud and claims that in the future that consciousness could be downloaded into a robotic body, allowing for a form of immortality that sounds more like a prison. Peter Thiel, the crypto-fascist former business partner of Musk, is famous for having a "blood boy," a young man whom Thiel uses for regular blood transfusions under the belief that it will keep him young and healthy.

Under the system of capitalism, death is the end of productivity and importance. This was not always the case, as, for much of human history, the dead traveled with us and embodied spiritual powers and forces within nature or ourselves. Of course, anyone who has lost someone important or close to them knows that capitalist logic is wrong. We always carry the memory of the dead with us; with that memory, our lives are constantly transformed. The connection does not end after death; each life ripples through and touches countless people, shaping them for better or worse. But, since the capitalist logic of productivity lingers and haunts us just as much as those we have lost, the fear of death is one of modern life's most profound and vital qualities. We might know its troubles and pitfalls—from ecological collapse to genocidal wars—but to imagine the end of our World is even hard to imagine than our own individualized death. This is partly why moralizing and guilting of politicians around extinction, like Extinction Rebellion has been doing, has not successfully mobilized militant resistance to global capitalism. Those who are destroying the planet know exactly what they are doing. We can't guilt them into acting with compassion. We cannot plead with our oppressors and shame them to do what is right. We must, instead, act in concert, and tear the whole thing down.

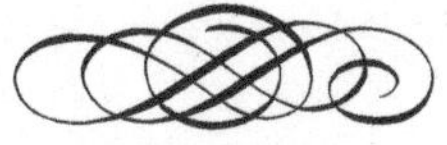

Works Cited

Abram, David. (1996). *The Spell of the Sensuous: Perception and Language in a More-than-Human World*. New York: Pantheon books.

Adams, Carol J. (2017). *The Sexual Politics of Meat: A Feminist-Vegetarian Critical Theory*. Bloomsbury revelations edition, reprinted. New York; London; Oxford; New Delhi; Sydney: Bloomsbury Academic, an imprint of Bloomsbury Publishing Inc.

Adorno, Theodor W. (2003). "34 'Cultural Criticism and Society.'" In *The Holocaust*, 280–1. Edinburgh University Press. https://doi.org/10.1515/9781474470230-045.

Agamben, Giorgio. (1998). *Sovereign Power and Bare Life*. Stanford, CA: Stanford University Press.

Agamben, Giorgio. (2005). *State of Exception*. Chicago: University of Chicago Press.

Albert, Michael. (2010). "Anarchism = Zerzan?" *The Anarchist Library*. https://theanarchistlibrary.org/library/michael-albert-anarchism-zerzan (September 8, 2023).

Allinson, Jamie, China Miéville, Richard Seymour, and Rosie Warren. (2021). *The Tragedy of the Worker: Towards the Proletarocene*. London: Verso Books.

Anderson, Kevin. (2020). *Class, Gender, Race & Colonialism: The "intersectionality" of Marx*. Ottawa: Daraja Press: Monthly Review Essays.

Anker, Elisabeth R. (2022). *Ugly Freedoms*. Durham: Duke University Press.

Anonymous. (2018). *What Is Gender Niihilism?: A Reader*. Contagion Press.

Bakunin, Mikhail. (1953). "Man as Conquorer of Nature." In G. P. Maximoff (eds.), *The Political Philosophy of Bakunin: Scientific Anarchism*. Los Angeles: The Free Press.

Bastani, Aaron. (2019). *Fully Automated Luxury Communism: A Manifesto*. London; New York: Verso.

Bataille, Georges. (1986). *Erotism: Death & Sensuality*. 1st City lights ed. San Francisco: City Lights Books.

Baudrillard, Jean. (1983). *In the Shadow of the Silent Majorities, or, the End of the Social, and Other Essays*. New York, NY: Semiotext(e).

Baudrillard, Jean. (1994). *Simulacra and Simulation*. Ann Arbor: University of Michigan Press.

Baudrillard, Jean. (1995). *The Gulf War Did Not Take Place*. Bloomington: Indiana University Press.

Baudrillard, Jean. (2012). *The Ecstasy of Communication*. Los Angeles, CA: Semiotext(e).

Baudrillard, Jean. (2016). *Symbolic Exchange and Death*. Rev. edition. Thousand Oaks, CA: Sage Ltd.

Baudrillard, Jean. (2019). *For a Critique of the Political Economy of the Sign*. London; New York: Verso.

Beddington, Emma. (2023). "The Orca Uprising: Whales Are Ramming Boats – But Are They Inspired by Revenge, Grief or Memory?" *The Guardian*. https://www.theguardian.com/environment/2023/jul/11/the-orca-uprising-whales-are-ramming-boats-but-are-they-inspired-by-revenge-grief-or-memory (September 26, 2023).

Benjamin, Walter, Hannah Arendt, and Harry Zohn. (1986). *Illuminations*. New York: Schocken Books.

Benjamin, Walter, Marcus Paul Bullock, and Michael W. Jennings. (2004). *Selected Writings. 1: 1913 – 1926 / Ed. by Marcus Bullock and Michael W. Jennings*. 6. print., 1. paperback ed. Cambridge, MA: Belknap Press of Harvard University Press.

Benjamin, Walter, Howard Eiland, and Michael W. Jennings. (2006). *Selected Writings. Volume 4: 1938 – 1940 / Ed. by Howard Eiland and Michael W. Jennings*. 1st pbk ed. Cambridge, MA: Belknap Press of Harvard University Press.

Benjamin, Walter, Peter D. Fenves, and Julia Ng. (2021). *Toward the Critique of Violence: A Critical Edition*. Stanford, CA: Stanford University Press.

Berardi, Franco. (2018). *Breathing: Chaos and Poetry*. South Pasadena, CA: Semiotext(e).

Berardi, Franco, Gary Genosko, and Nicholas Thoburn. (2011). *After the Future*. Oakland, CA; Edinburgh: AK Press.

Berkman, Alexander. (2003). *What Is Anarchism?* Edinburgh, Scotland; Oakland, CA: AK Press.

Berlant, Lauren Gail. (2011). *Cruel Optimism*. Durham: Duke University Press.

Bestley, Ross, Mike Dines, Paula Guerra, and Alastair Gordon, eds. (2021). *Trans-Global Punk Scenes: The Punk Reader Volume 2*. Bristol; Chicago, USA: Intellect Books.

Bogdanov, Alexander, Loren R. Graham, Richard Stites, and Charles Rougle. (1984). *Red Star: The First Bolshevik Utopia*. Bloomington, IN: Indiana University Press.

Bonanno, Alfredo. (2022). *Anarchy and Insurrection*. Detritus Books.

Bond, David. (2022). *Negative Ecologies: Fossil Fuels and the Discovery of the Environment*. Oakland, CA: University of California Press.

Borges, Jorge Luis, and Andrew Hurley. (1998). *Collected Fictions*. New York, NY: Penguin Books.

Boyle, Louise. (2022). "Experts Eviscerate Joe Rogan's 'Deadly' Interview with Jordan Peterson on Climate." *The Independent*. https://www.independent.co.uk/climate-change/news/joe-rogan-jordan-peterson-spotify-b2001368.html (September 12, 2023).

Brown, Wendy. (1995). *States of Injury: Power and Freedom in Late Modernity*. Princeton, NJ: Princeton University Press.

Brown, Wendy. (1999). "'Resisting Left Melancholy.'" *Boundary*, 26 (3): 19–27.

Brown, Wendy. (2015). *Undoing the Demos: Neoliberalism's Stealth Revolution*. Brooklyn, NY: Zone Books.

Brown, Wendy. (2017). *Undoing the Demos: Neoliberalism's Stealth Revolution*. First paperback edition, this edition corrects errors in previous printings. New York: Zone Books.

Bunyard, Tom. (2023). "History and Revolution in Debord's 'The Society of the Spectacle.'" *Radical Philosophy* (214): 36–48.

Butler, Judith. (2004). *Undoing Gender*. New York; London: Routledge.

Butler, Judith. (2006). *Gender Trouble: Feminism and the Subversion of Identity*. New York: Routledge.
Calichman, Richard, ed. (2005). *Contemporary Japanese Thought*. New York, NY: Columbia University Press.
Chantal Da Silva. (2023). "A Tale of Two Disasters: Missing Titanic Sub Captivates the World Days after Deadly Migrant Shipwreck." *NBC News*. https://www.nbcnews.com/news/world/syria-migrants-boat-sinking-titanic-submersive-missing-rcna90336 (September 12, 2023).
Chernyshevsky, Nikolay Gavrilovich, and Michael R. Katz. (1989). *What Is to Be Done?* Ithaca, NY: Cornell University Press.
Chuang. (2021). *Social Contagion: And Other Material on Microbiological Class War in China/ by Chuang*. Chicago, IL: Charles H. Kerr Publishing Company.
Chumbawamba. (1987). *Never Mind the Ballots*. Agit-prop.
Chumbawamba. (1994). *Anarchy*. No Masters.
Ciccariello-Maher, George. (2012). "The Dialectics of Standing One's Ground." *Theory & Event*, 15 (3). https://muse.jhu.edu/article/484431/pdf
Ciccariello-Maher, George. (2016). *Decolonizing Dialectics*. Durham: Duke University Press.
Connolly, William E. (2017). *Facing the Planetary: Entangled Humanism and the Politics of Swarming*. Durham; London: Duke University Press.
Coulthard, Glen Sean. (2014). *Red Skin, White Masks: Rejecting the Colonial Politics of Recognition*. Minneapolis, MN: University of Minnesota Press.
Cronon, William. (1996). "The Trouble with Wilderness: Or, Getting Back to the Wrong Nature." *Environmental History*, 1 (1): 7–28. https://doi.org/10.2307/3985059.
Culp, Andrew. (2022). *A Guerrilla Guide to Refusal*. Minneapolis, MN: University of Minnesota Press.
Danchev, Alex, ed. (2011). *100 Artists' Manifestos: From the Futurists to the Stuckists*. London: Penguin Books.
Davidovic, Ivana. (2022). "'Lying Flat': Why Some Chinese Are Putting Work Second." *BBC News*. https://www.bbc.com/news/business-60353916 (September 13, 2023).
Debord, Guy. (1994). *The Society of the Spectacle*. New York: Zone Books.
Debord, Guy. (2011). *Comments on the Society of the Spectacle*. London; New York: Verso.
Debord, Guy, Donald Nicholson-Smith, and Guy Debord. (2008). *A Sick Planet*. London: Seagull.
Defiance. (1996). *No Future, No Hope*. Mind Control.
Deleuze, Gilles, Félix Guattari, and Gilles Deleuze. (1994). *What Is Philosophy?* New York, NY: Columbia University Press.
Derrida, Jacques. (1986). "Declarations of Independence." *New Political Science*, 7 (1): 7–15. https://doi.org/10.1080/07393148608429608.
Dolinšek, Sašo. (2022). "Desire Versus Ego: On How Kaneko Fumiko Transcended Stirnean Egoism." *Asian Studies*, 10 (3): 241–72. https://doi.org/10.4312/as.2022.10.3.241-272.
Donaghey, Jim. (2020). "The 'Punk Anarchisms' of Class War and CrimethInc." *Journal of Political Ideologies*, 25 (2): 113–38. https://doi.org/10.1080/13569317.2020.1750761.

Edie, James, James Scanlan, and Mary-Barbara Zeldin, eds. (1976). *Russian Philosophy, Volume 2: The Nihilists, the Populists, Critics of Religion and Culture*. Nashville, TN: University of Tennessee Press.

Eiliprin, Juliet, Dennis Brady, and Chris Mooney. (2018). "Trump Administration Sees a 7-Degree Rise in Global Temperatures by 2100." *The Washington Post*. https://www.washingtonpost.com/national/health-science/trump-administration-sees-a-7-degree-rise-in-global-temperatures-by-2100/2018/09/27/b9c6fada-bb45-11e8-bdc0-90f81cc58c5d_story.html (October 13, 2022).

Emma Goldman. (1917). "Address to the Jury in U.S. v. Emma Goldman and Alexander Berkman." https://www.marxists.org/reference/archive/goldman/works/1917/address-to-the-jury.html (September 12, 2023).

Emre, Merve. (2022). "The Illusion of the First Person." *The New York Review of Books* 69(17). https://www.nybooks.com/articles/2022/11/03/the-illusion-of-the-first-person-merve-emre/ (September 8, 2023).

Errico Malatesta. (2015). *Life and Ideas: The Anarchist Writings of Errico Malatesta*. Oakland, CA: PM Press.

Escalante, Alyson. (2015). "Gender Nihilism: An Anti-Manifesto." In *What Is Gender Nihilism? A Reader*, 307–18. Contagion Press, 2018.

Fanon, Frantz. (2008). *Black Skin, White Masks*. 1st ed., new ed. New York : [Berkeley, CA]: Grove Press; Distributed by Publishers Group West.

Federici, Silvia Beatriz. (2014). *Caliban and the Witch*. 2, rev. ed. New York, NY: Autonomedia.

Felch, Jason, and Doug Smith. (2008). "Inflated Art Appraisals Cost U.S. Government Untold Millions." *Los Angeles Times*. https://www.latimes.com/local/la-me-irs2mar02-story.html (September 12, 2023).

Fisher, Mark. (2009). *Capitalist Realism: Is There No Alternative?* Winchester; Washington, DC: Zero Books.

Foucault, Michel. (1990). *The History of Sexuality. 1: An Introduction*. New York: Vintage Books.

Foucault, Michel. (1995). *Discipline and Punish: The Birth of the Prison*. 2nd Vintage Books ed. New York: Vintage Books.

Foucault, Michel, and Michel Foucault. (2010). *The Archaeology of Knowledge*. New York: Vintage Books.

Gable, Nicolette. (2017). "'Willful Sadness': American Decadence, Gender, and the Pleasures and Dangers of Pessimism." *Journal of Gender Studies*, 26 (1): 102–11. https://doi.org/10.1080/09589236.2016.1267611.

Gabrielson, Teena, ed. (2016). *Oxford Handbook of Environmental Political Theory*. 1st ed. Oxford: Oxford University Press.

Gates, Bill. (2022). "A Scary but Hopeful Novel about Climate Change." *gatesnotes.com*. https://www.gatesnotes.com/The-Ministry-for-the-Future (September 12, 2023).

Geifman, Anna. (1995). *Thou Shalt Kill: Revolutionary Terrorism in Russia, 1894 – 1917*. 2. print, and 1. paperback print. Princeton, NJ: Princeton University Press.

Gordon, Uri. (2008). *Anarchy Alive! Anti-Authoritarian Politics from Practice to Theory*. London; Ann Arbor, MI: Pluto Press.

Graeber, David, and David Wengrow. (2021). *The Dawn of Everything: A New History of Humanity*. First American ed. New York: Farrar, Straus and Giroux.

Gray, John. (2013). *The Silence of Animals: On Progress and Other Modern Myths*. 1st ed. New York, NY: Farrar, Straus and Giroux.

Grindon, Gavin. (2015). "Poetry Written in Gasoline: Black Mask and Up Against the Wall Motherfucker." *Art History*, 38 (1): 170–209. https://doi.org/10.1111/1467-8365.12129.

Groïs, Boris, and David Fernbach. (2012). *Introduction to Antiphilosophy*. London; New York: Verso Books.

Gruppo di nun. (2022). *Revolutionary Demonology*. Falmouth: Urbanomic.

Hahne, Ron, and Ben Morea. (2011). *Black Mask & Up against the Wall Motherfucker: The Incomplete Works of Ron Hahne, Ben Morea, and the Black Mask Group*. Oakland, CA: PM Press.

Haiven, Max. (2020). *Revenge Capitalism: The Ghosts of Empire, the Demons of Capital, and the Settling of Unpayable Debts*. London: Pluto Press.

Hane, Mikiso, ed. (1993). *Reflections on the Way to the Gallows: Rebel Women in Prewar Japan*. 1. California paperback print. Berkeley: University of California Press.

Hardt, Michael, and Antonio Negri. (2003). *Empire*. 1. Harvard University Press paperback ed., [Nachdr.]. Cambridge, MA: Harvard University Press.

Hemmens, Alastair, and Gabriel Zacarias, eds. (2020). *The Situationist International: A Critical Handbook*. London: Pluto Press.

Hobbes, Thomas, and John C. A. Gaskin. (2008). *Leviathan*. Oxford: Oxford University Press.

Horkheimer, Max, Theodor W. Adorno, and Gunzelin Schmid Noerr. (2002). *Dialectic of Enlightenment: Philosophical Fragments*. Stanford, CA: Stanford University Press.

Hunt, Elle. (2016). "Pair of Glasses Left on US Gallery Floor Mistaken for Art." *Guardian UK*. https://www.theguardian.com/us-news/2016/may/27/pair-of-glasses-left-on-us-gallery-floor-mistaken-for-art (November 6, 2022).

Jorn, Asger, and Guy Debord. (1959). "Asger Jorn | Mémoires." *The Metropolitan Museum of Art*. https://www.metmuseum.org/art/collection/search/727492 (September 12, 2023).

Kaneko, Fumiko, Jean Inglis, and Fumiko Kaneko. (1991). *The Prison Memoirs of a Japanese Woman*. Armonk, NY: Sharpe.

Karatani, Kōjin, and Seiji M. Lippit. (2012). *History and Repetition*. New York: Columbia University Press.

Kinna, Ruth. (2016). *Kropotkin: Reviewing the Classical Anarchist Tradition*. Edinburgh: Edinburgh University Press.

Klinkner, Philip A., and Rogers M. Smith. (1999). *The Unsteady March: The Rise and Decline of Racial Equality in America*. Chicago: University of Chicago Press.

Knabb, Ken, ed. (2006). *Situationist International Anthology*. Rev. and expanded ed. Berkeley, CA: Bureau of Public Secrets.

Kohso, Sabu. (2020). *Radiation and Revolution*. Durham: Duke University Press.

La Dialectique Peut-Elle Casser Des Briques? 1973.

Lem, Stanislaw. (2002). *Solaris*. Boston, MA: Mariner Books.

Lévi-Strauss, Claude. (1963). *Structural Anthropology*. New York: Basic Books.

Lilley, Sasha. (2012). *Catastrophism: The Apocalyptic Politics of Collapse and Rebirth.* Oakland, CA: PM Press.

Lockett, Christopher. (2015). "'We Are Not Who We Are': Lovecraftian Conspiracy and Magical Humanism in The Cabin in the Woods." *Horror Studies*, 6 (1): 121–39. https://doi.org/10.1386/host.6.1.121_1.

Lovecraft, H. P. (2014). *The Complete Fiction of H.P. Lovecraft.* New York, NY: Race Point Publishing.

Lovecraft, Herbert P. (1927). "'Supernatural Horror in Literature' by H. P. Lovecraft." https://www.hplovecraft.com/writings/texts/essays/shil.aspx (September 12, 2023).

Luke, Timothy W. (1997). *Ecocritique: Contesting the Politics of Nature, Economy, and Culture.* Minneapolis, MN: University of Minnesota Press.

Luxemburg, Rosa, and Paul Le Blanc. (2010). *Socialism or Barbarism: Selected Writings.* London: Pluto Press.

Mackay, Robin, and Armen Avanessian, eds. (2019). *#accelerate#*. 3rd ed. Falmouth: Urbanomic.

Malm, Andreas. (2021a). *How to Blow up a Pipeline: Learning to Fight in a World on Fire.* First edition paperback. London; New York: Verso.

Malm, Andreas. (2021b). *White Skin, Black Fuel: On the Danger of Fossil Fascism.* London; New York: Verso.

Marcuse, Herbert. (1969). "An Essay on Liberation." https://www.marxists.org/reference/archive/marcuse/works/1969/essay-liberation.htm (September 12, 2023).

Martel, James R. (2022). *Anarchist Prophets: Disappointing Vision and the Power of Collective Sight.* Durham: Duke University Press.

Martin Luther King Jr. (1960). "Outline, The Philosophy of Nonviolence." https://kinginstitute.stanford.edu/king-papers/documents/outline-philosophy-nonviolence (September 12, 2023).

Marx, Karl. (1853). "The British Rule in India by Karl Marx." *New-York Daily Tribune.* https://www.marxists.org/archive/marx/works/1853/06/25.htm (September 12, 2023).

Mbembe, Achille, and Steve Corcoran. (2019). *Necropolitics.* Durham: Duke University Press.

Merchant, Carolyn. (1989). *The Death of Nature: Women, Ecology, and the Scientific Revolution.* New York: Harper & Row.

Meyer, Robinson. (2022). "The Climate Art Vandals Are Embarrassing." *The Atlantic.* https://www.theatlantic.com/science/archive/2022/10/vermeer-glue-soup-climate-protest-outrage/671904/ (November 6, 2022).

Miéville, China. (2004). *Iron Council.* 1st ed. New York: Del Rey/Ballantine Books.

Mignolo, Walter. (2011). *The Darker Side of Western Modernity: Global Futures, Decolonial Options.* Durham: Duke University Press.

Morton, Timothy. (2013). *Hyperobjects: Philosophy and Ecology after the End of the World.* Minneapolis, MN: University of Minnesota Press.

Morton, Timothy. (2016). "Frankensteinand Ecocriticism." In Andrew Smith (ed.), *The Cambridge Companion to 'Frankenstein'*, 143–57. Cambridge: Cambridge University Press. https://doi.org/10.1017/CBO9781316091203.012.

Mumford, Lewis. (1974). *The Pentagon of Power.* New York: Harcourt Brace Jovanovich.

Murphy, Bernice M. (2013). "The Cabin in the Woods: Order versus Chaos in the 'New World.'" In *The Rural Gothic in American Popular Culture*, 15–47. London: Palgrave Macmillan UK. https://doi.org/10.1057/9781137353726_2.

Mussap, Christian J. (2019). "The Plague Doctor of Venice." *Internal Medicine Journal*, 49 (5): 671–76. https://doi.org/10.1111/imj.14285.

Nechayev, Sergey. (1869). "The Revolutionary Catechism by Sergey Nechayev 1869." https://www.marxists.org/subject/anarchism/nechayev/catechism.htm (September 12, 2023).

Newitz, Annalee. (2006). *Pretend We're Dead: Capitalist Monsters in American Pop Culture*. Durham: Duke University Press.

Newman, Saul. (2000). "Anarchism and the Politics of Ressentiment." *Theory & Event*, 4 (3). https://muse.jhu.edu/article/32594

Nietzsche, Friedrich Wilhelm, and Douglas Smith. (2008). *On the Genealogy of Morals: A Polemic: By Way of Clarification and Supplement to My Last Book, Beyond Good and Evil*. Oxford: Oxford University Press.

Nixon, Rob. (2013). *Slow Violence and the Environmentalism of the Poor*. First Harvard University Press paperback edition. Cambridge, MA; London: Harvard University Press.

Novak, David. (2013). *Japanoise: Music at the Edge of Circulation*. Durham: Duke University Press.

Olson, Joel. (2007). "The Freshness of Fanaticism: The Abolitionist Defense of Zealotry." *Perspectives on Politics*, 5 (4). https://doi.org/10.1017/S1537592707072179.

Panagia, Davide. (2021). "On the Possibilities of a Political Theory of Algorithms." *Political Theory*, 49 (1): 109–33. https://doi.org/10.1177/0090591720959853.

Paperno, Irina. (1988). *Chernyshevsky and the Age of Realism: A Study in the Semiotics of Behavior*. Stanford, CA: Stanford University Press.

Parson, Sean. (2019). *Cooking up a Revolution: Food Not Bombs, Homes Not Jails, and Resistance to Gentrification*. Manchester: Manchester University Press.

Perlman, Fredy, ed. (1983). *Against His-Story, against Leviathan! An Essay*. Detroit, MI: Black & Red.

Petrov, Kristian. (2019). "'Strike out, Right and Left!': A Conceptual-Historical Analysis of 1860s Russian Nihilism and Its Notion of Negation." *Studies in East European Thought*, 71 (2): 73–97. https://doi.org/10.1007/s11212-019-09319-4.

Phillips, Leigh, and Michal Rozworski. (2019). *The People's Republic of Walmart: How the World's Biggest Corporations Are Laying the Foundation for Socialism*. London; New York: Verso.

Pinker, Steven. (2012). *The Better Angels of Our Nature: Why Violence Has Declined*. New York, NY; Toronto, Ontario; London: Penguin Books.

Poison Harvest. (2023). *Pinnacle of Ectasy*. Relapse Records.

Raddeker, Hélène Bowen. (2016). *Treacherous Women of Imperial Japan: Patriarchal Fictions, Patricidal Fantasies*. Paperback edition. Abingdon; New York: Routledge.

Rancière, Jacques, and Steven Corcoran. (2016). *Dissensus: On Politics and Aesthetics*. Reprinted. London; New York; Oxford; New Delhi; Sydney: Bloomsbury Academic.

Ray, Emily. (2021). "Creature Comforts: Neoliberalism and Preparing for Disaster." *New Political Science*, 43 (2): 171–88. https://doi.org/10.1080/07393148.2021.1906584.

Richter, Hans. (2016). *Dada: Art and Anti-Art*. Data centenary edition. New York, NY: Thames & Hudson.

Rimbaud, Penny. (2005). "You're Not Punk." *Vice*. https://www.vice.com/en/article/bndgnw/fuck-v12n3 (September 8, 2023).

Robinson, Idris. (2023). "The Destituent Urge Is Also a Destructive Urge: Agamben, Aristotle, and Benjamin on the Potentiality for Destitution." *South Atlantic Quarterly*, 122 (1): 137–56. https://doi.org/10.1215/00382876-10242714.

Robinson, Kim Stanley. (2020). *The Ministry for the Future*. 1st ed. New York, NY: Orbit.

Rousseau, Jean-Jacques, and Donald A. Cress. (2019). *On the Social Contract*. 2nd ed. Indianapolis, IN: Hackett Publishing Company, Inc.

Saba Hamedy. (2023). "Search for Titanic Submersible Unleashes 'Eat the Rich' Sentiment Online." *NBC News*. https://www.nbcnews.com/news/titanic-submersible-memes-social-media-anti-billionaire-sentiment-rcna90520 (September 12, 2023).

Sahlins, Marshall. (2017). *Stone Age Economics*. London; New York, NY: Routledge Classics.

Saitō, Kōhei. (2017). *Karl Marx's Ecosocialism: Capitalism, Nature, and the Unfinished Critique of Political Economy*. New York: Monthly Review Press.

Saitō, Kōhei. (2022). *Marx in the Anthropocene: Towards the Idea of Degrowth Communism*. Cambridge; New York, NY: Cambridge University Press.

Saitō, Tamaki. (2019). "Japan's 'Hikikomori' Population Could Top 10 Million." *nippon.com*. https://www.nippon.com/en/japan-topics/c05008/japan's-hikikomori-population-could-top-10-million.html (September 13, 2023).

Saitō, Tamaki, and Jeffrey Angles. (2013). *Hikikomori: Adolescence without End*. Minneapolis, MN: University of Minnesota Press.

Sakai, Naoki. (2005). "Two Negations: The Fear of Being Excluded and the Logic of Self-Esteem." In *Contemporary Japanese Thought*, edited by Richard Calichman. New York, NY: Columbia University Press.

Schmitt, Carl. (2005). *Political Theology: Four Chapters on the Concept of Sovereignty*. University of Chicago Press ed. Chicago: University of Chicago Press.

Schmitt, Carl, Russell A. Berman, and Samuel Garrett Zeitlin. (2015). *Land and Sea: A World-Historical Meditation*. Candor, NY: Telos Press Publishing.

Schmitt, Carl, and Carl Schmitt. (2006). *The Nomos of the Earth in the International Law of the Jus Publicum Europaeum*. First paperback edition. New York: Telos Press.

Schmitt, Carl, and Carl Schmitt. (2007). *The Concept of the Political*. Expanded ed. Chicago: University of Chicago Press.

Skov, Marie Arleth. (2023). *Punk Art History: Artworks from the European No Future Generation*. Bristol; Chicago, IL: Intellect.

Solnit, Rebecca. (2016). *Hope in the Dark: Untold Histories, Wild Possibilities*. Chicago, IL: Haymarket Books.

Srnicek, Nick, and Alex Williams. (2016). *Inventing the Future: Postcapitalism and a World without Work*. Revised and updated edition. London; New York, NY: Verso.

Staff, VICE. (2014). "Penny Rimbaud on How Crass Nearly Started World War III." *Vice*. https://www.vice.com/en/article/5gkbn3/penny-rambaud-on-how-crass-nearly-started (September 8, 2023).

Stern, Jacob. (2023). "Killer Whales Are Not Our Friends." *The Atlantic*. https://www.theatlantic.com/science/archive/2023/06/orca-killer-whale-attacking-boats/674438/ (September 26, 2023).

Stirner, Max. (2018). *The Unique and Its Property*. Berkeley, CA: Ardent Press.

Subhumans. (1985). *Someone Is Lying*. Bluurg Records.

Táíwò, Olúfẹmi O. (2022). *Elite Capture: How the Powerful Took over Identity Politics (and Everything Else)*. Chicago, IL: Haymarket Books.

Tattersall, Nick. (2008). "Nigeria Oil Rebels Reject Niger Delta Summit." *Reuters*. https://www.reuters.com/article/idUSL17190258 (September 10, 2023).

Theweleit, Klaus. (1987). *Male Fantasies*. Minneapolis, MN: University of Minnesota Press.

Thompson, Peter. (2017). "The Chemical Subject: Phenomenology and German Encounters with the Gas Mask in the World War I." *History and Technology*, 33 (3): 249–71. https://doi.org/10.1080/07341512.2018.1449712.

Thompson, Peter. (2020). "Wardens of the Toxic World: German Women's Encounters with the Gas Mask, 1915–1945." *German Studies Review*, 43 (2): 353–76. https://doi.org/10.1353/gsr.2020.0041.

Thorstensson, Victoria. (2016). "Nihilist Fashion in 1860s–1870s Russia: The Aesthetic Relations of Blue Spectacles to Reality." *Clothing Cultures*, 3 (3): 265–81. https://doi.org/10.1386/cc.3.3.265_1.

Too Many Cooks. (2014). Adult Swim.

Truscello, Michael. (2020). *Infrastructural Brutalism: Art and the Necropolitics of Infrastructure*. Cambridge, MA: The MIT Press.

Tucker, Robert C., Karl Marx, and Friedrich Engels, eds. (1978). *The Marx-Engels Reader*. 2nd ed. New York: Norton.

Tully, John Andrew. (2011). *The Devil's Milk: A Social History of Rubber*. New York: Monthly Review Press.

Turgenev, Ivan Sergeevich, and Richard Freeborn. (2008). *Fathers and Sons*. Oxford; New York: Oxford University Press.

Tyner, James A. (2019). *Dead Labor: Toward a Political Economy of Premature Death*. Minneapolis, MN: University of Minnesota Press.

Vaneigem, Raoul. (2012). *The Revolution of Everyday Life*. Oakland, CA: PM Press.

Virilio, Paul. (2003). *Unknown Quantity*. London; New York: [Paris]: Thames & Hudson; Fondation Cartier pour l'art contemporian.

Waits, Tom. (1992). *Bone Machine*. Island Records.

Wallace-Wells, David. (2022). "Opinion | Air Pollution Kills 10 Million People a Year. Why Do We Accept That as Normal?" *The New York Times*. https://www.nytimes.com/2022/07/08/opinion/environment/air-pollution-deaths-climate-change.html (September 10, 2023).

Wark, McKenzie. (2013). *The Spectacle of Disintegration*. 1st ed. Brooklyn, New York: Verso.

Watson, David. (1998). *Against the Megamachine: Essays on Empires and Its Enemies*. Brooklyn, NY: Autonomedia.

Weisenfeld, Gennifer. (2014). "Gas Mask Parade: Japan's Anxious Modernism." *Modernism/modernity*, 21 (1): 179–99. https://doi.org/10.1353/mod.2014.0015.

Whedon, J., Goddard, D., Connolly, K., Hemsworth, C., Hutchison, A., Kranz, F., Williams, J., Jenkins, R., Whitford, B., Deming, P., Lassek, L., and Julyan, D. (2012). *The Cabin in the Woods*. Lionsgate.

Williams, David. (2021). "John Stuart Mill and the Practice of Colonial Rule in India." *Journal of International Political Theory*, 17 (3): 412–28. https://doi.org/10.1177/1755088220903349.

Williams, Evan Calder. (2011). *Combined and Uneven Apocalypse*. Winchester: Zero Books.

Wolin, Sheldon S., and Chris Hedges. (2017). *Democracy Incorporated: Managed Democracy and the Specter of Inverted Totalitarianism*. New edition. Princeton, NJ: Princeton University Press.

Worley, Matthew. (2017). *No Future: Punk, Politics and British Youth Culture, 1976–1984*. Cambridge: Cambridge University Press.

Yoder, Kate. (2019). "Can Art Museums Survive without Oil Money?" *Grist*. https://grist.org/climate/can-art-museums-survive-without-oil-money/ (September 12, 2023).

Zerzan, John. (2012). *Future Primitive Revisited*. Port Townsend, WA: Feral House.

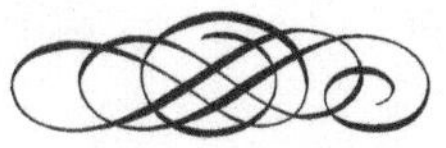

Index

Note: Page umbers followed by "n" refer to notes.